DATE DUE

JUDICIAL POLITICS
IN TEXAS

TEACHING TEXTS IN LAW AND POLITICS

David A. Schultz
General Editor

Vol. 36

PETER LANG
New York • Washington, D.C./Baltimore • Bern
Frankfurt am Main • Berlin • Brussels • Vienna • Oxford

Kyle Cheek • Anthony Champagne

JUDICIAL POLITICS
IN TEXAS

Partisanship, Money,
and Politics in State Courts

PETER LANG
New York • Washington, D.C./Baltimore • Bern
Frankfurt am Main • Berlin • Brussels • Vienna • Oxford

Library of Congress Cataloging-in-Publication Data
Cheek, Kyle.
Judicial politics in Texas: partisanship, money, and politics in state courts /
Kyle Cheek, Anthony Champagne.
p. cm. — (Teaching texts in law and politics; v. 36)
Includes bibliographical references and index.
1. Judges—Texas—Elections. 2. Texas—Politics and government—1951–
I. Champagne, Anthony. II. Title. III. Series.
KFT1725.5.N6C48   347.764'014—dc22   2003027712
ISBN 0-8204-6767-7 (paperback)
ISBN 0-8204-7644-7 (hardcover)
ISSN 1083-3447

Bibliographic information published by Die Deutsche Bibliothek.
Die Deutsche Bibliothek lists this publication in the "Deutsche
Nationalbibliografie"; detailed bibliographic data is available
on the Internet at http://dnb.ddb.de/.

Cover design by Dutton & Sherman Design

The paper in this book meets the guidelines for permanence and durability
of the Committee on Production Guidelines for Book Longevity
of the Council of Library Resources.

© 2005 Peter Lang Publishing, Inc., New York
275 Seventh Avenue, 28th Floor, New York, NY 10001
www.peterlangusa.com

Printed in the United States of America

Table of Contents

Preface   vii

Chapter I   Introduction   1

Chapter II   History and Overview of Judicial Selection   17

Chapter III   Plaintiff-Defense Wars: Money Enters the Picture   37

Chapter IV   Voter Awareness of Texas Judges   55

Chapter V   Judicial Elections by the Numbers   69

Chapter VI   The Difficulty of Reform   83

Chapter VII   Coming to a Judicial Election Near You:
                 The New Era in Texas Judicial Elections   117

Chapter VIII   Judicial Elections: Present and Future   171

Index   183

Preface

This research really began in the mid-1980s when Texas was going through remarkable changes in its state judiciary. Most notably, huge sums of money were being contributed to judicial candidates, and major battles were occurring over the selection of judges, primarily at the state supreme court level, between trial lawyers and business interests and the lawyers who represent them. One of the authors was approached by the Texas Bar Foundation to do a report on the new developments in Texas judicial politics. That report, published in 1986 as part of a special issue of Southern Methodist University's Southwestern Law Journal, represented one of the first efforts to identify the new developments in judicial elections that have later been described as "nastier, noisier, and costlier." And changes in Texas judicial politics continued. For one thing, at about the same time Texas became a battleground between plaintiffs and defense interests the state's politics changed. The Republican Party emerged as a major force in the state. Beginning with the election of Republican Governor Bill Clements in 1978, within a few years Republicans were running for and winning seats on the state supreme court. And, in the 1990s the Republican Party became the dominant party on the court.

Texas judicial politics became a focus of national attention as the battles between the parties and competing economic interests led to vigorous and expensive judicial campaigns in the state. Incumbent judges, who in the past had been secure in judicial office, began to be defeated, sometimes for simply having an unpopular political party affiliation. Million-dollar campaigns for the state supreme court became common as did huge donations to judges and judicial candidates from individual lawyers, law firms, and litigants. The question began to be asked of the Texas judicial system, "Is justice for sale?"

By the 1990s, it also became clear that the Texas situation was not an anomaly, but rather that Texas judicial politics was heralding the future of judicial politics in other states as well. States as diverse as North Carolina, Mississippi, Alabama, Louisiana, Illinois, Michigan, Ohio, New York, and Idaho began experiencing many of the problems Texas faced, especially high-dollar and highly competitive judicial campaigns. It became clear that the story of the Texas judiciary was more than just a story of the judicial system in one state; it was the story of what was happening in many states, especially those with partisan judicial elections.

This book concentrates on Texas judicial politics because we do believe the Texas judicial scene was the harbinger of events in the judiciaries of other states. However, we do try to connect what has happened to Texas to the broader national pattern of elected judiciaries. In examining the new politics of judicial elections in the states, we are indebted to a number of journals for allowing us to reprint substantial parts of these previously published articles: "Judicial Reform in Texas," 72 *Judicature* 146 (1988); "Awareness of Trial Court Judges," 75 *Judicature* 271 (1991); "Campaign Contributions in Texas Supreme Court Races," 17 *Crime Law and Social Change* 91 (1992); "Coming to a Judicial Election Near You: The New Era in Texas Judicial Elections," 43 *South Texas Law Review* 9 (2001); "Political Parties and Judicial Elections," 34 *Loyola of Los Angeles Law Review* 1411 (2001); "Interest Groups and Judicial Elections," 34 Loyola of Los Angeles Law Review 1391 (2001); "The Cycle of Judicial Elections: Texas as a Case Study," 29 *Fordham Urban Law Journal* 907 (2002); and "Partisan Judicial Elections: Lessons from a Bellwether State," 39 *Willamette Law Review* 1357 (2003).

Chapter I

Introduction

Electing Judges

Elected state courts, especially state supreme courts, have become a new battleground for competing interest groups. Increasingly, millions of dollars are being spent in state judicial campaigns that are funded by lawyers, litigants, and interests with concerns over the outcomes of litigation. Judges are being challenged in judicial elections with increasing frequency and more are being defeated as well. Interestingly, until about twenty-five years ago, judicial elections were sleepy affairs where judges were seldom challenged and rarely defeated. And, judicial campaigns were decidedly low budget affairs. Beginning in the late 1970s, however, several developments occurred that led to a new era of "nastier, noisier, and costlier" judicial campaigns.[1] One development was the demise of the solid Democratic South. With several Southern states having partisan judicial elections, as the Republican Party became increasingly powerful, judicial races between Democrats and Republicans became increasingly hard fought. The popularity of Ronald Reagan in particular allowed for the election of Republican governors who began to appoint Republicans to state benches in the South. Thus, Republican judges began to have an incumbency advantage in running for office. And the Republican Party became increasingly competitive in Southern judicial races in the 1980s.[2] At the same time, the legal profession was increasingly specialized and fractured, with large firms representing business interests and smaller plaintiffs' firms representing those suing business, insurance companies and professionals. The era of the generalist lawyer was coming to an end. In place of the generalists were lawyers whose clients represented a narrow base and whose economic interests were closely tied to the economic success of that narrow base of clients. Plaintiffs' lawyers were paid by contingent fees and had to win to receive compensation. Lawyers representing business and insurance companies tended to be paid by the hour, and, while their economic survival was not as closely tied to victory as plaintiffs' lawyers, they had to have a good success rate in lawsuits to maintain their value to their employers. And both sides in the legal profession knew that it was not just the law that was important—it was also the attitudes and values of the judges who interpreted the law.[3] No better evidence of that was the increasing activism of state courts in a variety of areas of law ranging from criminal justice, to school finance, to tort reform. As the activism of the Warren Court era filtered down to state supreme courts, it was clear that the justices on those courts could significantly impact public policy in the states.[4] Nor was it just lawyers who noted the impact of state courts on public policy. Interest groups could also see the value of judges favorable to their points of view. Most interesting to those groups was that there were relatively few justices on state courts compared to the numbers of state legislators, and campaign contributions given to a handful of judicial candidates could elect judges who benefited those groups' interests just like campaign contributions to governors or state legislators could benefit interest groups. Added to that was that judicial campaigns rarely came close to the costs of gubernatorial campaigns and the small number of judicial campaigns in any election cycle meant that an interest group could use its contributions to sway a court more easily and cheaply that it could sway a state legislature.[5]

Thus, by the late 1970s the state courts were ripe for a new more competitive era in judicial politics. That new competition did not happen everywhere all at once, of course. Even today many state supreme court elections retain the sleepy characteristics of an earlier era.[6] But there were states that proved to be bellwether states in terms of the new era in judicial elections. In 1978 some Los Angeles assistant district attorneys organized against trial judges they believed were soft on crime. That marked the beginning of the new era in judicial politics. Shortly thereafter the Texas Supreme Court became a battleground between plaintiff and defense interests. That was quickly followed by a battle in California's Supreme Court retention elections that defeated three incumbent justices.[7] In the early 1980s, California showed that retention elections can be "nasty, noisy, and costly." However, partisan elections are structurally more raucous because candidates have opponents and those opponents carry an opposing party label.[8] Thus, Texas quickly became the model for what can go wrong in judicial races. This book is the story of Texas judicial politics—a story of money, partisanship, failed reform efforts, and sometimes corruption. But it is also the story of a bellwether state—a story of what can happen to elected judiciaries in the modern era in judicial politics.

Background on Judicial Elections

Unlike the federal model of judicial selection, the prevailing model for the selection of state judges has undergone significant change throughout American history.[9] Until the mid-1800s, state judicial selection generally adhered to the federal model's emphasis on the appointment of judges. Typically, judges were selected by gubernatorial appointment often coupled with confirmation by the legislature. In some cases, judges were appointed directly by a state legislature.[10] The emergence of Jacksonian egalitarian democratic ideals early in the nineteenth century brought about a growing belief that judges, like other public officials, should be accountable to the voting public.[11] As that ideal gained strong acceptance among reformers, states began to move away from legislative and gubernatorial appointment toward the selection of judges by popular election. In 1832, Mississippi became the first state to provide for the selection of all its judges by popular election. New York followed in 1846 and for the next 65 years, from Iowa in 1847 through Arizona in 1912, every new state to enter the Union provided for some or all of its judges to be chosen by popular election.[12]

From the time that Mississippi and New York first led the way with popular judicial elections, judges typically ran on partisan ballots, campaigning alongside their fellow party candidates. In the latter part of the nineteenth century, Progressive reformers became concerned with the influence that party bosses were asserting on the makeup of state judiciaries, often providing nominations for judicial office as a reward to the party faithful rather than to the most qualified. As a means of removing judicial selection from the influence of party leaders, reformers pressed for nonpartisan judicial elections as a means of encouraging the election of judges based on their qualifications rather than their partisan affiliation.[13] In the closing decades of the 1800s the legal profession also responded to the extraordinary influence that parties wielded over judicial selection by organizing into bar associations—largely in an effort to promote the selection of judges on the basis of qualifications rather than through party patronage.[14]

Then, in the twentieth century, reformers began to press for the adoption of the so-called Missouri Plan, which removed the initial selection of judges from popular control but retained a mechanism for maintaining the Jacksonian ideal of electoral accountability.[15] Under this plan, judges were to be appointed by a governor from a list prepared by a judicial nominating committee. The judges appointed under this plan would then run in periodic, uncontested "retention" elections in which the voters would be allowed to determine whether the judge would continue in office.[16]

That twentieth century move to eliminate contested elections from the judicial selection process has been far from universal though. In fact thirty-nine states still select some portion of their judiciary through popular election. Eleven states select their state supreme court justices in partisan elections.[17] In spite of the initial popularity of the Missouri Plan, the wave of reform that accompanied its early years has waned.

A better understanding of judicial elections provides a clearer understanding of how that process of selecting judges may be improved. It is the Texas experience with judicial elections, a history that has often foreshadowed the experience of other states, to which we now turn.

Framing the Normative Debate: Judicial Independence versus Electoral Accountability

The various concerns surrounding the increased politicization of Texas Supreme Court elections and the reform proposals that have followed are but a reflection of a larger debate surrounding judicial selection. The underlying theme that drives the judicial selection debate in Texas and elsewhere is a centuries-old question of whether judges, who are expected to be impartial decision-makers and fair administrators of justice, should be periodically subjected to the electorate for its approval.

Those involved in this debate can be divided into two general camps whose view of judicial selection derives largely from contending views of the judicial function. On one side of the debate are those who argue that the function of the judge is merely to serve as the neutral voice of the law. It follows from this view that judges should be insulated from public pressures in their official capacities so that they can apply the law fairly without fear of repercussions from the electorate, especially when a fair decision is made which is counter to the preference of the majority. This argument is usually accompanied by support for the appointment of judges and long tenure on the bench. Through appointment, able judges may be selected, and long terms ensure that judges will not be swayed in their decisions by looking to the possible ramifications on a reelection bid or a decision concerning reappointment.

The other side of the debate consists of those who hold that judges not only interpret and apply the law but also make law and, therefore, public policy. Because judges may exercise a wide range of discretion in this law-making function, this camp adheres to the axiom that judges should routinely go before the voters in order to be made accountable for their decisions and to ensure that they remain aware of public preferences. If a judge is found by the electorate to have exhibited preferences in his decisions that are counter to the desires of the majority, he may be replaced by a candidate who is expected to conform more closely to the preferences of the majority.

This dialogue surrounding judicial selection predates the birth of the American nation. While the early American experience highlighted the need for a judiciary independent of political pressures, later experiences were to heighten the desire for some form of electoral control over this branch of government. The history of judicial selection is a story of contending values, independence and accountability, and various attempts to reconcile the judicial function with the democratic process. Independence held sway as the dominant ideal in early America but gradually gave way to the desires of the public to have a voice in the selection of those who would hold judicial office. Accountability won out at least for a while as the dominant ideal and has been sought through different institutional arrangements for selection—some even attempting to reinstate a measure of the independence that judges once knew.

The Case of Texas

In its first five years of statehood, Texas was a microcosm of the early national experience with state judicial selection, providing originally for the appointment of judges by the governor with consent of the Texas Senate. Then, in 1850, the influence of Jacksonian democracy led to the adoption of judicial selection by popular election. Under Reconstruction, Texas returned to the gubernatorial appointment of judges. However, largely in response to the abuses of the gubernatorial appointment power during Reconstruction, Texas included a provision in its current constitution, adopted in 1876, for the selection of its judges in popular elections.[18] While the Texas Constitution does not specify that judicial candidates must run on partisan ballots, Texas election law encourages judicial candidates to run as party nominees.[19]

Although judicial elections in Texas are conducted on partisan ballots, the first 100 years of judicial elections under the 1876 state constitution reflected the one-party state of Texas politics. Judicial races were seldom contested and, when a contested race did occur, incumbent judges were typically very secure.[20] One study of judicial selection in Texas found that from 1952 through 1962, death, resignation or retirement more often signaled the end of a judicial tenure than did electoral defeat.[21] During the era of one-party politics, contested elections seldom occurred in the general election. Instead challengers were more likely to appear in the Democratic primary.

Texas' provision for gubernatorial appointments to fill mid-term vacancies also became an important means of accession to the bench. Mid-term resignation was common among judges who planned to leave the bench, allowing the governor to name a replacement.[22] Judges initially appointed by the governor then enjoyed the benefit of incumbency when facing election for the first time. This arrangement was so common in the first 100 years of the 1876 constitution that one study concluded that the Texas judicial selection system was primarily appointive.[23]

Only in the 1970s, with the newly emerging two-party political landscape, did meaningful contests begin to appear in judicial elections. Beginning with races for district courts in urban areas, Republican candidates began to break the stranglehold that Democrats had held over the Texas judiciary for over a century.[24] As competitive partisan contests became more common, so did the nature of the campaigns that were waged, with perhaps the most important developments being the new role of the parties and the escalating cost of judicial races.

Courts as Policy-Making Institutions

There exist a wide range of views on the efficacy of the courts as policy-making institutions; however, few political scientists would disagree today that courts do make policy.[25] The implications of this view of the judicial function continue to have broad implications for the judicial selection debate. To understand these implications, though, it is useful to address the ways in which courts serve as policy-making institutions.

Courts at both the state and national level are called upon to interpret the U.S. Constitution, state constitutions and legislation that has been passed to further certain governmental objectives. By its very nature, the interpretation of the law defines the scope of policy and, in some cases, may totally redefine policy.[26] State appellate courts serve an especially important role in the making of policy as they are routinely called upon to clarify and develop the common law in areas that have not been codified or that are beyond the scope of legislative definition.[27] The decisions that appellate courts make in matters of common law and statutory interpretation serve in turn as precedents that guide the decisions of trial court judges who dispose of the bulk of litigation in the court systems.

The arguments in favor of the popular election of judges often stress the discretion that individual judges exercise in the decisions they make. Dubois has argued that the nature of the judicial process at the state level is characterized by the policy-making activities of the courts where judges make choices which are influenced by the personal values they carry to the bench:

> Whether engaged in the resolution of constitutional, statutory, or common law cases, judges are required to make choices in their determination of the relevant facts. These choices are pregnant with underlying questions of equity, justice, and public policy, which are inevitably influenced by the judges' personal attitudes and values.[28]

These choices often involve the allocation of resources among individuals or groups; they may entail the redistribution of resources in decisions concerning damage awards, for example, or they may involve regulatory decisions which affect the uses of property, such as in a case determining the constitutionality of a zoning ordinance. No matter the nature of the case, though, the decisions of courts often have a direct impact on resource allocation with valuable implications for the parties involved. Some groups, perhaps even the public, will be made better off as a result of these decisions while some will be left in a position less favorable than that from which they began.

Popular control over the judiciary receives much of its legitimacy from recognition of this role of judges as allocative decision-makers, similar to the desire for the electoral control that the voting public has over its legislators and other representative decision-makers. The popular selection of judges allows the voting public to choose a judiciary that can be expected to make allocative decisions consistent with the desire of the majority.

Dubois furthers this argument by noting that the vast majority of the work of state courts, consisting of the development of the common law and in statutory interpretation, involves the further definition of majoritarian public values that have been left ambiguous or imperfectly detailed in the legislative process. Dubois contends that as the courts make and interpret law that they should remain mindful of the societal goals from which the law emerged.

Therefore, the need for judicial accountability to the voting public again emerges as the courts are often in a position to further societal values and goals.[29]

This is held to be the case especially for the members of the appellate courts in a state's judicial system who "are less frequently called upon to implement narrow procedural rules" but are "more frequently asked to answer questions with importance beyond the immediate case at hand." [30] In other words, the need for accountability increases as the decisions of the court become more encompassing.

Selecting Judicial Policy-Makers

The role played by the courts in shaping and defining public policy is important when considering the implications of the various judicial selection systems. In the early nineteenth century, spurred by the ideals of Jacksonian democracy, the staffing of state courts was often turned over to the voting public in the states. The move toward electoral accountability for judges was, in large part, a response to the patronage appointment of individuals to long terms of office on the bench. Once appointed, judges were free to support the policies of the appointing governor or legislature, even after those policies may have been rejected by the voters. Instead, the voters wished to be able to pass on individual judges on the basis of the policy positions they may have taken on the bench.[31]

The ideal of accountability remained strong, with some modification in the early twentieth century, until the middle of the twentieth century when a number of states began to remove judicial selection from the electorate in favor of merit appointment systems, with the hope of removing judges from the partisan political process and improving the quality of the judges who were selected.[32] In spite of this most recent trend, though, and coupled with evidence that appointive systems do not provide for more qualified state judiciaries,[33] there has remained strong support in many quarters for elective selection systems. Adamany and Dubois have summed the argument in favor of holding judges accountable to the elected public as follows:

> Since no persuasive argument can be advanced for indirect accountability of judicial policymakers, direct accountability through elections is a preferable means for giving the public control over the third branch of government. And partisan elections seem preferable to nonpartisan ballots. At the simplest level, partisan elections are much more likely to assure the existence of opposition, vigorous criticism of those in power, and

effective presentation of alternative policies. Political party leaders feel an obligation to recruit qualified candidates for each partisan office contested in an election, if for no other reason than to fill out and balance the party ticket.[34]

Judicial Accountability in Texas

The arguments set forth in favor of popular control over the judiciary speak directly to the position of the Texas court system and, particularly, the Texas Supreme Court. As the court of last resort for all civil cases in the state,[35] the Texas Supreme Court is responsible for establishing legal and state constitutional principles that could affect the interests of a vast majority of the citizens of the state, either directly or indirectly. Therefore, it is of particular interest to the public-at-large that some measure of control resides in the hands of the public whose values are to be allocated and whose interests are to be protected by the decisions of the court.

The selection of Texas' judges through partisan election and questions about the impartiality of judges that have arisen through the dynamics of this system have become the focus of attention in both political and academic circles. The perceptions of the Texas judiciary are generally an effect of the partisan elections through which judges are selected in Texas. The emergence of the Republican party in the state produced meaningful two-party judicial contests for the first time in the state's history. The heightened competition was accompanied, in turn, by an increase in special-interest activity in judicial elections—especially in Texas Supreme Court races. Races that were relatively staid affairs only twenty years ago became some of the most expensive races in the state, with a substantial portion of the funding for these races contributed by special-interest groups that stand to be most affected by the decisions of the court. As a result of the involvement of clearly defined special interests in the financing of these candidates, these races came to be perceived as the battleground for special-interest groups who are able to arm their preferred candidates with the financial support to run highly visible and effective campaigns.

Repeated calls have been issued for reform in the way that judges are selected in Texas.[36] Concerns about both the impact of the courts on public policy as well as appearances of impropriety that stem from campaign contribution practices under the current method of selection have become central issues around which the debate has grown. The Supreme Court of Texas has come to be at the center of these arguments for selection reform because of its influence on policy issues through constitutional, statutory and common law interpretation and because of the attention that several of its members have received for actions that have raised questions about their impartiality. As the involvement of organized interests has increased, concern has grown that members of the Court have become overly sensitive to and dependent upon the interest groups that have contributed substantial amounts to their campaigns. Texas judges have been accused of being unfairly biased in favor of one of several competing special-interest groups.

In spite of Texas' continuance with a system which stresses the accountability of judges to the public, concerns about the current method of selection are heightened by research which suggests that the public may be poorly equipped to hold its judges accountable. Survey research has shown Texas voters' knowledge of judicial candidates is exceedingly low.[37] As a result, voters rely upon cues such as name familiarity and party affiliation when identifying the judicial candidate for whom they will cast their ballot.[38] In turn, judges are evaluated largely on the basis of the strength of their party rather than their individual qualifications and performance.

Also, as a result of heightened competition and the increased need to generate name-recognition, judicial candidates have been forced to become much more active in campaigning. The reliance of judicial candidates upon large financial contributions in an era of increasingly costly campaigns has led to concerns that judges have become responsive to the special interests that finance their campaigns and have compromised the impartiality that has been deemed essential for the proper maintenance of an effective judiciary. So, while Texas has maintained a judicial selection system that emphasizes the desire for an accountable judiciary, the question has become: to whom are judges accountable?

Ultimately, these various concerns have led to repeated calls for change in the state's method of selecting its judges. Reform proposals have been introduced at various times which seek to remove the influence of special interests in judicial selection. These reform proposals have included calls for various modifications of the electoral process through which judges are selected, reforms in campaign finance practices, and have even included plans for replacing the electoral process with an appointment plan.

In spite of these calls for reform, the judicial selection process in Texas has remained virtually unchanged since 1876 when the current state constitution was adopted. Texas Supreme Court justices are still elected in partisan statewide races although constraints have been placed upon campaign contribution practices.[39] The various judicial selection reform proposals that have been formulated have never survived long enough to emerge from the state legislature and go before the electorate for approval.

As a result of failed reform attempts and continued criticisms of the campaign contribution practices involved in Texas Supreme Court elections, important questions remain to be answered concerning the nature and effects of judicial elections in Texas. Races for seats on the Texas Supreme Court provide an opportunity for an empirical analysis of the factors that determine their outcome and the subsequent effects that these factors have on the behavior of the Court and its justices.

Ultimately, answers to these questions speak to the larger issue of accountability as well. Recent experience suggests that accountability will remain the dominant theme in Texas judicial selection. While it certainly remains within the province of the state to demand accountability of its judicial office-holders, a closer look at the process is in order to ensure that the ideal is attained.

Over two centuries ago Edmund Burke, in his commentary on the French Revolution, penned a passage that still offers insight into the concerns of those who are critical of subjecting the members of the judicial branch to the pressures of the electoral process:

> ...elective, temporary, local judges...exercising their dependent functions in a narrow society, must be the worst of all tribunals. In them it will be vain to look for any appearance of justice towards strangers, towards the obnoxious rich, towards the minority of routed parties, towards all those who in the election have supported unsuccessful candidates. It will be impossible to keep the new tribunals clear of the worst spirit of faction.[40]

While extreme concerns, such as those expressed by Burke, have been largely silenced by over a century of experience with elected judiciaries,[41] the basis of Burke's critique still offers a useful perspective from which to consider the nature of an elected judiciary. To subject a judiciary to the electoral process virtually ensures that judicial candidates of differing ideologies will be pitted against one another and will garner support from contending interests. This raises the concern that a judge will come to the bench with a predisposition that might favor one class of litigants over another and, therefore, that he or she might not display the impartiality that many consider to be fundamental to the effective dispensation of justice.

This theme resounds particularly loudly in Texas Supreme Court elections in which candidates for the bench typically receive a great deal of financial support from either the trial lawyers' group or from the organized defense interests.[42] The intense involvement of these interest groups has generated a concern that the accountability of the judiciary to the public has been compromised.

The concerns surrounding the Texas Supreme Court—especially those concerns about the dramatic increase in the politicization of campaigns for the court—indicate that the justices of the court have reason to be more cognizant of the special interests that financially enable them to mount a successful campaign than of the interests of the public at large. This concern is sharpened by the general perception of the judicial electorate as a generally acquiescent group of voters who cast their ballot not on the basis of opinions formed about substantive issues but, rather, on the basis of some general cue such as party affiliation or name familiarity.[43] This perception of voters indicates that special interests may need only provide the monetary resources for judicial candidates to gain a sufficient level of familiarity with the voters in order to achieve electoral success. The following chapter explores money and interest groups' involvement in Texas judicial elections.

Notes

[1] Schotland wrote, "The greatest current threat to judicial independence is the increasing politicization of judicial elections. They are becoming nastier, noisier, and costlier." Roy Schotland, Comment, *Law & Contemporary Problems* 149 at 1509 (1988).

[2] Anthony Champagne, Political Parties and Judicial Elections, *34 Loyola of Los Angeles Law Review* 1411 at 1415 (2001).

[3] Anthony Champagne, Interest Groups and Judicial Elections, 34 *Loyola of Los Angeles Law Review* 1391 at 1394–1396 (2001).

[4] For an excellent treatment of the importance of the Warren Court's activism on public policy, see, Mark Silverstein, *Judicious Choices* 48–62 (1994).

[5] For a general discussion of interest groups in state judicial politics, see Champagne, supra note 3.

[6] Anthony Champagne, Modern Judicial Campaigns, 41 *Judges' Journal* 17 (2002).

[7] Champagne, supra note 3 at 1394–1396.

[8] Champagne, supra note 2.

[9] See Mary L. Volcansek and Jacqueline L. Lafon, *Judicial Selection: The Cross-Evolution of French and American Practices* (1988) for a full treatment of judicial selection in the states.

[10] Phillip Dubois, *From Ballot to Bench: Judicial Elections and the Quest for Accountability* 3 (1980).

[11] "The concept of an elected judiciary emerged during the Jacksonian era as part of a larger movement aimed at democratizing the political process in America. It was spearheaded by reformers who contended that the concept of an elitist judiciary...did not square with the ideology of a government under popular control." Burton M. Atkins, Judicial Elections: What the Evidence Shows, 50 *Florida Bar Journal* 152 (1976).

[12] Dubois supra note 10 at 3

[13] Id. at 4

[14] Id. at 4

[15] Richard A. Watson and Rondal G. Downing, *The Politics of the Bench and the Bar: Judicial Selection Under the Missouri Nonpartisan Court Plan* 7–9 (1969).

[16] Id. at 7–9.

[17] Roy Schotland, Introduction: Personal Views, 34 *Loyola University of Los Angeles Law Review* 1361, 1362 (2001) and American Judicature Society, Judicial Selection Methods in the States, http://www.ajs.org/select11.html. Lists of states with partisan elections will differ simply because of varying definitions of partisanship. The American Judicature Society list includes: Alabama; Illinois; Louisiana; Michigan; Ohio; Pennsylvania; Texas; and West Virginia. Arkansas moved from partisan to nonpartisan elections in 2000. North Carolina will do so in 2004. Michigan and Ohio ostensibly have nonpartisan elections since the party label does not appear on the ballot, but the parties are so involved that the American Judicature Society now considers them to be partisan states. Recently Idaho has had very high levels of partisanship in its nonpartisan elections as well.

[18] Anthony Champagne, The Selection and Retention of Judges in Texas, 40 *Southwestern Law Review* at 55 (1986).

[19] Susan Douglas, Selection and Discipline of State Judges in Texas, 14 *Texas Tech Law Review* at 674–675 (1977).

[20] Bancroft Henderson and T.C. Sinclair, The Selection of Judges in Texas 5 *Houston Law Review* at 430–498 (1968).

[21] Only 4.9 percent of all trial judges and 6.6 percent of appellate judges suffered electoral defeat between 1952 and 1962, while 40.8 percent of all changes in judicial office during that same time resulted from retirement or resignation. Id. at 441.

[22] "Of all the judges who served during the period 1940–1962, a total of 66 percent were appointed. Just how meaningful appointments were is shown by reference to the period 1952–1962 for which primary election statistics were available. In the first election following appointment, 86.2 percent of the judges were unopposed and only 4 percent were defeated." Id. at 442.

[23] Id. at 442.

[24] Champagne, supra note 18 at 53–117 (1986).

[25] Generally, see Donald Horowitz, *The Courts and Social Policy* (1977).

[26] Id. See also David Adamany and Phillip Dubois, Electing state judges, 1976 *Wisconsin Law Review* 731 (1976).

[27] Phillip Dubois, Accountability, Independence, and the Selection of State Judges: The Role of Popular Judicial Elections, 40 *Southwestern Law Journal* 31–52 (1986).

[28] Id. at 38.

[29] Id.

[30] Id. at 40.

[31] Volcansek and Lafon, supra note 9.

[32] Watson and Downing, supra note 15.

[33] Henry Glick and Craig Emmert, Selection System and Judicial Characteristics: The Recruitment of State Supreme Court Judges, 70 *Judicature* 229 (1987).

[34] Adamany and Dubois, supra note 26 at 770.

[35] Texas employs a dual Supreme Court system. The Texas Supreme Court is the court of last resort for all civil and juvenile cases in the state while the Court of Criminal Appeals is the court of final appeal for criminal cases only.

[36] John Hill, Taking Texas Judges out of Politics: An Argument for Merit Election, 40 *Baylor Law Review* 339 (1988).

[37] Charles Johnson, Roger Shaeffer & Neal McKnight, The Salience of Judicial Candidates and Elections, 50 *Social Science Quarterly* 371 (1978); Barbara Johnson, Voter Survey: Judges Unknown, *Texas Lawyer* Nov. 10–14, 1986, at 1, 8–9; Anthony Champagne & Greg Thielemann, Awareness of Trial Court Judges, 74 *Judicature* 271 (1991).

[38] Dubois, supra note 10; Dubois, supra note 27.

[39] Kyle Cheek and Anthony Champagne, Money in Texas Supreme Court Elections: 1980–1998, 84 *Judicature* 20 (2000).

[40] Edmund Burke, *Reflections on the Revolution in France* at 223 (Anchor Books edition, 1973).

[41] Jack Ladinsky and Alan Silver, Popular Democracy and Judicial Independence, 1967 *Wisconsin Law Review* 128 (1967).

[42] Champagne, supra note 14.

[43] Ladinsky and Silver, supra note 41; Dubois, supra note 10; Mary Volcansek, Money or Name? A Sectional Analysis of Judicial Elections, 8 *The Justice System Journal* 46 (1983).

Chapter II

History and Overview of Judicial Selection

Introduction

There is great variation in the way judges are selected in the United States. With each method of judicial selection, problems do exist. Nevertheless, one of the major themes found in the study of judiciaries over the years is the theme of judicial reform—and the main goal of judicial reform is to improve the process by which judges are selected.

Judicial reform has existed since the founding of the United States. Prior to the American Revolution, there was such resentment against the King's power to appoint and remove judges that one of the grievances mentioned in the Declaration of Independence was that the crown had made judges dependent on his will alone. Judges were dependent on the crown for their tenure in office and for their salaries. As a result, at the earliest moments in the country's history, the concern was with developing a mechanism that would insure the independence of judges from political pressures. In that way, it was believed that judges would be free to interpret the law without fear of political reprisal. The Framers were familiar with appointment of judges since that had been their experience under the King. Election of judges was unknown to the Framers. As a result, debate was over how judges should be appointed, whether by the President or by the Senate. The compromise was that the President appoint judges with the advise and consent of the Senate. Judicial independence was then insured by providing judges with life tenure.[1]

With the writing of state constitutions, appointment was also the method of selecting judges, although some states allowed the state legislature to choose judges and some states provided that the governor appoint judges with approval by the legislature.[2] Even today there are three states that have gubernatorial appointment (without the nomination commission found in merit selection states) and two states that have legislative selection of judges (although one of those states now has a merit selection nominating committee to screen the candidates for legislative selection).[3]

In the first third of the 1800s, there was a movement for a new way to select judges. One reason may have been dissatisfaction with federal judges such as John Marshall, who reflected the views of the Federalist Party at a time when the Jeffersonians were dominant. Thomas Jefferson, for example, though once an advocate of life tenure for judges, had come to support six-year judicial terms. And, with the growth of popular democracy in the era of Andrew Jackson, support developed for election of judges. Judicial elections also developed due to efforts by members of the legal profession to provide the judiciary with its own base of legitimacy. Since appointed judges were patronage positions, electing judges was seen as a reform that would remove judges from the politics and corruption associated with political patronage. Georgia provided that the judges of inferior courts be elected as early as 1812. In 1816, Indiana entered the Union with a Constitution that provided for the election of associate judges on its circuit court. It was 1832, however, before Mississippi became the first state to elect all its judges. When New York adopted an elective system for judges in 1846, it was a clear signal that judicial elections were the new trend in the judicial reform effort. In 1850, seven states adopted election of judges and by the beginning of the Civil War, twenty-four of thirty-four states had elected judges.[4]

However, it was not long until concerns developed over judicial elections. In the late 1800s, one of the concerns was that political machines selected and controlled judges, thus leading to a common perception that judges were often political party hacks who were corrupt and incompetent. It did not appear that electing judges had achieved the goal of an independent and impartial judiciary.[5]

The failures of judicial elections led to a reform in the way judges were elected. Generally, judges had been elected the way other candidates on the ballot were chosen in that time period—with a party label. Thus, judicial candidates, like other candidates, ran with the support of political parties. As early as 1873, judicial candidates in Cook County, Illinois, voluntarily agreed to run on a nonpartisan basis. Although Cook County later returned to partisan election, it was the beginning of a new movement in judicial reform politics. By 1927, twelve states chose judges in nonpartisan elections. Like appointment of judges and partisan election of judges, the promise of the nonpartisan election of judges was too great. Although twelve states elected judges on a nonpartisan basis in 1927, by that date three states had already tried and rejected nonpartisan elections.[6] The problem was that party leaders still selected judicial candidates even in nonpartisan elections, and voters were even less knowledgeable of the candidates in nonpartisan elections since they did not have the guidance provided by party labels.

Reformers then proposed still another system of judicial selection, claiming that under the new system judges would be selected on the basis of merit rather than partisanship or patronage. The idea behind merit selection plans was that a nonpartisan commission would recruit and evaluate candidates for judgeships and recommend several possible candidates to the governor. The recommended candidates would be chosen without regard to political considerations, but on the basis of their ability and qualifications. The governor would then appoint one of those recommended candidates who would serve for a period of time and then run for retention in office. That election, however, would not be a contested election such as existed with partisan or nonpartisan elective systems. Instead, it would be a retention election where the incumbent judge would run without an opponent. The question on the ballot would simply be "yes" or "no" on whether the judge should be retained in office. The commission plans essentially merged an appointive system with an elective system. The idea was that the blue ribbon commission would limit a governor's choices to able and qualified judges, and the voters would still have a voice, after observing the appointed judge's performance for a period of time, in determining whether the judge should continue in office. In 1940, Missouri became the first state to put a commission selection plan into effect. As a result, commission or merit selection is often called the "Missouri Plan." There are thirty-four states that use commission plans to select at least some judges.[7]

In reality, most states have hybrid systems for selecting judges where various selection systems are used. Variations in selection systems within states depend on the level of court, whether it is initial selection of judges or selection for midterm vacancies or the region of the state. Some states have also merged systems of selection in unique ways that defy more general classifications. The result is that any simple scheme that classifies judges should be interpreted cautiously. For example, in Texas almost all judges run in partisan elections, but municipal court judges are often appointed by the local governing body. In rural counties in Missouri, trial judges are still elected in partisan elections even though the state is the originator of the Missouri Plan. Although Illinois uses retention elections for determining if incumbent judges should be retained in office, judges are initially chosen in partisan elections. In New Mexico, judges are initially appointed to the bench, and then in their first election after appointment they run in partisan elections. If elected, the judges run in retention elections for subsequent terms.[8] With these cautions about the problems associated with oversimplifying systems of judicial selection within the states, Table 1 presents a rough classification of the systems of selection for the initial selection of judges in the states.

Table 1				
Initial Judicial Selection Methods in the States (Oct. 2002)				
Merit Selection	Appointment Governor (G) Or Legislature (L)	Partisan Election	Nonpartisan Election	Merit Selection Combined with Other System
Alaska	California (G)	Alabama	Arkansas	Arizona
Colorado	Maine (G)	Illinois	Georgia	Florida
Connecticut	N. Jersey(G)	Louisiana	Idaho*	Indiana
Delaware	Virginia (L)	Michigan	Kentucky	Kansas
DC	S. Carolina(L)	Ohio	Minnesota	Missouri
Hawaii		Pennsylvania	Mississippi	N. York
Iowa		Texas	Montana	Oklahoma
Maryland		W. Virginia	Nevada	S. Dakota
Massachusetts			N. Carolina	Tennessee
Nebraska			N. Dakota	
New Hampshire			Oregon	
New Mexico			Washington	
Rhode Island			Wisconsin	
Utah				
Vermont				
Wyoming				
*A number of scholars would disagree with the American Judicature Society's classification of Idaho as nonpartisan and would consider it better classified as partisan. Source: American Judicature Society, www.ajs.org				

There are also variations in the operation of the various types of election systems. For example, although retention elections generally require a majority vote for judges to be retained in office, in Illinois a supermajority of

60% is required. And, although some states claim to have nonpartisan elections because the candidate does not appear on the ballot with a party label, party activity is so pervasive in states like Michigan, Ohio, and Idaho that in reality those states can be considered partisan election states.[9]

Valid criticisms exist for all the various systems of judicial selection. The problems with appointment of judges, for example, led to development of election of judges as a reform system. And, today partisanship remains in the appointment process. The most studied appointment process for judges is, of course, the system for selecting federal judges. In recent years, interest groups have become heavily involved in promoting their agendas by supporting or opposing the judicial nominees of Presidents. Prospective judges and their ideologies have been the targets for highly charged political battles during the Senate confirmation process. Ability and qualifications can easily be ignored in the partisan and ideological battles over membership on the bench. Nor does legislative selection of judges offer a more desirable alternative in judicial selection politics. When legislatures select judges, influential legislators are the ones who get selected. Thus, legislative selection—though far less studied than executive appointment of judges— appears to involve a highly political process as well.[10] The most heralded improvement in the selection of judges is, of course, merit selection of judges. However, problems even exist with this system. The commission decision-making process, for example, often results in highly partisan and political decision-making. And, membership on the commission can often involve intense campaigns among opposing segments of the bar. There are accounts of merit selection commissions stacking their nominations in ways that insure the governor will select certain persons as judges. There are also accounts of commissioners working in concert with the governor to insure the selection of the governor's friends.[11] Additionally, there is research suggesting that there are not many differences in the background characteristics of merit-selected compared to elected judges. There is also research suggesting that there is not much difference in the quality of merit-selected compared to elected judges.[12] Finally, although it is still rare, retention elections can be very expensive, highly partisan, political battles. One of the most expensive judicial elections in history was the 1986 California Supreme Court retention elections. In more recent times, a retention election in Tennessee saw heavy political party and interest group involvement. There was also unanticipated interest group activity in a

Nebraska retention election that defeated an incumbent state supreme court justice. Merit selection promises more than it delivers in removing partisanship and politics from the judicial selection process and in improving the quality of judges. However, reformers have been especially concerned in recent years with the problems of elected judges, particularly the problems of partisan election of judges.

The New Era in Judicial Selection

For many years, judicial elections tended to be low-key affairs. Candidates for judicial office would campaign largely on their qualifications and experience. They would seek to win bar polls and would use them in their campaigns if they were successful. They would visit newspaper editorial boards and try to obtain the newspaper's endorsement. And, they would give a few speeches before bar groups, civic groups, unions, and local medical societies. The campaigns of that era were inexpensive, low visibility, and low key.

Judicial campaigns, however, entered a new era in 1978 when deputy district attorneys in Los Angeles campaigned against judges they believed were soft on crime. Soon campaigns for the Texas Supreme Court heated up and became expensive pitched battles between plaintiffs' lawyers on one side and business interests and lawyers representing the defense in tort cases on the other. Then hard-fought judicial campaigns began to be waged in other states such as California, North Carolina, Ohio, and Alabama.[13]

In this new era of judicial elections, the hardest-fought races have tended to be in states with partisan elected judges. However, tough battles have also occurred in nonpartisan states and even in some retention elections. And, as judicial elections have heated up in the states, at the national level confirmation battles for federal judicial appointments have also become much tougher.

At the national level, in the aftermath of the judicial activism of the Supreme Court of the 1950s and 1960s and highly controversial decisions such as *Roe v. Wade*, the 1973 abortion decision, have meant that interest groups and the political parties now see federal judgeships as a way to have a vast influence on public policy in the nation. With an increasing number of organized interest groups and with parties more polarized ideologically than in earlier years, battles over judicial confirmations have simply become another arena for control over the public policy agenda. Additionally, the vast expansion of media coverage of national politics now discourages private political arrangements that once led to compromises and avoidance of open battles over judicial appointments. [14]

The battles over federal judgeships are exacerbated in an era of divided government where it is no longer rare for one party to control the Presidency and the other to control the Senate. Even where the same party controls both the Presidency and the Senate, the close party division in the modern Senate means that the President no longer has an easy time gaining confirmation for his nominees.

In the states, much of the battle over the selection of judges ultimately reflects battles over control of the state's tort law. As tort reform has become a major political issue in the states, the issue is being fought not only in state legislatures, but also in state supreme courts. Thus, many of the major battles in state judicial races in recent years can be seen as reflecting tort reform battles. The major players in these battles are often trial lawyers and unions who tend to promote the candidacies of plaintiff-friendly judges and business interests, lawyers who represent the defense side in civil cases, and professional groups such as physicians who tend to support the candidacies of judges favorable to the defense side in tort cases. In this battle for control of state courts, Democrats tend toward the plaintiff-friendly side and Republicans tend to favor the defense side in tort cases. As a result, the interest group battles over the courts also reflect battles between the political parties for control of the courts. [15]

There are, of course, issues other than tort law that can be important in state judicial races, although much of the money contributed in judicial races tends to be given by those with interests in the shape of tort law. One other issue that has had a major role in judicial elections is criminal justice. At times victims' rights groups have joined with prosecutors to support judicial candidates they believe will be tough on crime. In such situations, criminal defense lawyers often support the opposing candidate. [16] However, because of the popularity of judicial candidates being tough on crime, it is common for all candidates to claim some variation of crime toughness. It is also common, when crime is a major judicial campaign theme, for the campaign issue to be backed by interests concerned with tort reform. The reason is simply that a crime theme resonates better with voters than does a tort reform issue. Thus, groups with a tort law agenda may promote issues relating to crime because that issue may excite and mobilize their supporters in ways that tort reform does not.[17]

Regardless of the theme, however, the most notable development in judicial elections over the past twenty years has been harder fought battles over the selection of judges.

The Battles

In 1986, three California Supreme Court Justices were defeated in an expensive retention election battle. Their defeats are often ascribed to the activities of interest groups such as Crime Victims for Court Reform. However, there was also much partisan activity where Republican legislative incumbents campaigned against the three justices. Only some Democratic incumbents from safe districts supported them. The Republican governor announced his opposition to the Democratic chief justice because of her votes in capital cases that were unfavorable to the death penalty, and he publicly warned the two associate justices that he would also oppose their retention unless they voted to uphold more death penalty cases.[18] In 1996, Tennessee Supreme Court Justice Penny White was also defeated in a retention election because of opposition from leading Republicans and conservatives who opposed her views on the death penalty and because they thought her generally soft on crime.[19] In 1996 as well, Judge David Lanphier became the first Nebraska Supreme Court judge defeated in a retention election. His defeat was also the result of a series of decisions that redefined the state's second-degree murder statute that resulted in vacating several murder convictions. He also received well-funded opposition—amounting to about $200,000—because of his decisions unfavorable to term limits in Nebraska.[20]

In spite of such notable instances of defeats of incumbent judges in retention election, such defeats remain rare although well-funded interest group opposition can defeat judges in elections that are generally not known for large campaign expenditures.

The line between partisan and nonpartisan elections is sometimes blurry, but nonpartisan judicial elections have also seen an influx of money, interest group, and political party involvement. In Mississippi, for example, the Chamber of Commerce has spent enormous sums on television commercials that supported their pro-business candidates for the Mississippi Supreme Court.[21] In elections in the 1990s, the Mississippi Prosecutors' Association wielded great influence in the state's supreme court elections.[22] In Nevada, casino interests are heavily involved in the state's nonpartisan judicial elections.[23] And, political parties have become so active in Idaho's nonpartisan elections in recent years that some scholars now consider that state's supreme court elections to be partisan.[24] A recent race for chief justice of the Wisconsin Supreme Court came to $1.3 million. That was twice the spending record set two years previously and ten times the spending of a campaign twenty years earlier.[25] In Minnesota, although the U.S. Supreme Court chose not to rule on that particular issue in the case, the state's Republican Party sought the right to endorse candidates for judicial office in that state's nonpartisan elections.[26]

Clearly, nonpartisan judicial elections have seen a massive upswing in politics, parties, interest groups, and campaign costs in recent years. Nevertheless, the real increase in the political intensity of judicial campaigns has come in partisan judicial elections. And, it is in reference to partisan judicial elections where much of the focus of judicial reform efforts has occurred.

One of the reasons that partisan judicial elections have been the most intensely contested is that many partisan election states are in the South. As the South has moved from one-party Democratic to the Republican Party, judgeships in those states have become hard fought.[27] One of the first states where major political battles broke out in supreme court elections was Texas. In the 1980s, huge sums were spent in battles between Democratic and Republican candidates that also often reflected underlying battles between plaintiff-oriented Democratic candidates and business-oriented Republican candidates. In the Texas Supreme Court elections in 1988, for example, six seats on the nine-justice court were up for election. Altogether the twelve major candidates for those seats raised over $10 million and another $1.4 million was raised by an independent political action committee primarily for television commercials and get-out-the-vote campaigns. It was a major battle, not only between Democrats and Republicans, but between candidates backed by trial lawyers versus candidates heavily backed by the business community and by medical doctors seeking a court less supportive of medical malpractice claims. While three Democrats and three Republicans were elected to the Court, only one of the strongly pro-plaintiff candidates was elected to the Court. It was the beginning of the end of the pro-plaintiff Texas Supreme Court of the 1980s and the beginning point for Republican domination of the Court. By the mid-1990s, Republicans gained complete control of the Court. That was primarily due to a rapid switch in Texas politics. Traditionally a Southern state, Texas elected Democratic judges for a century, but then the state—like many other Southern states—began to move into the Republican column. During the time of the Republican Party's emergence, judicial elections were expensive and hotly contested. However, as Texas became a one-party Republican state, judicial elections became less contested and less expensive, although battles in the Republican primary have now increased.[28]

Partisan elections are also more hotly contested for other reasons. In truly nonpartisan states, judges are somewhat removed from the jockeying for power between the political parties. However, in partisan states, judgeships are part of the prizes of successful election campaigns—prizes of political conflict to be battled over between the competing parties. Additionally, since judges run with party labels, judicial candidates in partisan states are affected more by votes for or against candidates at the top of the ticket. A popular candidate for President, or Senator, or Governor can have political coat-tails for less visible candidates, such as judicial candidates whose offices are further down on the ballot. As a result, in some partisan judicial elections, there have been "party sweeps" where popular top-of-the-ticket candidates have swept judges of the opposing party out of office and elected judges of the popular candidate's party for no other reason than that the judges shared the popular candidate's party affiliation.[29] One study of state judicial selection provides important data on just how hotly contested partisan elections have become in comparison to other judicial selection systems. As Table 2 points out, Melinda Gann Hall found that partisan election systems led not only to far more judicial election contests than other systems for electing judges, she also found that incumbent judges in partisan election states were far more likely to be defeated.[30]

Indeed, one of the greatest criticisms of partisan elections is that voters tend to know little about judicial candidates, and so they vote on the basis of party affiliation, rather than for the candidate who is most experienced, most qualified, or most able to be a judge.[31] And, since partisan judicial elections tend to be the most contested elections, more money tends to be contributed in these judicial elections than in other forms of judicial elections. That money tends to come from lawyers, litigants, and interest groups concerned with the outcome of litigation. The result is a fear that there is too much dependency between judges and those with an interest in outcomes of cases.[32] And some of that money is not subject to disclosure rules. In an earlier, less-competitive era in judicial politics, judicial candidates raised little money. Now, however, judicial candidates in some states can have campaigns involving hundreds of thousands or even millions of dollars. If the money is given to the judicial candidate's campaign fund, at least the donors are reported so that it is possible to learn who is supporting judicial candidates and the amount of that support. In just the past few years, however, it has become popular in some states for interest groups to mount campaigns that are independent of the judicial candidate's campaign. These independent campaigns are often called "issue advocacy" efforts or "educational campaigns." However, the important aspect of these campaigns is that they are not generally subject to state disclosure laws. Thus, it is difficult (and often impossible) to identify the source and amounts of support for judicial candidates. In addition to avoiding campaign disclosure laws, these independent campaigns are free from the ethical constraints imposed by the Canons of Judicial Conduct on judicial candidates' campaigns. As a result, for example, statements about pending or likely future cases may be made in independent campaign ads that would be ethically improper if made in a candidate-funded campaign ad.[33]

Table 2 Percentage of State Supreme Court Incumbents Challenged and Defeated by Type of Election from 1980–1994			
	Retention Election	Nonpartisan Election	Partisan Election
% Challenged	NA	44.2	61.1
% Defeated	1.7	8.6	18.8
Source: Melinda Gann Hall, State Supreme Courts in American Democracy: Probing the Myths of Judicial Reform, 95 *American Political Science Review* 317, 319 (2001).			

One of the criticisms of judicial elections has been that voters are often unaware of judicial candidates' views. In part, that lack of knowledge is because most judicial races are relatively low visibility when compared to other offices. Another reason for that lack of voter knowledge is because judicial candidates have been restricted in what they may say in a campaign. In order to maintain judicial objectivity, states have limited judicial candidate speech in various ways through codes of judicial conduct. These restrictions on judicial candidate speech have led to a series of recent court cases which have great potential to increase the level of controversy in judicial campaigns.

The Courts and the Codes

Several state codes of judicial conduct have included a ban on judicial candidates' announcing views on controversial issues. In 1996, Gregory Wersal ran for associate justice of the Minnesota Supreme Court. In the course of his campaign, he distributed literature criticizing several Minnesota Supreme Court decisions relating to crime, welfare, and abortion. A complaint against Wersal challenging the propriety of this literature was filed with the Office of Lawyers Professional Responsibility, the agency which investigates and prosecutes ethical violations of lawyer candidates for judicial office. The complaint was dismissed with regard to the charges that his campaign materials violated the announce clause, and the agency expressed doubt whether the clause could constitutionally be enforced. However, fearing that further ethical complaints would jeopardize his ability to practice law, Wersal withdrew from the election. In 1998, Wersal again sought the same office. Early in that race, he sought an opinion from the agency with regard to whether it planned to enforce the announce clause, and the agency only offered an equivocal response.

Shortly thereafter, Wersal filed a lawsuit in Federal District Court seeking a declaration that the announce clause violates the First Amendment and an injunction against its enforcement. Wersal alleged that he was forced to refrain from announcing his views on disputed issues during the 1998 campaign to the point where he declined response to questions put to him by the press and public out of concern that he might run afoul of the announce clause. Other plaintiffs in the suit, including the Minnesota Republican Party, alleged that, because the clause kept Wersal from announcing his views, they were unable to learn those views and support or oppose his candidacy accordingly. Ultimately, the case was heard by the U.S. Supreme Court, which struck down the announce clause as an unconstitutional restriction on freedom of speech. Justice Scalia, writing for the Court, did not believe the announce clause was narrowly tailored or that it served a compelling governmental interest.

On the one hand, elimination of that ban allows voters to learn more about judicial candidates' views. However, on the other hand, judicial candidates now have greater ability to curry the favor of voters and interest groups by announcing views in campaigns that practically amount to pre-judging cases. Some advocates of judicial reform believe that this Court decision, *Republican Party of Minnesota v. White* (2002),[34] will exacerbate the problems with judicial campaigns, making them even nastier contests with candidates vying for interest group support by announcing their views in future cases. Such concerns have led a reform group, the Constitution Project, to work with several bar and civic groups in an effort to maintain quality control over judicial candidates by asking candidates to sign commitments to maintain decorum in their campaigns.[35]

Contrary to the pattern during much of the 20th century, modern judicial campaigns now allow much more open discussion of judicial candidates' views though independent campaign advertisements or through judicial campaign speech in the wake of *Republican Party of Minnesota v. White.*

Republican Party of Minnesota v. White has not been the only judicial attack on codes restricting judicial campaign speech. Several courts have held that prohibitions on misleading statements in the codes violate the First Amendment. In a Michigan case, for example, the state's Judicial Tenure Commission held that a judicial candidate's strategy had been to "wage a 'brass knuckles' campaign" to retain judicial office and that the candidate had even violated a revised canon in the Code of Judicial Conduct that held that a judicial candidate "should not knowingly, or with reckless disregard, use or participate in the use of any form of public communication that is false." That provision of the code had been revised due to First Amendment considerations from a prohibition against "false, fraudulent, deceptive, and misleading" statements. In a further modification of the canon, the Michigan Supreme Court held that judicial campaign speech "that can be reasonably interpreted as communicating hyperbole, epithet, or parody is protected" under the canon. It further held that expressions of opinion are protected under the canons "as long as it does not contain probably false factual connotations." If judicial campaign speech does set forth objectively factual matters, the communication is to be analyzed to determine if the statements are literally true. Literal truth means there is no violation of the canon. On the other hand, even if there is an untrue statement, that is insufficient to show a violation of the canon because the communication as a whole must be examined to see if "the substance, the gist, the sting" of the communication is true in spite of the false statement. If it is then determined that there has indeed been a false public communication, there must then be an inquiry as to whether the communication was knowingly made or made with reckless disregard of the truth.[36] To put the matter in less legalistic terms, the Michigan Supreme Court effectively eviscerated the canon against "false, fraudulent, deceptive, and misleading" statements and has opened judicial campaigns to a level of controversy approaching campaigns for the political branches of government.

A federal court of appeals decision has recently stuck down a Georgia canon that is virtually identical to the canon the Michigan Supreme Court declared unconstitutional. In 1998, George Weaver ran for election to the Georgia Supreme Court and was defeated by the incumbent. During his campaign, he distributed a brochure that characterized his opponent as wishing to "require the State to license same-sex marriages." He also claimed his opponent "has referred to traditional moral standards as 'pathetic and disgraceful.'" He also claimed his opponent had referred to the electric chair as 'silly' and the words "THE DEATH PENALTY" were published in an adjacent column. The Special Committee on Judicial Election Campaign Intervention found this brochure to be "false, misleading, and deceptive" in violation of Georgia's Code of Judicial Conduct. Weaver then revised his brochure although similar charges about his opponent's views were made. Weaver and his campaign committee then aired a television advertisement that included the following:

> (1) The narrator states: 'What does Justice Sears stand for? Same sex marriage.' This statement is made while a graphic shows: 'Same Sex Marriage.'
> (2) The narrator states: 'She's questioned the constitutionality of laws prohibiting sex with children under fourteen.' This statement is made while a graphic shows: 'Questioned Laws Protecting Our Children.'
> (3) The narrator states: 'And she called the electric chair silly.' This statement is made while a graphic shows: 'Called Electric Chair Silly.'

The Special Committee concluded that the television advertisement had violated its previous cease and desist order regarding the first brochure. It issued a public statement to the media that stated that Weaver had "intentionally and blatantly" violated the original cease and desist request and deliberately engaged in "unethical, unfair, false and intentionally deceptive" campaign practices. In the court challenge to the Special Committee's actions, the federal court of appeals held that while Georgia had a compelling interest in "preserving the integrity, impartiality, and independence of the judiciary" and "ensuring the integrity of the electoral process and protecting voters from confusion and undue influence," the canon that Weaver had violated was not narrowly tailored. Restrictions on the speech of judicial candidates, the court said, must be limited to false statements that are made with actual knowledge of falsity or with reckless disregard as to whether the statement is false. A restriction that is on negligently made false statements would not meet the narrowly tailored test and there would be a violation of the First Amendment. Still another canon provision prohibited judicial candidates from personally soliciting campaign contributions and personally soliciting publicly stated support, although it did allow the candidate's election committee to engage in such activities. The court held that ban on personal solicitation by judicial candidates chilled a candidate's speech while "hardly advancing the state's interest in judicial impartiality at all." Interestingly the court emphasized their view that judicial campaigns were akin to other political campaigns. "We agree," wrote the court, "that the distinction between judicial elections and other types of elections has been greatly exaggerated, and we do not believe that the distinction, if there truly is one, justifies greater restrictions on speech during judicial campaigns than during other types of campaigns."[37]

Although a federal court of appeals has recently overturned the federal district court decision on grounds that the court should have abstained from action pending state actions,[38] the federal district court decision had effectively blocked enforcement of New York's rules that regulate the off-the-bench conduct of the state's judges. What makes the case of continuing importance is that it probably is not yet concluded, and there is considerable concern that the district court decision portends the demise of conduct rules regarding judicial off-the-bench activities. Judge Thomas Spargo drew national attention when he joined a demonstration by Republicans in Florida during the contested 2000 presidential election. He was also charged with giving a keynote speech at an upstate Conservative Party dinner and with courting voters with coupons for free doughnuts, coffee, and gasoline when he ran for a town court justice in 1999. The federal judge held that a conduct code that prohibited an elected judge or judicial candidate from participating in politics was "not narrowly tailored to serve a state's interest in an independent judiciary." And, added the federal judge, provisions of the code such as the one requiring judges to "uphold the integrity and independence of the judiciary" were too vague to be meaningful. The federal judge wrote, "How would anyone know that handing out donuts would constitute a failure to uphold the integrity and independence of the judiciary while serving cake would not?"[39] Decisions such as this one will allow judges greater involvement in the political process than is already the case in elective judicial systems.

Systemic Change or Incremental Change

In spite of the problems with partisan (and sometimes nonpartisan) judicial elections, they have remained a major system of judicial selection. For the initial terms of appellate judges, 40% face partisan elections and 13% face nonpartisan elections. For the initial terms of trial judges, 43% face partisan elections and 33% face nonpartisan elections.[40] One reason is that major political changes are almost always difficult. The political parties, for example, at least as long as they are successful in a state, tend to support partisan election of judges. And, key interest groups that are successful in electing their candidates in a state will tend to continue supporting partisan election of judges. Since incumbent judges generally gained their offices through partisan politics, they will tend to support the existing system. Thus, groups that benefit from partisan elections will continue to support it. However, there is another reason for the persistence of partisan election of judges. In the absence of other information about the attitudes and values of judicial candidates, voters can use the candidate's party affiliation as a crude cue to the judges' ideology—their liberalism or conservatism—such that voters may reasonably infer that Democratic judicial candidates tend to be more "liberal" than are Republican judicial candidates. Of course, while that is not the case in every judicial election, it is enough of a pattern that voters, absent other information, can and do rely on party labels.

One of the criticisms of nonpartisan elections, in fact, is that voters have no cue at all to ideology and so will vote without knowledge of a candidate—being forced to rely even more than voters in partisan elections on things like the attractiveness of candidates' names. Possibly freer judicial campaign speech will reduce the reliance on such cues to candidates' views as party affiliation, but freer candidate speech also adds to the danger of judicial candidates behaving more like legislators in stating their policy preferences and soliciting public support.

Until recently, judicial reformers tended to promote merit selection of judges as the best system of selection, and in the process they downplayed the flaws of that system. Partisan election was often seen by reformers as the least desirable system, ignoring research that showed notable similarities between merit-selected judges and partisan elected judges.[41] And, the usefulness of the party cue to voters was often overlooked if merit selection proved impossible in a state, but if nonpartisan election seemed viable. Recently, however, some advocates of judicial reform have recognized that judicial elections—even partisan judicial elections—are here to stay. That recognition has led some judicial reformers to adopt a new reform strategy. They have argued that the appropriate reform strategy is not to move toward merit selection but to move toward more incremental judicial reforms that are more achievable. Many of the recommendations of the National Summit on Improving Judicial Selection,[42] for example, propose reforms that will improve judicial selection in a more incremental fashion than major changes in the system of selection. Terms of judges might be lengthened, for example. Simply lengthening terms would reduce the number of judicial elections, thus reducing the role of money, parties and interest groups in judicial campaigns. Similarly, judges appointed to fill a vacancy on the bench commonly can only serve briefly before they then must run for office. Often they may only run for the time left in the unexpired term to which they have been appointed. By simply lengthening the time that judges appointed to mid-term vacancies served before an election and by allowing them to serve a full term before a second election, one could reduce the number of elections and therefore the number of battles for control of a court. Similarly, the role of money in judicial races could be better managed. There might be public funding of judicial campaigns, rapid filing and disclosure of campaign contributions perhaps through the Internet, and reasonable limitations on campaign contributions to judicial candidates. Voters may be made more aware of judicial candidates by state provision of voter information pamphlets, and the cost of these pamphlets could be greatly reduced by free mailing privileges being provided for distribution of the pamphlets. And, judicial campaign conduct could be monitored by civic organizations and the bar, which would try to discourage inappropriate campaign tactics and advertisements.

Conclusion

The long-standing goal of judicial reformers has been to improve the selection of judges. For much of the twentieth century reformers have concentrated on changing the system of selection away from elective—and especially partisan elective—systems. Achieving that goal of systemic change has been a slow one. In part, success has not been achieved because change in the system of judicial selection has been opposed by entrenched interests. In part, the promise of merit selection in improving the judiciary has exceeded its performance. Increasingly, many reformers view the goal of merit selection as being one that is unrealistic in many states. As a result, some advocates of judicial reform are working for more incremental reforms that maintain elective systems but improve judicial selection within the existing system of selection.

Both the systemic reformers and the incremental reformers are both working to improve judicial selection at a time when judicial selection is undergoing major changes at both the state and national levels. Federal judicial confirmations are becoming more politicized. State judicial elections are increasingly becoming hard fought, expensive battles between competing parties and interest groups. At the same time, the traditional restrictions on judicial campaign behavior are rapidly being eroded. It is a period of rapid changes in judicial selection politics. It is also a period where thoughtful reforms are clearly needed.

Notes

[1] Anthony Champagne & Judith Haydel, Introduction in Champagne & Haydel, eds., *Judicial Reform in the States* 2–4 (1993).

[2] Id., 3–4

[3] American Judicature Society, *Judicial Selection in the States: Appellate and General Jurisdiction Courts* (2004), www.ajs.org/js/JudicialSelectionCharts.pdf. The American Judicature Society also classifies California as a gubernatorial appointment state. This is correct, although California has a unique commission with the power to veto gubernatorial appointments.

[4] Larry C. Berkson, updated by Seth Anderson, *Judicial Selection in the United States: A Special Report*, www.ajs.org/js/berkson.pdf.

[5] Id.

[6] Id.

[7] Id.

[8] American Judicature Society, *supra* note 3.

[9] Roy Schotland wrote: While the ballots in Michigan and Ohio carry no party labels for judicial candidates, nominations in those states are made in totally partisan ways (party conventions in Michigan, party primaries in Ohio), and candidates campaign as partisans. Also, in Idaho since 1998, the official and strong tradition of nonpartisan judicial races (going back to 1932) has eroded. See Roy Schotland, "To the Endangered Species List, Add: Nonpartisan Judicial Elections," 39 *Williamette Law Review* 1397, note 2 (2003)

[10] *For example, see* John V. Crangle, *Judicial Reform*, www.scvotersforcleanelections.com/point/9507/s04.html.

[11] The best treatment of the problems associated with merit selection remains Richard A. Watson & Rondal G. Downing, *The Politics of the Bench and the Bar: Judicial Selection Under the Missouri Nonpartisan Court Plan* (1969).

[12] This research is discussed in Daniel W. Shuman & Anthony Champagne, Removing the People from the Legal Process: The Rhetoric and Research on Judicial Selection and Juries, 3 *Psychology, Public Policy, and Law* 242, 247–248 (1997).

[13] Anthony Champagne, Interest Groups and Judicial Elections, 34 *Loyola of Los Angeles Law Review* 1391, 1394–1396 (2001).

[14] A superb treatment of the judicial selection process at the national level is Mark Silverstein, *Judicious Choices: The New Politics of Supreme Court Confirmations* (1994).

[15] Anthony Champagne, Political Parties and Judicial Elections, 34 *Loyola of Los Angeles Law Review* 1411, 1423–1425 (2001).

[16] Champagne, *supra* note 13, 1393–1394, 1399–1401.

[17] Interestingly, a number of television ads in the 2000 state supreme court elections were sponsored by the U.S. Chamber of Commerce and yet stressed crime control themes. See Anthony Champagne, Television Ads in Judicial Campaigns, 35 *Indiana Law Review* 669, 688–689 (2002).

[18] Champagne, *supra* note 15, 1420.

[19] Id., 1420–1421.

[20] Traciel V. Reid, The Politicization of Judicial Retention Elections: The Defeat of Justices Lanphier and White, in *Research in Judicial Selection* 1999 (2000).

[21] Roy Schotland, Financing Judicial Election 2000: Change and Challenges, 2001 *Law Review Michigan State University-Detroit College of Law* 849, 877 (2001).

[22] Champagne, *supra* note 13, 1399.

[23] Id., 1401–1402.

[24] Schotland, *supra* note 9.

[25] Champagne, *supra* note 13, 1403.

[26] Indeed, that is the reason the Republican Party of Minnesota is a party to the case. The Republican Party opposed the ban on judicial candidates appearing at party functions and seeking party endorsements. See Schotland, *supra* note 9, 1415.

[27] Champagne, *supra* note 15, 1415–1416.

[28] Anthony Champagne & Kyle Cheek, The Cycle of Judicial Elections: Texas as a Case Study, 29 *Fordham Urban Law Journal* 907, 909–910, 937 (2002).

[29] Id., 919.

[30] Melinda Gann Hall, State Supreme Courts in American Democracy: Probing the Myths of Judicial Reform, 95 *American Political Science Review* 317, 319 (2001).

[31] Champagne, *supra* note 28, 919–920.

[32] Id., 933.

[33] Deborah Goldberg & Mark Kozlowski, Constitutional Issues in Disclosure of Interest Group Activities, 35 *Indiana Law Review* 755 (2002).

[34] 536 U.S. 765 (2002)

[35] "The Higher Ground: Standards of Conduct for Judicial Candidates" is available on The Constitution Project's website, www.constitutionproject.org.

[36] The discussion of this case is taken from, *In re Chmura*, 464 Mich. 58 (2001), 626 N.W.2d 876 (2001).

[37] This discussion is from *Weaver v. Bonner*, 309 F3d 1312 (C.A. 11 (Ga.) 2002).

[38] *Spargo v. New York State Commission on Judicial Conduct*, 351 F.3d 65 (C.A. 2 (N.Y.) 2003).

[39] This discussion is from *Spargo v. New York State Commission on Judicial Conduct*, 244 F. Supp. 2d 72 (N.D. N.Y., 2003).

[40] These data are from Roy Schotland, Introduction: Personal Views, 34 *Loyola of Los Angeles Law Review* 1361, 1365 (2001).

[41] *For example*, Shuman & Champagne, *supra* note 12.

[42] National Summit on Improving Judicial Selection, *Call to Action*, Expanded Edition with Commentary by David B. Rottman, *et al* (2002).

Chapter III

Plaintiff-Defense Wars:
Money Enters the Picture

Introduction

Prior to 1980, judicial races in Texas and elsewhere were sleepy affairs that garnered little attention and even less excitement. That changed when special interests began to infuse judicial campaigns with large contributions in an attempt to promote the election chances of candidates with judicial philosophies favorable to those interests. On a larger scale, interest groups viewed their involvement in judicial elections as a way to sway the composition of state judiciaries and, in turn, achieve a long-term effect on the shape of the law. These efforts have been especially pronounced in appellate court races where decisions can have a more significant and lasting impact on the overall tenor of the law. Special interests in Texas, especially the plaintiffs' bar, were the first to gamble on this strategy of influencing the makeup of a state's bench. The end result, however, has been more than just a shifting composition on Texas' highest courts as the locus of power has shifted among competing interest groups. Rather, the intense involvement of interest groups in Texas judicial races has ushered in a new era of judicial politics in which the integrity of elected courts has come under greater criticism than ever before.

As seen in Table 1, the amount of money that has been infused into judicial campaigns in Texas has been substantial. Since 1980, the first year in which special interests waged a wholesale effort to influence judicial election outcomes in Texas, million-dollar campaigns have become commonplace. In the early 1980s, special interest funding initially came from trial lawyers. As trial lawyer candidates became more successful, defense interests began to counter by backing their own preferred candidates. By 1988, an exceptional year in which six Texas Supreme Court seats were up for election, special interest battles for the court had become so intense that record amounts of money were poured into those elections. Since 1988, as Texas has become a one-party Republican state, the battles between interest groups have waned.

Table 1		
Average Contributions to Texas Supreme Court Candidates[a]		
Year	Average for All Candidates[b]	Average for Winning Candidates[b]
1980	$155,033 / ($360,681)	$298,167 / ($693,679)
1982[c]	$173,174 / ($332,391)	$332,998 / ($639,158)
1984[c]	$967,405 / ($1,718,354)	$1,922,183 / ($3,414,280)
1986	$519,309 / ($857,618)	$1,024,817 / ($1,692,444)
1988	$859,413 / ($1,344,458)	$842,148 / ($1,317,448)
1990	$970,154 / ($1,378,319)	$1,544,939 / ($2,194,929)
1992	$1,096,001 / ($1,436,468)	$1,096,687 / ($1,437,367)
1994	$1,499,577 / ($1,856,521)	$1,627,285 / ($2,014,628)
1996	$656,190 / ($769,238)	$1,277,127 / ($1,497,150)
1998	$521,519 / ($584,127)	$829,794 / ($929,410)
2000	NA[d]	$584,719[e] / ($626,238)
2002[f]	$425,474 / ($434,844)	$568,430 / ($580,948)

[a] Averages are reported for candidates from contested races featuring both a Republican and Democratic candidate.

[b] Averages reported without parentheses are for nominal dollar amounts received while those in parentheses are in 2003 dollars. The inflation calculator is at http:cgi.money.cnn.com.

[c] The 1982 and 1984 elections each featured only 1 contested race with both a Democratic and Republican candidate.

[d] No Democrats ran in the three Supreme Court elections in 2000.

[e] Average campaign contributions for the three victorious Republicans; none with a Democratic opponent

[f] Chief Justice Tom Phillips ran for re-election and refused to accept any campaign contributions beyond his cash on hand, which amounted to $19,433. His Democratic opponent, however, raised almost no funds—$12,815. Phillips was the victor in this race, which lowers the average contributions for this year. Three of the other successful Republican candidates raised between $910,837 and $953,573. The fifth successful Republican candidate, however, raised only $15,828.

Still, it is not uncommon for large sums to be contributed to the campaigns of candidates who are virtual shoo-ins to win their elections. How then, did money become so important in Texas judicial races? Who are the interests that have supported these million-dollar campaigns? Why does big money still appear in general election contests whose outcome is a foregone conclusion? What is the future of money in judicial races?

Plaintiff-Defense Wars and Big Money

Like other states that elect judges, Texas judicial elections were not always contested.[1] Texas justices traditionally were, like the majority of elected officials in the state, conservative Democrats. One journalist well described the pre-1978 Court:

> ...justices' names seldom appeared in the press and were known only to the legal community. Most justices had been judges in the lower courts; a few had served in the Legislature. At election time, sitting justices almost never drew opposition. Some justices resigned before the end of their terms, enabling their replacements to be named by the governor and to run as incumbents. In the event that an open seat was actually contested, the decisive factor in the race was the State Bar poll, which was the key to newspaper endorsements and the support of courthouse politicians. In effect, the legal and political establishment begat generations of justices who reflected the assumption of their progenitors that preservation of a "good bidness climate" is the highest aim of government. Part of that climate was a legal system in which oil companies, hospitals, insurers, and other enterprises didn't have to live in constant fear of lawsuits.[2]

The sleepy, low-key affairs that were judicial elections and that resulted in the election of pro-civil defense Democratic judges did not begin to change until the late 1970s. At that time, a remarkable event in the history of the Texas judiciary occurred.

An unknown lawyer named Don Yarbrough ran for the Texas Supreme Court and won. Not only was he an unknown, but he had numerous ethical complaints that had been filed against him, and he ran against a highly respected incumbent who had won the State Bar poll by a 90 percent margin. Yarbrough served only a few months before criminal charges and the threat of legislative removal led to his resignation. Why did he win the election? At the time, Yarbrough was a well-known political name in Texas, and voters probably confused him with either the long-time U.S. senator, Ralph Yarborough, or with Don Yarborough who had twice run for governor.[3] But most importantly, the election of Don Yarbrough showed that literally anyone could get elected to the Texas Supreme Court, at least if they had name identification.

In 1978, a little-known plaintiffs' lawyer, Robert Campbell, from Waco made his try for the Texas Supreme Court, running against an incumbent judge. Campbell was also a great name with which to run for the Court. The previous fall, University of Texas running back Earl Campbell had won the Heisman Trophy.[4]

Having a great name could allow a judicial candidate to break the tradition of election of justices who reflected the old tradition of a pro-civil defense philosophy and low-key election campaigns. But name identification can come about naturally through the Yarbrough or Campbell name, or it can be created through significant campaign expenditures. And plaintiffs' lawyers began pouring significant amounts of money in Texas Supreme Court campaigns to elect justices with pro-plaintiff philosophies. In 1982, for example, a good election year for Democrats since the popular Democratic Senator Lloyd Bentsen headed the ticket, one highly successful plaintiffs' lawyer in San Antonio and one of his wealthiest and most litigious clients, Clinton Manges, poured $350,000 into three Supreme Court races and two of their candidates were elected.[5]

By 1983, justices who had significant backing from the plaintiffs' bar had gained a majority on the Texas Supreme Court.[6] And, with the election of a pro-plaintiffs' court came the movement of Texas tort law in a plaintiffs' direction. But the creation of a plaintiffs' court was not done without damage to the reputation of the Court. A jury had found that Clinton Manges had violated his obligations to the Guerra family while acting as executive manager of mineral leases on 70,000 acres and had awarded the Guerras $382,000 in actual damages and $500,000 in exemplary damages, and Manges was removed as executive manager. The verdict was upheld on appeal to the intermediate appellate court, and appeal was taken to the Supreme Court of Texas. With the Supreme Court appeal, Manges hired Pat Maloney, Sr. as his attorney.

There the case was assigned to Justice C.L. Ray, the recipient of large sums in campaign contributions from Manges and Maloney. Ray initially proposed an opinion supporting Manges. And, when that opinion was rejected by the Court, Ray tried again. In a June conference, one of the justices, who had been sued by Manges over a campaign statement the justice had made, recused himself. With eight justices participating, one of the justices, Ted Z. Robertson, who had received $100,000 in campaign money from Manges and Maloney, recused himself. With that recusal, the vote was 4–3 for Manges and for reversal of the lower court. The Chief Justice ruled that five votes were required for reversal, and so the Court of Appeals was affirmed. Justice Robertson immediately changed his recusal to a vote in favor of reversal.[7] The attorney for the Guerras filed a motion for a rehearing and asked that Justices Kilgarlin and Robertson and, later, Justice Ray recuse themselves.[8] It was the beginning of a major Supreme Court scandal, but only the beginning.

In 1984, Justice Ray held a fund-raiser where he told a man who was a litigant before the court that his case was a tough one and that if he did not win that case, he would win the next. Justice Ray then discussed the court's deliberations and told the litigant he would see what could be done back in Austin. Then in 1985 Justice Ray attempted to transfer two cases in one court of appeals to another court of appeals at the request of Pat Maloney, Sr. Those and other matters led to a scandal that ultimately led to a public reprimand against Justice Ray[9] and a public admonition against another justice, William Kilgarlin.[10] Nor did challenges to the prestige and integrity of the court cease. Around the time that the court refused to review an $11 billion judgement against Texaco, large campaign contributions flowed into the court's campaign coffers from both Texaco lawyers and particularly from the plaintiff and the plaintiffs' attorneys.[11]

Confronted with a crisis on the Court, Chief Justice John Hill, proposed merit selection of judges in Texas in 1986 and offered himself as the leader of a movement for judicial reform. That created a rebellion against Hill's leadership on the Court, and there was unprecedented intra-court conflict.[12] Fifteen months after proposing merit selection, Hill resigned from the court after serving only half of his six-year term. His replacement, appointed by a Republican governor, was Tom Phillips, a Houston trial judge and a Republican. And when Hill used Phillips' swearing-in ceremony to plead for merit selection of judges, Justice Robert Campbell resigned so that, claimed Campbell, he could campaign against Hill's reforms.[13]

The result of the scandal and Hill's reform movement was not only unprecedented conflict within the Texas Supreme Court but also an opening wedge for Republican penetration of the court. And, by 1988, it was time for an effective counter-attack by the civil defense forces. With the 1988 elections, two-thirds of the Court was up for grabs—the three scheduled seats and three other seats caused by mid-term vacancies. Associate Justice Ted Z. Robertson chose to run against Phillips for the Chief Justice's position. Justice Kilgarlin, admonished by the State Commission on Judicial Conduct, was challenged by Republican Nathan Hecht. Democratic incumbent Raul Gonzalez was challenged by Republican Charles Ben

Howell. New appointee to the Court, Republican Barbara Culver, was challenged by Democrat Jack Hightower; new appointee Republican Eugene Cook was challenged by Democrat Karl Bayer and there was a battle over an open seat between Democrat Lloyd Doggett and Republican Paul Murphy. It was the political equivalent of war between plaintiffs' and civil defense interests.[14]

The twelve major candidates for the Texas Supreme Court raised $10,092,955. A political action committee primarily funded by trial lawyers raised another $1.4 million for independent expenditures for television commercials and for get-out-the-vote campaigns. Several, though not all of the races, clearly divided between plaintiffs' lawyer-funded candidates and candidates funded by civil defense interests. That was especially true of the race for Chief Justice between Phillips and Robertson in which Phillips raised slightly over $2 million and Robertson raised nearly $1.9 million. Other heavily funded races involving clear differences between plaintiff and civil defense-backed candidates included the Kilgarlin-Hecht race where Kilgarlin raised over $2 million and Hecht raised about $650,000 and the Doggett-Murphy race, where Doggett raised about $660,000 to Murphy's $438,000.[15]

The Texas Medical Association was heavily involved in that year's Supreme Court elections, having been angered by the recent pro-plaintiff tinge of the Court's decisions. Its political action committee gave over $181,000 in direct contributions and encouraged individual doctors to give at least $250,000 more.[16]

One great strength of the Republican candidates was that they could campaign against the plaintiff-backed candidates on the grounds that they were reformers who wished to bring integrity back to the Court. Indeed, Chief Justice Phillips headed a bipartisan "Clean Slate" of candidates who were opposed to the incumbent Democrats who were backed by the trial lawyers.[17]

It was the reform message coupled with the financial backing from civil defense interests and the increasing strength of the Republican Party that led to the defeat of all the plaintiff-backed incumbents. The only strongly pro-plaintiff justice elected was Lloyd Doggett, a non-incumbent who had run for an open seat. Democrat Raul Gonzalez, backed by civil defense interests against a largely unfunded Republican, won as did Hightower, a moderate Democrat who defeated an incumbent Republican who had angered the

Medical Association by opposing medical malpractice caps. Republicans Phillips, Hecht and Cook won with Phillips and Hecht defeating the most heavily funded plaintiff-backed Democrats. The result was the beginning of Republican domination of the Court.[18] And, civil defense interests learned that in head-on battles with heavily funded plaintiff-backed candidates such as Kilgarlin and Robertson, the civil defense candidates could win. The election of 1988 was also the beginning of the end of the pro-plaintiff court of the 1980s.

Perhaps the last gasp of the plaintiff-civil defense wars was in 1994 when pro-civil defense Democratic justice Raul Gonzalez was up for reelection. If a trial lawyer-backed Democrat could not beat a civil defense-backed Republican, then the venue for battle needed to change, and it did in the Gonzalez case. Gonzalez was challenged in the Democratic primary by trial lawyer and trial lawyer-financed Rene Haas in one of the most vicious judicial campaigns in Texas history. It was clearly an effort by trial lawyers to defeat a conservative Democrat who was strongly supportive of civil defense interests.[19] That primary campaign turned into one of the most expensive judicial races in history. Total candidate expenditures in that race totaled $4,490,000 in a battle that went in Gonzalez's favor.[20] And, when Gonzalez won the run-off primary against Haas, the Republican candidate conveniently withdrew from the race, in effect giving the office to Gonzalez.

In the aftermath of the Gonzalez-Haas race, serious challenges for the Texas Supreme Court were no longer mounted by trial lawyers who seemed to deem it fruitless to expend resources for those offices. In some cases, trial-lawyer money moved to other courts, such as some courts of appeals where it seems plaintiff-backed candidates had a chance, but the big battles within the bar over the Texas Supreme Court were at an end.[21]

The great plaintiff-defense battles on the Texas Supreme Court are not, however, unique to Texas judicial elections. Similar battles have occurred in other states, such as Alabama[22] and Ohio.[23] Indeed, where there are judicial elections, some of the most common interests battling for control of the court are the plaintiff-defense interests.

Who Gives, Who Gets, and in What Amounts?

The Texas Research League produced an analysis of the size and number of campaign contributions in contested appellate races in 1980, 1982, 1984, and 1986, which found a very small number of very large contributors to

these races and a relatively small base of contributors overall (Table 2). Patti
Kilday in a major *Dallas Times Herald* story examined the contributions of
all justices who were sitting on the Court in 1987. The contributions were
examined from 1980 or from the first post-1980 election campaign of the
justices. Kilday found that eight Texas law firms or lawyers contributed
17.7% of those funds. All the firms except for one were plaintiffs' firms.
Three of the eight firms contributed over $200,000 each.[24]

Table 2 Number of Contributions for Texas Contested Appellate[a] Court Races.				
Size of contribution	No. in 1980	No. in 1982	No. in 1984	No. in 1986
< $500	2,519	3,039	3,319	6,054
$500–< $5,000	707	512	773	1,605
$5,000–> $5,000	37	23	26	169
Source: Texas Research League [a] Supreme Court, Court of Criminal Appeals, and Courts of Appeals.				

It is virtually impossible to peg a precise number of dollars in
contributions from a firm. Often the contribution lists are long enough that
analysts exclude individual contributions of under $500. Thus, several
separate contributions of slightly less than $500 will not be picked up in an
analysis. Texas disclosure laws then did not require information on
occupations of contributors or firm/business associations of contributors.
Family members with a name different from that of a major contributor or
staff members who report their home address rather than the firm's address
can easily be excluded from an analysis. The high mobility of attorneys can
make it difficult to trace contributions from a particular firm. It is possible
for a contributor to make the tracing of contributions difficult simply by
using a different name and address for different contributions. Using a full
name and a firm address for one contribution and initials or a nickname and a
home address for another contribution can make tracing contributions almost
impossible, especially when the surname is a common one or when the city
where the law office is located is different from the home city. Judicial
contributions can also be hidden from all but some of the more diligent
research efforts when an individual gives to a political action committee
which gives to another political action committee which then gives to the
candidate. Thus, one has to find the records of the candidate, then look up the
records of the second political action committee to find the name of the first

one. Then one has to locate the first political action committee's records to find the individuals who actually contributed money.[25] If expenditures are independent contributions, they can be made virtually untraceable since they will not appear on the candidate's contribution statement and will only appear on the political action committee records. There the expenditures can be masked as money for receptions for several people, publication expenses, or television expenses. If the political action committee supported several candidates with independent expenditures, it is impossible to break down the amount of time, energy and effort put into the candidacy of one candidate over another candidate.

The firms identified by Patti Kilday were still major players in the 1988 elections, although generally their contributions to winning candidates were far less in 1988 since the plaintiffs' firms tended to back candidates who lost in that election. From 1980–1986, they tended to back winning candidates. It was plaintiffs' attorney contributions that were to become a major issue in the 1988 Supreme Court elections, where it was argued that "big bucks" had too much influence in electing Supreme Court justices and that there was a need to remove the role of "big bucks" from judicial selection.

Candidates who ran as reformers in 1988 had a ready-made issue. Not only had the court been the subject of bad publicity and an ethical probe by both the legislature and the State Commission on Judicial Conduct, but there were lawyers practicing before justices who were giving huge sums to those justices. If some way could be found to raise smaller amounts of money from more people, that "big bucks" issue could win a lot of votes. Still some alternative way of raising large amounts of money had to be developed in order to present the issue to the voters.

The 1988 Supreme Court elections saw two-thirds of the Court up for grabs and a chance in one election to set the tone of tort law at least until 1990 and possibly for years to come. As one might expect, a plaintiff-defense conflict emerged in the Supreme Court races. The old "big money crowd" which had so heavily funded Supreme Court races in the past was on the scene again. But some new big players appeared—particularly money from the Texas Medical Association to support physicians' interests. Additionally, several candidates, most notably Chief Justice Tom Phillips, imposed campaign contribution limitations of $5,000. Phillips, a Republican appointee who had practiced law with a major defense firm, was unlikely to generate the big-dollar contributions from plaintiffs' lawyers. Thus, he gave up little in very large individual contributions by imposing a $5,000 limitation. At the same time, he was able to generate considerable political appeal as a reformer. Unlike previous justices, including his opponent Ted Z. Robertson, he was not dependent upon a handful of lawyer contributors. As is shown in Table 3, Phillips generated many small contributions and many contributors, far more than typically give money to a Texas Supreme Court candidate. He also broke $2,000,000 in total contributions.

Table 3
Contributions to Tom Phillips.

Amounts contributed	No. of contributors	Percent of total contributors
$100 or less	6,182	68.2%
$101 to $500	2,160	23.8%
$501 to $1,000	537	5.9%
$1,001 to $2,500	120	1.3%
$2,501 to $5,000	64	0.7%
Total	9,063	

Sources: Calculated from Tom Phillips' contribution statement, Office of the Texas Secretary of State.

The 1988 Supreme Court elections were the most expensive in Texas history. One reason that the twelve general election candidates for the court were able to raise $10,092,955 in direct contributions was because 1988 was a year when there were few statewide races in Texas. The major state offices, governor, lieutenant-governor, comptroller, land commissioner, agriculture commissioner, and attorney general were all up in 1990. While there was one interesting Railroad Commissioner race involving Republican incumbent Kent Hance's successful effort to win a low-level state race for the Republican Party and to try to maintain his political viability, nothing much was going on in state elective politics. Even the U.S. Senate race pitting Beau Boulter and Lloyd Bentsen was a foregone conclusion. There was some excitement over the presidential race, largely because Lloyd Bentsen was on the national ticket, but that was national politics and involved different interests and also different players. Still, what brought in the money for the Texas Supreme Court in 1988 was that 1988 was the year money mattered. It was the year when one side in the conflict over the tone of tort law in Texas could say that one general election led to control of the Court. That itself was rare; six seats had never before become available on the Court all at once.

Table 4 shows direct campaign contributions to those Democratic and Republican candidates in the general election, and it identifies the amounts of major contributions and whether the major contributors were plaintiff or defense oriented. In addition to these amounts, two organizations, the Fund for a Democratic Texas and the Texas Medical Association, made independent expenditures which benefited the candidates for the Court. The Fund for a Democratic Texas was a plaintiffs' lawyer PAC whose goal was the election of Democratic candidates and especially a Democratic Court. The Texas Medical Association backed a Supreme Court slate of candidates that included Tom Phillips, Paul Murphy, Nathan Hecht, Raul Gonzalez, Jack Hightower and Gene Cook.

The big money still came from lawyers, even the money for the candidates who imposed $5,000 contribution limitations. That is because, while candidates imposed limitations upon money donated by individual lawyers, they did not impose any limitation on the amounts donated by firms.

The top ten contributors to the Supreme Court races gave $1,414,021. The twelve major candidates for the Texas Supreme Court raised $10,092,955. When the amounts raised by primary opponents are added to this sum, a total of $10,374,442 was raised by all candidates for the Texas Supreme Court. Some of the top contributors also gave to the unsuccessful primary candidates, and so the $1,414,021 raised from the top ten contributors was 13.6% of all contributions. The top twenty contributors to the Texas Supreme Court primary and general election races contributed over one out of every five dollars raised, a total of 20.7% of total contributions. The top fifty law firm contributors plus the Texas Medical Association contributed over 1/3 of all funds raised in the 1988 Texas Supreme Court races, $3,467,669 or 33.4% of total funds raised[26]

The Fund for a Democratic Texas raised another $1.4 million in independent contributions, almost all of which was contributed by a small group of plaintiffs' lawyers. This money was spent on Texas Democratic Party get-out-the-vote campaigns and on air purchases for three television commercials, two of which were directed at the Supreme Court races.

The PAC of the Texas Medical Association gave $181,355 in direct contributions to candidates for the Texas Supreme Court. In addition, the TMA urged doctors to give individual contributions. TMA's legislative

Table 4				
Top Contributors to Texas Supreme Court Candidates.				
Candidate Party Incumbent	No. of Defense firms Among top 10 Contributors	No. of Plaintiff firms among top 10 contributors	Name of PACS among top 10 Contributors	Non-lawyer Contribution
Phillips R, I	10	0		$22,394
Robertson D	0	10		$43,008
Doggett D	0	10		$14,639
Murphy R	8	0	Texas Medical Ass'n; Texas & SW Cattle Raisers	$10,832
Kilgarlin D, I	0	10		$43,214
Hecht R	9	0	Texas Medical Ass'n	$10,409
Gonzalez D, I	7	0	Texas Medical Ass'n; Texas Real Estate; Texas Ass'n Defense Counsel	$19,260
Howell[a] R	0	0	Irving GOP Dallas Rep. Men's Club	-
Culver R, I[b]	8	1	Dow Chemical Employees	$5,477
Hightower D	5	2	Texas Medical Ass'n; Texas Dental Ass'n; Texas Real Estate	$12,582
Cook R, I	9	1		$8,865
Bayer[a] D	0	10		$4,160

Continued from previous page

| Table 4 | | | | |
| Top Contributors to Texas Supreme Court Candidates. | | | | |
Candidate Party Incumbent	Range of contributions of top 10 contributors	No. of plaintiff firms among top 10 contributors	Total $ given by of top 10 contributors	Total contributions of top 10 contributors
Phillips R, I	$10,525 – $45,433	0	$223,937	$2,005,305
Robertson D	$30,000 – $65,100	10	$430,081	$1,883,690
Doggett D	$10,500 – $21,250	10	$146,393	$658,135
Murphy R	$5,000 – $50,030	0	$108,315	$438,013
Kilgarlin D, I	$27,000 – $65,100	10	$432,144	$2,038,902
Hecht R	$6,350 – $19,850	0	$104,085	$653,254
Gonzalez D, I	$7,000 – $63,620	0	$192,603	$826,038
Howell[a] R	$100	0	-	$447
Culver R, I[b]	$3,450 – $9,873	1	$54,773	$548,425
Hightower D	$5,500 – $45,770	2	$125,820	$449,290
Cook R, I	$5,375 – $16,565	1	$88,653	$460,867
Bayer[a] D	$2,500 – $7,500	10	$41,595	$130,589

Source: Calculated from data provided by Walt Borges, then of The Texas Lawyer.
[a] Excludes personal loans.
[b] One firm had a mixed practice.

director, Kim Ross, estimated that effort brought in another $250,000 to the TMA-endorsed candidates. Chief Justice Tom Phillips' analysis of his contributions indicated that individual doctors contributed $166,000 to his race alone so Ross' estimate may be an underestimate. In addition, indirect contributions of the TMA amounted to $166,000 which was spent on polls, slate cards, and local advertisements backing the TMA slate of candidates. Doctors also became active in working in TMA-backed candidates' campaigns. It was, claimed TMA's Ross, "a textbook grassroots campaign."[27]

A New Era and a Conclusion

Huge sums were part of the Texas Supreme Court elections in the 1980s, reflecting the battle for control of the court fought by plaintiffs' and defense interests. It was a new era of big-money judicial politics. But quickly, new developments emerged in judicial politics which reduced the role of money in judicial races. As the 1980s gave way to a new decade, Texas judicial politics (and state politics in general) became more Republican and less competitive. The result was that the Republican party label gained new importance.

In 1994, for the first time, Democrats could not win any contested Texas Supreme Court races. Nor were Democrats able to win any of the seven contested races in 1996 or 1998. In 2000, Democrats did not even mount a challenge for the Texas Supreme Court. Incumbency, at least Republican Party incumbency, seemed to be asserting itself as a definitive explanation for Texas Supreme Court election results by the 1990s.

Does this mean that money will have a declining role in Texas Supreme Court politics? After all, if Republican Party candidates and especially Republican incumbents can not be defeated by Democrats, one would expect money to be vastly less important in these elections.

There are two problems with this assessment. One is that money may move from Texas Supreme Court elections to the Republican primary.[28] The other possibility is that Republican nominees will be the recipients of large contributions, but their opponents will receive minimal contributions. Money will, in other words, flow to obvious winners, and donors will be reluctant to give to obvious losers. At the same time, Republican nominees will not reject large contributions that will be viewed as further insurance of success. In the 1996 and 1998 elections, for example, for every dollar that the Democratic candidates raised, Republican candidates were able to raise $7.46. Money will continue to be the dark side of Texas Supreme Court politics. In the future, it may not continue to be the determining factor in judicial races, but it will continue to play a role.

Notes

[1] Roy Schotland, Statement of Roy A. Schotland before the Joint Select Committee on the Judiciary of the Texas Legislature Austin, Texas, March 25, 1988, 72 Judicature at 154 (1988).

[2] Paul Burka, Heads, We Win, Tails, You Lose, *Texas Monthly*, May 1987, 138 at 139.

[3] Id. at 139. Prior to Yarbrough's election in 1976, a State Bar grievance committee had filed a disbarment suit against him, alleging fifty-three violations. Later, twenty more allegations were added. Tape recordings of Yarbrough's plans to murder and mutilate enemies did not result in indictments, but Yarbrough was indicted and convicted for aggravated perjury in reference to a forged automobile title. Finally, Yarbrough resigned from the Court and in 1977 gave up his law license. This extraordinary story is well told in Paul Holder, That's Yarbrough—Spelled with One "O": A Study of Judicial Misbehavior in Texas, in *Practicing Texas Politics* 447–453 (Eugene Jones, et al., eds., 1980).

[4] Burka, supra note 2 at 139.

[5] Ken Case, Blind Justice, *Texas Monthly*, May, 1987, 136 at 138.

[6] Texans for Public Justice, Payola Justice: How Texas Supreme Court Justices Raise Money from Court Litigants, at http://www.tpj.org/reports/payola/intro.html.

[7] The case is *Manges v. Guerra*, 27 Tex. Sup. Ct. J. 421 (1984).

[8] Motion for Recusal of Justice C.L. Ray, *Manges v. Guerra*, 26 Tex. Sup. Ct. J. 430 (1983) and Motion for Recusal of justices Ted Z. Robertson and William W. Kilgarlin, *Manges v. Guerra*, 26 Tex. Sup. Ct. J. 430 (1983).

[9] State Commission on Judicial Conduct, Findings, Conclusions and Public Reprimand Relating to Certain Activities of Justice C.L. Ray of the Supreme Court of Texas (1987). Ray was disciplined for the appearance of favoritism in the transfer of cases, for the improper receipt of air transportation, for the receipt and consideration of ex parte communication, for the improper solicitation of funds, for the ex parte disclosure of confidential information to a litigant, and for the initiation of an ex parte private communication. Sadly, the timing of the release of the findings was terrible, occurring when Ray was caring for his terminally ill daughter. See, Robert Elder, Jr., Sanctions Spark More Feuding, *Texas Lawyer*, June 15, 1987, 1 at 17.

[10] State Commission on Judicial Conduct, Findings, Conclusion and Public Admonishment Relating to Certain Activities of Justice William Kilgarlin of the Supreme Court of Texas, (1987). Two of Justice Kilgarlin's briefing attorneys had accepted a weekend trip to San Antonio from Pat Maloney, Jr., a member of a well-known plaintiffs' firm. Kilgarlin was admonished to "make certain in the future that all staff working under him be required to observe the standards of fidelity and diligence that apply to him." Kilgarlin was also "admonished that solicitation of funds by a judge to prosecute a suit against a former attorney who had testified before the House Committee is violative of the Code of Judicial Conduct." Interestingly, Justice Kilgarlin blamed the sanction on the civil defense bar. Robert Elder wrote, "Kilgarlin placed the blame for the sanctions on Larry Thompson, who in 1985 formed the Supreme Court Justice Committee. Thompson has said the group was set up to counter the success of the plaintiffs' bar....Kilgarlin called the pro-defense committee

'19 lawyers who hate my guts' and said 'one of the expressed purposes of that group was to create a scandal involving me.'" See, Elder, supra note 9 at 15.

[11] "Lawyers representing Pennzoil contributed, from 1984 to early this year, more than $355,000 to the nine Supreme Court justices sitting today....Lawyers representing Texaco have also been contributors, but they have given far less." See Thomas Petzinger, Jr. and Caleb Solomon, Texaco Case Spotlights Questions on Integrity of the Courts in Texas, *Wall St. Journal*, November 4, 1987, at 1.

[12] Anthony Champagne, Judicial Reform in Texas, 72 *Judicature* (1988), 146 at 151–152.

[13] Id. at 158.

[14] Anthony Champagne, Campaign Contributions in Texas Supreme Court Races, 17 *Crime, Law and Social Change* (1992) 91 at 95.

[15] Id. at 97, 99.

[16] Id. at 99.

[17] Id. at 94–96.

[18] Id. at 96–99.

[19] Walt Borges, Gonzalez-Haas Fight Pushes Others Aside, *Texas Lawyer*, March 14, 1994, at 1.

[20] The Haas-Gonzalez primary election is just barely the record holder for judicial campaign expenditures. In 1996, in Alabama there was a Supreme Court race where the two candidates spent $4,488,504. We are grateful to Roy Schotland for providing us with these figures.

[21] One of the earliest examples large amounts of trial lawyer money going to courts of appeal races was in 1994 in the San Antonio Court of Appeals. There five plaintiffs' firms kept the court from going Republican when Democrats were being badly beaten in other areas of the state. The five firms contributed over $366,000 directly and through their PACs, and they raised another $254,000 from other personal injury lawyers. Those five firms contributed nearly 37% of the Democratic candidates total funds, and all four Democratic incumbents for the San Antonio court of appeals won in contrast to defeats of 10 of the 11 Democratic incumbents running for other courts of appeals in the state. Democrats running for the San Antonio court of appeals raised twice as much money as the average candidate in a Texas appellate race in 1994. See, Mark Ballard and Amy Boardman, 5 Firms Swung 4th Court Races, *Texas Lawyer*, March 20, 1995, 1, 28.

[22] Indeed, Alabama has been described as "a battleground between businesses and those who sue them." That battle, one scholar wrote, "is often fought in elections for the Supreme Court of Alabama." See, Stephen J. Ware, Money, Politics and Judicial Decisions: A Case Study of Arbitration Law in Alabama, 15 *Journal of Law and Policy* 645, 656–657 (1999).

[23] See Catherine Candisky, High Court Races, Once Dignified, Now Down, Dirty, *Columbus Dispatch*, Nov. 1, 2000, at 1A.

[24] Patti Kilday, Lawyers Fill Judges' Election Coffers, *Dallas Times Herald*, November 2, 1987, at 1.

[25] Clinton Manges' contributions in 1982 to Ted Z. Robertson were to a PAC which gave to a PAC which gave to Robertson. See the campaign disclosure statements for 1982.

[26] Perhaps because Dubois studied the funding of trial court races, he found a varied contributor base and relatively small contributions. It may also be that state judicial elections vary significantly from state to state due to state laws, state political culture, and extent of party competition. See Phillip Dubois, Financing Trial Court Elections: Who Contributes to California Judicial Campaigns?, 70 *Judicature* 8 at 12 (1986); and Phillip Dubois, Penny for Your Thoughts? Campaign Spending in California Trial Court Elections, 1976–1982, 39 *Western Politics Quarterly* 265 (1986).

[27] Walter Borges, Select Group Bankrolled '88 Supreme Court Races, *Texas Lawyer*, April 24,1989, 1 at 18–19.

[28] In the 1998 primaries, for example, Republicans raised nearly $2.5 million, while Democratic candidates raised slightly less than $148,000. We are grateful to Walt Borges of Texas Courtwatch for providing this information.

Chapter IV

Voter Awareness of Texas Judges

Introduction

Conventional wisdom, supported by some empirical work, suggests that voters tend to be unaware of the judges they elect.[1] As a result, in partisan election jurisdictions, voters may rely on cues such as political party affiliation or name recognition in casting their votes for judicial candidates. It is largely understood in the voting literature that the further down the ballot a race is, the less widespread the interest. As a result, fewer people vote in these races, and those who do are more likely to rely on the simple cues of party and the sound of the name. This phenomenon has led to pointed questions about the wisdom of the election process in down-ticket races, including judicial contests which are always found down on the ballot. As a result, proponents of merit selection argue that these voters are uninterested and/or uninformed and that merit selection would offer a better judiciary. In Texas, a central point in the debate over merit selection versus partisan election has been that judges are not known by voters, and therefore voters are uninformed in casting their ballots. The lack of awareness, it is argued, makes the objective of judicial accountability a questionable one. If voters do not know judges, it is argued, they cannot remove "bad" ones. Election supporters, on the other hand, argue that greater efforts should be undertaken to inform voters.

The Literature

The literature on judicial voting is sketchy at best, particularly in Texas. One study was done during the 1976 general election in Lubbock. It was based on polling place exit interviews and was at a time when Texas judicial races tended to be noncompetitive. Only 14.5 per cent of the Lubbock sample could recall the name of one state supreme court or court of criminal appeals candidate, compared to 43.7 per cent who could do so for one senator and 50.7 per cent who could recall a U.S. House of Representatives candidate. Only 2.5 per cent could name county court candidates, and only 4.9 per cent could name district court candidates.

Most interestingly, Don Yarbrough was pitted against two write-in candidates in the general election. He had a Democratic primary opponent, Charles Barrow, who was the overwhelming choice of the state bar's preferential poll. Media attention for this race was relatively high compared to other judicial races of the time period. Nevertheless, 75.2 per cent of the sample of voters was unaware of the Yarbrough controversy. All together, 85.8 percent of the sample could not recall the name of even one judicial candidate. However, 68 per cent of the sample supported the election of judges.[2]

In 1986, *Texas Lawyer* commissioned a poll based on polling place exit interviews with a cross section of precincts in Dallas and Harris (Houston) counties. Over 450 voters were questioned—259 in Dallas County and 195 in Harris County. Among other questions, Harris County voters were asked whether they had heard of George Godwin, who was the unsuccessful Republican candidate running for a district court seat. Seventy-seven per cent of those who claimed they voted in all or most judicial races said they had not heard of Godwin. In Dallas County, 81 per cent of the voters claimed they did not know the name Paul Light, who was a Democratic candidate in an open race for a Dallas County district court seat.[3]

The Dallas Case

The most detailed study of voter awareness of judicial candidates was done in 1988 in Dallas County, Texas. While the previous two surveys indicated that candidates had low name recognition on election day, this analysis explores name recognition during the term on the bench or name recognition after a recent defeat. The Lubbock study was done prior to the time that judicial elections were competitive in Texas and was done in a far smaller community than Dallas County. Unlike the *Texas Lawyer* survey, awareness of several district judges and a former district judge is explored, rather than being limited to only one judicial candidate in Dallas County who had never served as a district judge.

When this study was done, there were 37 district judges in Dallas County who were elected county-wide and who served four-year terms. Some of the courts are specialized courts which concentrate in criminal, juvenile, or family law cases. Other district courts have general civil jurisdiction. The district courts are the major trial courts in Texas. Of the six district judges in the survey, Larry Baraka was a Republican who ran unopposed for his second term as a judge in 1988. He had recently figured very prominently in publicity over the release of Randall Dale Adams, the individual about whom the movie *The Thin Blue Line* was made. Both the movie and the Adams release from prison figured prominently in the Dallas press.

Adolph Canales was a Republican who was first elected in 1986 and had not been involved in any widely publicized matters. Ron Chapman was first elected to the bench in 1978. At that time, he was the only Democrat to win election in Dallas County since the 1982 elections. After the 1988 elections, Chapman was the only Democrat on the district court bench. Jesse Oliver was a former state representative. He was a Democrat and an appointee of a Democratic governor, Mark White. He was the loser in a hotly contested state senate race in 1986 in the Oak Cliff area of Dallas, and in 1988 he was defeated by Joe B. Brown in the only contested district court election in Dallas County. Joe B. Brown was a former Democratic district court judge who was defeated in 1978 by a Republican. He changed his party affiliation and successfully ran as a Republican against Jesse Oliver in 1988. Jack Hampton was elected to the district bench as a Republican in 1986 and sought reelection in 1990. During the spring and summer of 1989, he generated immense publicity in Dallas County, and to a lesser extent in the nation, because of a sentence he gave to the murderer of two gay men as well as some comments he gave to the press about the two victims. At the time, considerable press attention was given to Hampton in Dallas, and there were calls not only for an investigation of Hampton by the State Commission on Judicial Conduct but for his impeachment or resignation.

Methodology

In order to test voter awareness of judges in Dallas County, a random sample was drawn from the universe of registered voters in Dallas County, Texas. The overall sample was 1000 registered voters. The result was a random sample with an error rate of three per cent.

The interview technique involved a telephone survey during the second week of June, 1989, which asked voters questions about officials' name and office recognition. In order to provide some points of comparison for state district judge name recognition, other officials were included. Additionally, some judges were selected in the study who had, as a result of their judicial or extra-judicial activities, been involved in matters of considerable notoriety; other judges, however, had not been involved in such instances.

The study was not conducted at the time of an election. In spite of the fact that the survey occurred in the summer of 1989, it allowed for the comparison of trial judges among themselves in a similar time frame, as well as for the comparison with U.S. Senator Lloyd Bentsen, Texas Supreme Court Justice Raul Gonzales, and Dallas Mayor Annette Strauss. In addition, while the norm is for elected officials to get media attention in the days immediately preceding the election, judicial candidates at the trial court level rarely engage in major media campaigns and rarely mount significant campaigns at all. They usually get little in the way of public attention. In this case, Jack Hampton received considerably more attention than most elected officials as a result of his gaffe during the spring of 1989. Larry Baraka's role in the Adams case also generated more publicity than is characteristic of judicial campaigns at election time.

In this survey, all persons were identified as "public officials." In addition, the names in the survey were selected to provide ethnic balance and a distribution of ticket placement. Bentsen and Strauss were selected because Bentsen was a statewide official who had been on the ballot in 1988 near the top of the ticket. Comparison of district judge recognition with Bentsen allows one to examine the extent of recognition drop-off from high-visibility top of the ticket office-holders to district judges who are nearer the bottom of the ballot. Strauss, while running on a nonpartisan ballot in the spring of 1989, represented a geographic area (the City of Dallas) similar to the area from which the district judges are elected (Dallas County). Strauss is an example of a high-visibility local level official, although Dallas mayors are elected on a nonpartisan ballot. The third non-district judge was Raul Gonzalez, a Democrat and a justice on the Texas Supreme Court. Gonzalez received the highest percentage of votes of any of the candidates in the six contested state supreme court races in 1988.

The Analysis

The overall result confirms the work in the previous two studies that found the voters unable to identify judicial candidates. An interesting finding is the difference between the control cases and the state district judges. The results not only confirm a fade factor for down-ticket offices but lend some credence to the uninformed voter hypothesis. Table 1 shows very high name recognition for Lloyd Bentsen and Annette Strauss. Over 98 per cent of registered voters recognized Bentsen and over 96 per cent recognized

Strauss. Supreme Court justice Raul Gonzalez, in contrast, was recognized by only about 46 per cent of the voters.

In spite of the generally low name recognition, there is also wide variability in the recognition of judges. Three of the six district court judges had very low name recognition. Adolph Canales was recognized by only 12.6 per cent of registered voters, the lowest name recognition of any of the nine persons used in the survey. Even though Jesse Oliver had been a state representative, had been in a highly publicized Democratic primary battle for state senator, and had been the incumbent judge in 1988 in the only contested race for Dallas County district judge, his name was recognized by slightly less than 29 per cent of the registered voters. His opponent in that 1988 race, Joe B. Brown, fared no better with only slightly more than 29 per cent name recognition. Perhaps due to the Randall Dale Adams case and the furor over the remarks about gays, Larry Baraka and Jack Hampton had considerably higher name recognition. Both Hampton and Baraka were recognized by about 41 percent of the voters, a recognition level not much lower than that for Supreme Court Justice Raul Gonzales. Amazingly, Ron Chapman had the third highest name recognition. With nearly 86 per cent of the registered voters recognizing his name, he was right behind the name recognition accorded Lloyd Bentsen and Annette Strauss.

Table 1	
Name Recognition in Dallas County	
(N=1000)	
Candidate	Percent Recognizing Name
Lloyd Bentsen	98.6
Annette Strauss	96.5
Raul Gonzales	46.1
Larry Baraka	41.7
Joe B. Brown	29.2
Adolph Canales	12.6
Ron Chapman	85.8
Jack Hampton	41.0
Jesse Oliver	28.7

Table 2 presents data on the percentage of respondents who recognized the name and also the office held by the nine persons mentioned or the office for which they ran in 1988. Over 77 per cent of the voters correctly noted that either Lloyd Bentsen was a U.S. senator, had run for U.S. senate, or that he had run for vice president. Annette Strauss had even higher office recognition with over 91 per cent recognizing that she was mayor. Interestingly, almost no voters recognized that Raul Gonzales was a justice or even that he held judicial office. They had heard of him but could not fit him with an office. Office recognition for district judges also tended to be quite low. Jack Hampton was correctly identified by about 26 per cent. This number is quite low considering the very high degree of publicity over his sentence of the killer of two gay men and his subsequent comments. Far fewer people could connect him with his office than could recognize his name. Larry Baraka's name and office were recognized by almost 21 per cent of the voters in the sample. Joe B. Brown's office was recognized by only 14.6 per cent of the respondents. Jesse Oliver had been a state representative and had campaigned for state senate. That may explain why he had correct office identification by only 2.7 per cent of those who recognized his name. Adolph Canales, who had not held legislative office in the past, had correct office identification by only 1 per cent.

Table 2 Office Recognition in Dallas County (N=1000)	
Candidate	Percent Recognizing Name & Office
Lloyd Bentsen	77.5
Annette Strauss	91.6
Raul Gonzales	1.2
Larry Baraka	20.7
Joe B. Brown	14.6
Adolph Canales	1.0
Ron Chapman	18.6
Jack Hampton	26.4
Jesse Oliver	2.7

Strangely, Ron Chapman, with the third highest name identification in the sample and the highest name recognition of the judges or justices, had low office recognition. Only 18.6 per cent of the registered voters who recognized his name could correctly identify him as a judge.

Most commonly, Ron Chapman was identified as a disk jockey even though the question asked registered voters to identify the "public office." There is another Ron Chapman who is a popular radio personality. At the time of this study, disk jockey Ron Chapman had led his station to the highest ratings in Dallas for well over a decade.

Remembering the hypothesis that in judicial elections voters tend to be uninterested as well as poorly informed, a separate analysis was performed that considered only the respondents who answered "yes" or "some" when asked if they voted in judicial elections. Table 3 shows these results and mirrors the results in Table 1 in regard to the relationship between the control cases and the district judges. Overall, there is only a slight increase in name recognition when the sample is limited to the 732 respondents who claimed to vote in judicial elections. This suggests that the abstainers in judicial contests are only slightly less informed than the voters.

Table 3	
Name Recognition in Dallas County	
Controlling for Those Who Vote in Judicial Elections	
(N=732)	
Candidate	Percent Recognizing Name
Lloyd Bentsen	99.3
Annette Strauss	98.2
Raul Gonzales	50.5
Larry Baraka	46.3
Joe B. Brown	34.6
Adolph Canales	13.8
Ron Chapman	88.5
Jack Hampton	46.0
Jesse Oliver	31.7

Table 4 is the same as Table 2 except that it shows the percentage of voters who actually vote in judicial elections who can recognize the office of the judge. As in Table 2, there is very high office recognition for Lloyd Bentsen and Mayor Strauss. Office recognition for Supreme Court Justice Gonzales is very low. Judge Canales and former Judge Oliver also have very low office recognition. The highest office recognition is for Judge Hampton, whose remarks about gays gave him a far greater degree of publicity than is normally accorded a judge. Judge Baraka also had relatively high office recognition, but only 23.5 voters in judicial elections were able to identify his office. Eighteen percent of the voters in judicial elections recognized Judge Joe B. Brown's office. However, Ron Chapman, the judge with the highest name recognition, did not have high office recognition due to the confusion with the disk jockey. In sum, even among those who vote for judges, there is low judicial office recognition. Even Jack Hampton, at the peak of his extreme media attention, had office recognition from less than one-third of the respondents who vote in judicial elections. The poll indicates that while the name recognition of judges is low, the ability to identify the judges by office is even lower.

Table 4 Office Recognition in Dallas County Controlling for Those Who Vote in Judicial Elections (N=732)	
Candidate	Percent Recognizing Name & Office
Lloyd Bentsen	81.0
Annette Strauss	94.4
Raul Gonzales	2.7
Larry Baraka	23.5
Joe B. Brown	18.0
Adolph Canales	1.4
Ron Chapman	21.2
Jack Hampton	31.0
Jesse Oliver	3.0

Ethnicity

Because the questionnaire asked the ethnicity of the respondents, it is also possible to compare recognition of judges across black, white, and

Hispanic respondents. Additionally, of the officials mentioned in the sample, Raul Gonzales is Hispanic, as is Adolph Canales. Both Larry Baraka and Jesse Oliver are black. Thus, it is possible to compare recognition by ethnicity of respondents, and it is also possible to determine whether black respondents are more likely to recognize black officials, Hispanic respondents are more likely to recognize Hispanic officials, and whether white respondents are more likely to recognize white officials.

Table 5 presents the recognition levels for the officials by ethnicity of the respondents. In the Dallas County case, it is interesting to note at the outset that, in general, voters from all ethnic groups were unable to recognize the names of the state district judges. While voters from all ethnic groups were able to recognize the names of Bentsen and Strauss, they slipped considerably when it came to judges. As is shown in Table 5, the major exception is Judge Ron Chapman who, as previously mentioned, shares the name of the most popular disk jockey in Dallas County.

Table 5 Percentage of Respondents Who Recognized Official's Name, by Race of Respondent			
Candidate	Hispanic	Black	White
	N=80	N=165	N=747
Lloyd Bentsen	91.3	98.2	99.5
Annette Strauss	90.0	96.4	97.3
Raul Gonzales	56.3	47.3	44.6
Larry Baraka	35.0	46.1	41.5
Joe B. Brown	15.0	24.8	31.6
Adolph Canales	37.5	12.7	9.8
Ron Chapman	78.8	74.5	88.9
Jack Hampton	25.0	32.1	44.3
Jesse Oliver	26.3	58.2	22.4

Texas Supreme Court Justice Raul Gonzales did better in name recognition than the bulk of the district judges. More interesting are the ethnic groups' recognition rates of officials who share their ethnicity.

Hispanics recognized the names of the two Hispanics in the survey at rates somewhat higher than the other judges. Gonzales and Canales were recognized more often than all others with the exception of the unusual case of Chapman. A similar pattern existed among black voters. The two black judges, Larry Baraka and Jesse Oliver, were recognized by 46.1 and 58.2 per cent of the black respondents; this, again, was more than recognition of any others except for the non-judges, Judge Chapman, and Supreme Court Justice Gonzales. White respondents in the survey did not tend to recognize whites more than others, although they recognized Bentsen, Strauss, and Chapman more than any other names.

Table 6
Percentage of Respondents Who Could Identify
the Office and the Name of the Official,
by Race of Respondent

Candidate	Hispanic	Black	White
	N=80	N=165	N=747
Lloyd Bentsen	56.3	60.0	83.4
Annette Strauss	81.3	86.1	93.6
Raul Gonzales	2.5	.6	2.8
Larry Baraka	20.0	30.0	18.6
Joe B. Brown	5.0	7.9	17.0
Adolph Canales	3.8	.6	.9
Ron Chapman	12.5	10.3	21.2
Jack Hampton	12.5	13.3	30.0
Jesse Oliver	1.3	3.6	2.4

Of course, name recognition can be misleading as it clearly was in the case of Ron Chapman, and the survey attempted to screen these problems out with a second question that asked the respondents to identify the office the person sought or held. Table 6 shows the percentage of the groups who recognized the name of the official and the office sought.

The first finding of importance confirms that respondents across all ethnic groups did not know who Chapman was. The most popular response

to this question was "disk jockey." Mayor Strauss was identified as the
mayor at higher rates than Bentsen was correctly placed as a vice-
presidential candidate or senator. In addition, Raul Gonzales was known as a
justice by virtually no one. White voters were more able to identify Judge
Hampton's office than were non-white voters. Black voters, on the other
hand, knew Baraka was a judge more than any other judges, but they were
unable to correctly identify the office of any other judge at a significant rate.
Hispanic voters did not tend to identify judicial offices. Judge Baraka was
correctly identified by only 20 percent; Justice Gonzales and Judge Canales
were correctly identified by 2.5 and 3.8 percent, respectively. Overall, the
levels of office recognition are quite low for all ethnic groups in the case of
judges.

Table 7 Respondents' Awareness of Candidate's Race, by Race of Respondent			
Candidate	Hispanic	Black	White
	N=80	N=165	N=747
Lloyd Bentsen	92.7	86.3	96.1
Annette Strauss	87.3	85.0	95.7
Raul Gonzales	57.6	68.8	50.2
Larry Baraka	30.3	18.8	14.3
Joe B. Brown	12.7	5.0	16.5
Adolph Canales	15.8	35.0	10.2
Ron Chapman	66.1	66.3	76.6
Jack Hampton	25.5	20.0	34.5
Jesse Oliver	40.6	11.3	9.1

As Table 7 shows, respondents from all ethnic groups appeared able to
identify the race of the non-judges in the sample. In the judicial offices the
ethnic backgrounds of two candidates were known. About two-thirds of each
of the groups knew that Ron Chapman was white—perhaps due to the
visibility of the DJ Chapman on billboards in Dallas County. The other
recognizable name was Raul Gonzales, who was known to be Hispanic by
over 50 per cent of all the groups; although more Hispanics and blacks knew

this than whites. For the remaining state district judges, respondents could not identify their ethnicity. Nevertheless, with the exception of Chapman, Hispanics tended to do better identifying Canales' ethnicity than the other district judges (35.0 per cent); blacks did better identifying Oliver's (40.6 per cent) and Baraka's (30.3 per cent) ethnicity than the other district judges; and whites knew Hampton's ethnicity (34.5 per cent) and Brown's (16.5 per cent) more than any non-white district judges.

Summary and Conclusions

Several points should be made about these findings. First, not surprisingly, judges do not have the name or the office recognition that more political officeholders have such as U.S. senator and mayor. This pattern holds across all ethnic groups studied. In general, voters were unable to recognize the name and provide the office of the judicial officials in the survey. Additionally, all ethnic groups tended to be unaware of the ethnicity of judges although voters of one ethnicity were somewhat more able to identify ethnicity of officials from their own ethnic group. Like Professor Lawrence Baum's study of awareness of Ohio Supreme Court justices, there is variation in awareness of judges.[4] However, some judges, such as Adolph Canales, have almost no name or office recognition, and no judge, except for Ron Chapman, had name recognition from even one-half of the county's registered voters. Only one judge, embroiled in a controversy that received national publicity, had office recognition from over one-quarter of the registered voters. Some judges, even a state supreme court justice, had almost no office recognition.

In order to have high name recognition at the trial court level, it appears that one must have a name with which people identify. Judge Ron Chapman seems fortunate to have had the name of a popular radio personality. Perhaps the popularity of the disk jockey explains why Judge Chapman could still win elections as a Democrat in Dallas County.

Republicans built on William Clements' power to make new and interim appointments to the bench, party-switching by formerly Democratic judges also occurred, and the Republican Party grew dramatically. The last year preceding this study in which the Democratic Party showed real strength in district court races in the county was in 1982 when Democrat Lloyd Bentsen was able to carry the county in his senatorial race with 50.8 per cent of the two-party vote, and even then only incumbent Democratic district judges could win.

Indeed, lacking other information, it appears that voters will use party as an imperfect voting cue. Race or ethnicity, on the other hand, does not seem a strong factor in explaining voting behavior in judicial races since voters have low awareness of the race or ethnicity of candidates for these offices. Information obtained by voters about individual judicial candidates (other than party affiliation which is readily available on the ballot) seems to result from significant media attention brought about either through name confusion as in Judge Chapman's case, handling an exceptionally controversial case that led to a movie as in Judge Baraka's case, or from immense publicity resulting from notably inappropriate comments about murder victims as in the case of Judge Hampton.

This study suggests that voters in judicial races are strongly influenced by party and by media attention even where that media attention is caused by confusion over names as in the case of Judge Chapman. And, of course, since media attention seems so important in affecting voter awareness, it should not be surprising that some judges or judicial candidates might use outrageous comments or behavior to garner that attention or might seek significant campaign contributions to buy the media advertisements necessary to gain voter attention.

Notes

[1] Allen Klots, The Selection of Judges and the Short Ballot, 38 *Journal of the American Judicature Society* 134 (1955). Low levels of voting participation in judicial elections provide indirect support for the claim that voters lack awareness of judicial candidates. Numerous scholars have reported relatively low levels of judicial voting participation, including Herbert Jacobs, Judicial Insulation—Elections, Direct Participation, and Public Attention to the Courts in Wisconsin, 1966 *Wisconsin Law Review* 801 (1966) and Kathleen Barber, Ohio Judicial Elections—Nonpartisan Premises with Partisan Results, 32 *Ohio State Law Journal* 762 (1971). Mixed results on awareness of Ohio Supreme Court candidates have been reported by Baum with very high awareness of the controversial Ohio Chief Justice race in 1986. See Lawrence Baum, Voters' Information in Judicial Elections: The 1986 Contests for the Ohio Supreme Court, 77 *Kentucky Law Journal* 645 at 664–67 (1988–89).

[2] Charles Johnson, Roger Shaeffer & Neal McKnight, The Salience of Judicial Candidates and Elections, 50 *Social Science Quarterly* 371 (1978).

[3] Barbara Johnson, Voter Survey: Judges Unknown, *Texas Lawyer* Nov. 10–14, 1986, at 1, 8–9.

[4] Baum, supra note 1.

Chapter V

Judicial Elections by the Numbers

Doing It By the Numbers: An Empirical Test

Taken separately, incumbency, party affiliation, money, ethical violations, race, ethnicity, and gender each represent but one dimension of the multidimensional environment in which judicial elections operate. If inferences are to be drawn about the influence of any of these variables on voter behavior in judicial elections, then a multivariate assessment of the election data is in order. For valid inference, it is important to consider these factors in light of any intercorrelations that may be present among them. In this way, judicial elections may be better understood for the factors that exert a real influence as well as those whose apparent influence is but an artifact of the influence of other covariants.

To better understand the dynamics of judicial elections in Texas, races for the Texas Supreme Court have been chosen for analysis. While judicial elections in Texas have become more politicized at all levels, competition for the Texas Supreme Court has been the most intense and perhaps best epitomizes the all-out battle waged among interest groups and political parties to shape the composition of the Texas judiciary. As the court of last resort for civil disputes in Texas, the Supreme Court of Texas routinely renders decisions that directly impact the deepest pockets in Texas and garner the most attention from those interest groups that wish to shape not only the composition of a single collegial court, but also the tenor of the law in the state over an extended course of time. Thus, the dynamics of Texas Supreme Court elections may be examined for insight into the most visible of all judicial races in Texas and also as an exemplar of what judicial elections in other states might become—or what they might already be.

The Data

The dynamics of Texas Supreme Court elections began to experience significant changes in 1980, the year that the first Republican justice on the court in over a century faced election for the first time. Associate Justice

Will Garwood had been appointed to fill out the remainder of an unexpired term and faced election in the next regularly scheduled contest in order to retain his seat on the court. It was in this 1980 election that plaintiffs' attorneys first organized a concerted effort to sufficiently fund a candidate to unseat an incumbent. Thus, our analysis will begin with the 1980 elections and end with the 2002 elections. In particular, only general election races featuring both a Republican candidate and a Democratic candidate are included in the analysis. In all, 33 such races occurred during that time. Third-party candidates (most commonly, Libertarian Party candidates) are not examined since the vote-drawing power of such candidates has been minimal in Texas. In the 2000 elections, no Democratic candidate ran for any seat on the Texas Supreme Court. Thus, the 2000 Supreme Court races are also excluded from the empirical analysis.

For each of the thirty-three races selected for analysis, data were collected on the percent of the vote received by each winning candidate,[1] the party affiliation of each candidate, the two-party vote at the top of the ticket,[2] the length of service on the Supreme Court for each candidate at the time of the election under analysis, the total campaign contributions to each candidate,[3] and the race, ethnicity and gender of each candidate. From these raw data, measures were constructed for each race to capture the differential in election dynamics between contending candidates. Specifically, those variables are:

1. the differential between the two candidates in the total two-party vote received (measured as percentage of the two-party vote received by the winner less the percentage of the two-party vote received by the unsuccessful candidate),
2. the differential between the two candidates' respective party's vote share at the top of the ballot (measured as the winning candidate's party's share of the two-party vote in the race at the top of the ticket less the unsuccessful candidate's party's share of the two-party vote in the top-of-ticket race),
3. the differential in the campaign funding of the two candidates relative to the size of the voting public (measured as the winning candidate's total campaign funding, in 2002 dollars, per registered voter less the unsuccessful candidate's total campaign funding, in 2002 dollars, per registered voter),

4. the differential between the candidates' length of service on the bench (measured as the winning candidate's length of service on the court at the time of election less the unsuccessful candidate's length of service on the court at the time of election[4]),

5. the differential between the candidates' minority and gender status (with each of the black, Hispanic and female variables measured as 1 if the winning candidate belongs to that demographic while her challenger does not, 0 if neither or both of the candidates belong to that demographic or -1 if only the unsuccessful candidate belongs to that demographic), and

6. An ethics variable has been constructed to denote those races where ethics issues figured prominently in the campaign. In one of those races, an incumbent candidate seeking reelection received a public admonishment from the State Commission on Judicial Conduct for ethics violations.[5] In another race, an associate justice sought the Chief Justiceship and faced significant ethical allegations dealing with his voting behavior in *Manges v. Guerra*.[6]

We now turn to an analysis of these data.

Party

Table 1 illustrates the effect of party strength at the top of the ticket on Texas Supreme Court races, showing the number of contested races in each election year and the corresponding number of Texas Supreme Court races that followed the partisan vote in the race at the top of the ticket. Given the importance that prior research has attached to the party label and its coattail effect on down-ballot judicial races,[7] one would expect to find that a substantial proportion of Texas Supreme Court races follow this pattern. The results in Table 1 do show that 63 percent of Texas Supreme Court races followed the outcome at the top of the ticket.

Interestingly, from 1980 through 1992, only seven of nineteen Texas Supreme Court races—37 percent—were won by the candidate of the same party as the winner of the race at the top of the ticket. Even including the elections held since the emergence of a Republican monopoly on statewide races, less than two-thirds of the contests since 1980 follow the coattail effect from the top of the ballot.

Table 1		
Year	Number of Contested Races	Winners with Coattail Advantage
1980	2	0
1982	1	1
1984	1	0
1986	3	0
1988	6	3
1990	3	2
1992	3	1
1994	2	2
1996	3	3
1998	4	4
2000	0	0
2002	5	5
TOTALS	33	21

Incumbency

Table 2 shows the relationship between incumbency and Texas Supreme Court election outcomes. Twenty of the contested races involved a challenge to an incumbent.[8] In fourteen of those races (70% of the races), the incumbent won. As expected, incumbents experienced a significant electoral advantage. Although incumbency probably does not generate much name familiarity among voters, it likely would do so among members of the legal community. Incumbency provides a judge the opportunity to demonstrate judicial abilities that lead to such things as high bar poll ratings and newspaper endorsements.

Still, when judicial elections in Texas were truly competitive from 1980 through 1992, only five of ten incumbents were successful in winning reelection. Most incumbent successes have occurred since 1994. Of the ten incumbents who have been challenged in the general election since 1994, nine were successful. Of course, those nine were also Republican candidates. The lone incumbent who was unsuccessful was the one remaining Democrat on the Court in 1998. It is difficult, therefore, to conclude that incumbency offers much advantage to contemporary judicial candidates independently of its interaction with the party variable.

Interestingly, only 60 percent of all the Texas Supreme Court races since 1980 have featured a challenge to an incumbent justice. Strong incumbents may not face challengers because of their name recognition, their funding, or other political factors. In 2000, for example, Democrats, facing the immense popularity of George W. Bush at the top of the ticket, did not contest any of the three Texas Supreme Court seats up for election.

Table 2			
Year	Number of Contested Races	Number of Contested Races with Incumbent	Winners with Incumbency Advantage
1980	2	1	0
1982	1	0	0
1984	1	0	0
1986	3	2	2
1988	6	5	2
1990	3	1	0
1992	3	3	1
1994	2	1	1
1996	3	3	3
1998	4	4	3
2000	0	0	0
2002	5	3	3
TOTALS	33	23	14

Campaign Finance

Table 3 shows the overwhelming advantage of candidates who receive more campaign contributions than their opponents do. Of the 33 contested races included in this analysis, the better-funded candidate won twenty-eight, or 85% of the time. Unlike the effect of party and incumbency on election, the correlation between money and electoral success is constant across time. From 1980 through 1992, the candidate with the largest campaign coffer won sixteen of nineteen contested races (84%). Since 1994, twelve of fourteen contested races (86%) have been won by the candidate who received the most in campaign contributions.

Although the relationship between money and electoral success appears strong, it is important not to look at these numbers in isolation from the other data. It is, for example, useful to note that campaign contributions have followed the party trend in Texas. From 1980 through 1986, years in which Democrats won every contested race for the Supreme Court, Democrats out-raised Republicans by a factor of 50 to 1. From 1988 through 1992, years in which both parties won at least one contested race, the dollars raised by each party's candidates were almost equal—Republicans had a marginal advantage of $1.04 to every Democratic dollar. Since 1994, the money has flowed again to the party in control of statewide offices. Since 1994, Republican candidates for the Supreme Court have out-raised their Democratic opponents by a margin of almost 2.5 to 1. So again, while a campaign funding advantage is a strong predictor of election outcomes, it also appears that the money variable is tied strongly to party trends in the state.

Table 3		
YEAR	Number of Contested Races	Winners with Money Advantage
1980	2	2
1982	1	1
1984	1	1
1986	3	3
1988	6	4
1990	3	3
1992	3	2
1994	2	1
1996	3	3
1998	4	4
2002	5	4
TOTALS	33	28

Candidate Demographics

It is also important to consider other variables that may impact voting behavior in judicial elections. In particular, race, ethnicity and gender may be important voting cues. Especially in elections in which voters have little substantive information about candidates' qualifications, voters might be expected to draw on other ballot cues such as a feminine given name or Hispanic surname. In the litigation brought against Texas in the late 1980s[9] it was alleged that Texas' single member district system of electing trial judges discriminated against minority candidates by diluting minority voting strength. Although that challenge to Texas' judicial elections was not successful, it was indicative of deeper concerns about the ability of minorities to win judicial elections in Texas. Similarly, going back to the days of the first woman judge in Texas, Judge Sarah Hughes, there have been concerns about the effects of gender on judicial election outcomes.[10]

The data, however, do not show much evidence of racial, ethnic, or gender-based voting patterns. Table 4 shows, for example, that of the eight women who have run against men, three have been successful.[11] Two of those victories have been by Republicans since 1994, and two of the losses were Democratic candidates who lost in 2002. It is difficult at best to disentangle the effect of gender on election outcomes from the influence exerted by the political party variable.

Table 4						
Year	Number of Contested Races	Races with Female v Male	Races Where Female Beats Male	Races with Hispanic v Non-Hispanic	Races Where Hispanic Beats Non-Hispanic	Races with Black v Non-Black	Races Won By Black Candidate
1980	2	0	0	0	0	0	0
1982	1	0	0	0	0	0	0
1984	1	0	0	0	0	0	0
1986	3	0	0	1	1	0	0
1988	6	1	0	1	1	0	0
1990	3	0	0	0	0	0	0
1992	3	1	1	0	0	0	0
1994	2	2	1	0	0	0	0
1996	3	1	0	0	0	0	0
1998	4	1	1	0	0	0	0
2002	5	2	0	1	0	2	2
	33	8	3	3	2	2	2

The same is true for African American and Hispanic candidates. The Hispanic candidate has won two of the three races pitting a Hispanic candidate against a non-Hispanic. Democratic Hispanic candidates won in

1986 and 1988 while Texas was in the midst of transition from Democratic to Republican dominance. The lone defeat suffered by a Hispanic candidate was in 2002 when a Democrat ran in a year that proved strongly Republican. Both African American candidates for the Court have won election. Both were Republican and both won in the 2002 elections.

Although the ethics issue only applied to two candidates for the Supreme Court, it is instructive to note that both of these justices were defeated. Both were well-funded and both were incumbent justices, though one sought to move from an associate justiceship to the Chief Justiceship.

Multivariate Analysis

A cursory inspection of the data shows that money, party (via the coattail effect), ethical questions and incumbency advantage correlate to some degree with the outcomes of judicial elections. However, it is also clear that there is significant correlation among those variables; e.g. the money and incumbency advantages follow party strength. So then, how do these variables working together influence voter behavior in judicial elections? Multivariate analysis may be employed to estimate the separate correlations of each independent variable on judicial election outcomes while also accounting for the observed intercorrelations among the predictors. In particular, logistic regression analysis[12] is a useful way to estimate the importance of party, money, ethics and incumbency along with other possible explanatory variables such as race, ethnicity, and gender in predicting the split in the two-party vote in each contested race.

Methodology

The familiar formulation for logistic regression with grouped data estimates a function (the 'logit') of the estimated probability of an event's occurrence as a linear combination of some set of variables. Namely,

$$\hat{L}_i = \ln\left(\hat{p}_i \big/ 1 - \hat{p}_i\right),$$

where

$$\hat{p} = \ln\left(\frac{1}{1 + e^{-X_i \hat{B}}} \right).$$

After rearranging terms it can easily be shown that

$$\hat{L}_i = X_i \hat{B}$$

and the parameters may be estimated for this linear model using a familiar weighted least squares approach.

In the case of contested elections, though, there are constraints that must be accounted for. Consider, for example, an election featuring two candidates. If p is the probability that a voter casts a ballot for the winning candidate, then the probability of a voter casting a ballot for the losing candidate must equal $1-p$, since the probability of any vote going for one of the two candidates must equal 1. Thus, the familiar logistic regression model specified above is not sufficient to model the probability that all candidates from a set of races will receive a given vote (or, more intuitively, the proportion of the total vote that a candidate will receive), as it does not impose the constraint that the total proportion of votes cast in a given race equal unity.

One straightforward approach that accounts for this constraint is to model only the vote share for winning candidates but to difference the independent variables. In this manner important information about the relative appeal of the candidates (vis-à-vis their opponent) is utilized while retaining the condition that the total proportion of votes in a given race equals unity. Thus, the model that we wish to estimate is:

$$\hat{L}_{W_i} = X_{D_i} \hat{B},$$

where X_{D_i} is the differenced value of each variable (taken as the value for the winner less the value for the losing candidate). The parameter estimates that are derived from this formulation, then, are suggestive of the degree of influence derived from any marginal advantage enjoyed by a candidate on any of the included explanatory variables.

Results of this specification of the logistic regression analysis are presented in Table 5. The party variable produces the strongest positive result, supporting the idea that judicial races tend to follow the division of the partisan vote at the top of the ballot. The money variable also shows a strong relationship with election outcomes, supporting the idea that the better-funded candidate has an electoral advantage. There is also evidence that the ethics variable has a significant negative correlation with voting behavior, suggesting that voters consider ethical problems as a negative voting cue. The relative influence of each of these variables, however, must be considered in light of their units of measurement. For example, the magnitude of the party variable is reflective of the fact that top-of-ticket voting is measured as a proportion rather than in percentage terms. Too, the magnitude of the money variable is relatively large in light of the unit of measurement employed to construct the variable. Since this variable is measured in dollars per registered voter, a marginal increase in money advantage has a far greater impact on judicial election outcomes than does a marginal change in the split in the two-party vote at the top of the ticket.

Table 5					
Variable	DF	Estimate	Error	t Value	Pr > |t|
MONEY	1	0.91409	0.21955	4.16	0.0003
PARTY	1	0.44699	0.19022	2.35	0.0267
INCUMBENCY	1	0.01251	0.00771	1.62	0.1170
SCANDAL	1	-0.25749	0.11610	-2.22	0.0355
HISPANIC	1	0.00264	0.11069	0.02	0.9812
BLACK	1	0.16067	0.12507	1.28	0.2102
FEMALE	1	0.00296	0.06196	0.05	0.9622
F Value	5.81			R-Square	0.6099
Pr > F	0.0004			Adj R-Sq	0.5049

Surprisingly, the incumbency variable returns no evidence of any correlation with the margin of victory in these judicial races. Neither do the race, ethnicity or gender variables show any explanatory significance. The lack of explanatory power from these variables strongly suggests that any correlation between them and election outcomes is actually the product of their interaction with the party and money variables. Overall, the logit model explains a significant amount of the variation in the vote share received by winning candidates—some 50%. Too, the predictive power of the regression estimates is also impressive, correctly predicting 28 of the 33 races in the study (see Table 6).[13]

Taken together, these results suggest that the factors that are influential in partisan judicial elections are top of the ticket voting, campaign funding, and ethics violations. Judicial races are swept up in the current that flows from the top of the ballot downward with the party coattail effect having a significant effect on election outcomes. Money is necessary to advertise and promote one's candidacy. Campaign money clearly has a significant sway over voter behavior. And, voters do have a concern with claims of ethics violations that, in turn, may have an effect on election outcomes.

However, incumbency does not appear to influence voting behavior in partisan judicial elections. While an incumbent judge may have years of distinguished service on the bench, success in judicial races does not seem to hinge on this factor. Neither do voters in these elections appear to rely to any significant degree on gender, race or ethnicity when deciding between candidates.

Together, these results suggest an interesting portrayal of the judicial voter. Although cues such as party affiliation are important determinants of judicial voting behavior, the data suggest that judicial voters, at least in Texas, do pay attention to judicial races—at least in the short term leading up to elections. While the judicial voter does appear to be influenced by the top of the ticket, the fact that the scandal and money variables are significant suggests that information presented during the course of a campaign (and the ability to convey that information via campaign funding) also influences the behavior of voters as they choose among the candidates for judicial office.

These findings are telling of the drastic shift in the dynamics of judicial campaigns. Prior to the emergence of the new politics of judicial elections and the corresponding proliferation of big money races and the use of more media-based campaigning strategies, the judicial voter had little to inform the vote outside of ballot cues such as party labels or name familiarity. The above analysis, however, suggests that the attempt of special interests to sway judicial elections by the infusion of campaign funds has been an effective strategy and, in fact, has a significant effect on voter behavior.

This is especially so given that the above findings suggest that the judicial electorate, although swayed by judicial campaigns, still does not attach a long-term attentiveness to the judiciary. The absence of any positive influence of an incumbency advantage on vote share earned suggests that the typical voter does not derive any informational cue from the name familiarity that would be expected to follow from an extended tenure on the bench.

Table 6					
Year	Winner	Loser	Predicted Share	Correctly Predicted?	Actual
1980	Wallace	Brady	0.51061	YES	0.54873
1980	Ray	Garwood	0.49702	NO	0.5029
1982	Robertson	Bates	0.54149	YES	0.57662
1984	Hill	Bates	0.56439	YES	0.54204
1986	Mauzy	Howell	0.56729	YES	0.55473
1986	Campbell	White	0.55023	YES	0.56391
1986	Gonzales	Bates	0.54707	YES	0.53149
1988	Phillips	Robertson	0.56737	YES	0.5663
1988	Doggett	Murphy	0.49514	NO	0.54937
1988	Hecht	Kilgarlin	0.50156	YES	0.50265
1988	Gonzalez	Howell	0.53417	YES	0.57947
1988	Hightower	Culver	0.47848	NO	0.55516
1988	Cook	Bayer	0.51942	YES	0.51717
1990	Phillips	Mauzy	0.58402	YES	0.59158
1990	Gammage	Howell	0.51269	YES	0.56439
1990	Cornyn	Kelly	0.56528	YES	0.55672
1992	Enoch	Mauzy	0.51091	YES	0.55298
1992	Spector	Cook	0.44772	NO	0.52226
1992	Hightower	Montgomery	0.51836	YES	0.56799
1994	Hecht	Oliver-Parrott	0.56826	YES	0.56189
1994	Owen	Carroll	0.51675	YES	0.56756
1996	Phillips	Kupper	0.57216	YES	0.58131
1996	Cornyn	Barron	0.5499	YES	0.53322
1996	Baker	Kelly	0.53575	YES	0.5572
1998	Enoch	Westergren	0.57033	YES	0.58181
1998	O'Neill	Spector	0.52521	YES	0.53523
1998	Abbott	VanOs	0.56456	YES	0.60108
1998	Hankinson	Scarbrough	0.56918	YES	0.56904
2002	Phillips	Baker	0.55978	YES	0.58737
2002	Schneider	Yanez	0.52239	YES	0.57454
2002	Wainwright	Parsons	0.56645	YES	0.57361
2002	Jefferson	Moody	0.5747	YES	0.56762
2002	Smith	Mirabal	0.49938	NO	0.54097

Notes

[1] This variable is measured as the percentage of the total votes received of all votes cast for the two major party candidates.

[2] Because of Texas' history of Presidential Republicanism—voting for the Republican candidate for president, while splitting the partisan vote in down-ballot races—the top of the ticket race in this analysis is defined in order as the Senate race, the gubernatorial race (in the absence of a Senate race) and, finally, the presidential race (in the absence of either a Senate or gubernatorial race).

[3] This variable is measured both in total dollar terms for the descriptive analysis in Table 3 and as the difference in dollars per registered voter for the analysis described in Table 4.

[4] In two races, an incumbent associate justice challenged an incumbent chief justice for the chief justice seat on the court. Every other race featured either an incumbent and a challenger with no prior service on the court or two challengers for an open seat, each with no prior service on the court.

[5] State Commission on Judicial Conduct, Findings, Conclusion and Public Admonishment Relating to Certain Activities of Justice William Kilgarlin of the Supreme Court of Texas (1987).

[6] Ken Case, Blind Justice, *Texas Monthly*, May 1987 at 136–138. The case is, *Manges v. Guerra*, 673 S.W.2d 180 (Tex. 1984).

[7] L. Douglas Kiel, et al., Two-Party Competition and Trial Court Elections in Texas, 77 *Judicature* 290 (1994).

[8] Two races that featured a challenge to the incumbent chief justice by incumbent associate justices are excluded from this total.

[9] *League of United Latin American Citizens, Council No. 4434 v. Clements*, 986 F.2d 728, 5th Cir. (Tex.), (1993).

[10] See, for example, the criticisms of the appointment of Sarah Hughes as Texas' first state district judge at http: //www.tsl.state.tx.us/governors/personality/allred-hughes-1.html and http://www.tsl.state.tx.us/governors/personality/allred-hughes-2.html.

[11] One incumbent female justice did win election against a minor party male candidate in 2000, a race not included in this study.

[12] For an introductory treatment of this statistical methodology, see N. Breslow & W. Day, *Statistical Methods in Cancer Research. Volume 1—The Analysis of Case-Control Studies* (1980).

[13] It is worth emphasizing that the model specification is not intended to model the probability that a candidate will win, but rather the voting behavior of voters that participated in the selected races.

Chapter VI

The Difficulty of Reform

Introduction

There have long been advocates for changing the system of judicial selection in Texas. There has been considerable support for the Missouri Plan for selecting judges at least since 1946 when the Texas Civil Judicial Council recommended its adoption. In 1949, a State Bar referendum favored the Missouri Plan over partisan election by a two to one vote. In 1953, the Texas Civil Judicial Council, the State Bar Committee on the Administration of Justice, the Advisory Committee on Revision of Judicial Selection of the Texas Constitution, and a majority of those voting in a State Bar poll all endorsed the Missouri Plan. In 1961, the Texas Civil Judicial Council again endorsed the Missouri Plan. In 1962, the Chief Justice of the Supreme Court of Texas, Robert Calvert, endorsed the Missouri Plan, and a survey of Texas lawyers showed a majority in favor of abandoning partisan election of judges and a plurality supporting the Missouri Plan. A commission selection plan for selecting judges was recommended in 1971 by the Task Force for Court Improvement. In 1972, the Texas Constitutional Revision Commission proposed merit selection for appellate judges.[1]

However, those reform efforts took on new life when Texas Supreme Court Chief Justice John Hill proposed merit selection of judges in 1986 and offered himself as the leader of the movement for judicial reform. Hill was no ordinary reformer. He had been a leading trial lawyer and had been Texas' Secretary of State under Governor John Connally as well as Texas' elected Attorney-General. An activist Attorney-General, Hill, a Democrat, challenged the incumbent Democratic Governor Dolph Briscoe in the 1978 primary and defeated him. Hill assumed that he was the next Governor. Democrats had been elected Governor since the end of Reconstruction, and Hill had prevailed against an incumbent Governor in the primary, obtaining 51.5% of the vote to Governor Briscoe's 42%. Described as "boldly overconfident," during his campaign speeches Hill would recognize local Democrats and talk about how he was looking forward to working with them when he took office. After a late October poll showed Hill leading his

Republican opponent Bill Clements by 11%, Hill stated, "There is no way I will lose. It's all over. We think we have enough votes to win regardless of the turnout. The polls show I'm going straight up." Hill was actually going straight down. He had lost the support of many of the more conservative Democrats who resented his defeat of Briscoe. And his Republican challenger not only had enormous personal wealth, but he had the willingness to spend huge sums in his campaign. Clements managed to win the race by a total of 16,909 votes out of 2.2 million cast. Hill became the first Democratic candidate for Governor defeated by a Republican in a century.[2]

It was not yet the end of John Hill's political career, however. In 1984, he ran for Chief Justice of the Supreme Court of Texas. Running the first million-dollar campaign for the Court with donated funds (Will Garwood had run a million-dollar campaign for the Court earlier but had mostly self-funded), Hill was elected. Interestingly, his politically unknown Republican opponent, John Bates, received nearly 46% of the votes even though Bates had roughly $12,000 in contributions to Hill's $1.4 million.[3] It was, however, a hint of the new strength of the Republican Party in the state, particularly because it was a presidential election year and Ronald Reagan was the Republican candidate.

In 1986, Hill announced his support for merit selection of justices and proposed himself as leader of the reform movement. Some suspected Hill was promoting judicial reform as a vehicle to make still another try for the governorship.[4] Nevertheless, Hill's advocacy of judicial selection change led to unprecedented conflict and tension on the Court. One associate justice went so far as to file an ethics complaint with the State Commission on Judicial Conduct against Hill.[5] When Hill created a group known as the Committee of 100 to advocate merit selection, a rival group known as the Committee of 250 was created to advocate continued judicial elections. Six associate justices became members of that group.[6]

Bitterness became so intense over Hill's advocacy of judicial selection reform that Hill increasingly was isolated from his colleagues on the Court, and some of the justices openly attacked him. Fifteen months after proposing merit selection, Hill resigned from the Court. As a private citizen, he argued, he could more effectively campaign for judicial selection reform. And, it should be noted, he could make much more money as a name partner of a major Houston law firm.[7]

His departure from the Court was gleefully welcomed by many of his colleagues on the bench. And, his resignation meant that Governor Bill Clements, the Republican who had defeated him in the 1978 election, could appoint his replacement. That replacement was Houston district judge Tom Phillips, a Harvard Law School graduate and former big-firm lawyer. At Phillips' swearing-in ceremony, Hill spoke and again issued a plea for merit selection. That speech led Robert Campbell, one of the associate justices on the Court, to resign claiming he was resigning to campaign against merit selection.[8]

Almost all the effort to change the way judges are selected in Texas has concentrated on the judges of the appellate and district courts, which are the major trial courts. It is in these courts, of course, where the stakes are the highest in terms of possible civil penalties and civil damages. Hill's proposals also focused on the major trial and the appellate courts. Hill argued that judges were now being defeated in Texas, often due to their political party affiliation. Other judges were resigning because of the "political hassle" involved in Texas judicial elections. And, voters did not know their judges anymore. In Harris County, for example, Hill pointed out that in 1982 over 106 judicial candidates were on the ballot. Hill pointed out that often judges were defeated simply because they did not have the party affiliation of popular presidential candidates. Some judges were changing their party affiliation to reflect the emergence of the Republican Party. Some judicial candidates were capitalizing on the popularity of their names in order to win office. Hill pointed out that the judiciary was not reflecting the demographics of the state's population. At the time of Hill's initial reform efforts, only one Hispanic and one female had served on the Texas Supreme Court in recent times, and no African American had done so. Hill also stressed that there was one issue that was "the big problem" in Texas judicial politics. It was the problem of money in judicial races. Judicial candidates, Hill argued, needed money to run in competitive races, and they could easily become "dependent upon the contributions of a very small group of special interest people." Merit selection—especially a plan called by Hill the "Texas Plan"—could lead to judges who took "non-political, non-partisan" approaches to their offices. Hill argued that merit selection would more likely produce judges who would not talk of issues before the court. Additionally, merit selection would prevent judges from becoming captives of groups or viewpoints, prevent judges from having constituencies, and avoid partisan politics and hints of favoritism.[9]

Of course, it was not just Hill who pushed for changes in the way Texas selected its judges. Hill was advocating changes at a time when there were the increased pressures for change from many sources. Most notably, Hill was advocating reform at a time when Texas was experiencing dramatic changes in its political parties, when the Republican Party, for a century virtually powerless in Texas politics, was becoming a major force in the state's politics. Another development affecting Hill's reform efforts was the increasing specialization of the bar and the intense competition between plaintiffs' lawyers and defense lawyers in civil cases that had developed in the early 1980s. Texas was also in the midst of dramatic growth where the urban counties had seen huge population surges leading to large numbers of judges and greater anonymity of those judges. With the dramatic growth of Texas, Texas was seeing significant demographic changes where Hispanic numbers were giving them more political power. And, African American concentration in urban areas of Texas provided the African American community with a significant political voice.

The Two-Party System

Although the partisan election system operates for all courts at the district level and higher, interim appointments are made by the governor for new courts and vacancies on the bench caused by death and resignation. These appointees serve until the next regular election, when they must run to retain their seats. As a result, the Texas partisan election system is actually a combination of an elective and appointive system. In 1987, when Hill was initially advocating merit selection, 59 per cent of district judges and 44 per cent of appellate judges initially gained their seats through appointment. The pattern is for a governor to appoint judges who are from his political party.[10] As a result, a watershed for a two-party Texas judiciary was the election of the first Republican governor since Reconstruction, William Clements, in 1978.

His appointment power, coupled with increasing Republican challenges to Democratic domination of judicial offices, led to partisan competition for judgeships in Texas by the early 1980s. Although the Texas system was one of partisan election, Democratic domination of the state for 100 years had meant that a Democratic governor would appoint Democrats to the bench, and any competition for judgeships would be limited to the Democratic primary. Although there was some competition within the Democratic primary, it was not widespread.[11] With Republican appointees to the bench and with Republican challenges for other judgeships, competition for offices became more widespread, and defeats of incumbent judges, something virtually unknown in previous years, began to occur. Those defeats tended to be primarily in Dallas and Harris Counties, which were also centers of Republican strength. Even today, many rural counties have never seen a contested judicial race.

There had been 57 challenges to Republican incumbents from 1980 through 1986, and 20 of those Republican incumbents have been defeated. Of 69 challenges to Democratic incumbents during the same time period, 25 of the Democratic district judges had been defeated. Seven of the 20 defeated Republicans and 20 of the 57 challenges to Republican incumbents were in Harris County (Houston). Nine of the 25 defeats of Democratic incumbents had also been in Harris County along with 28 of the 69 challenges to Democratic incumbents. Though Democrats had mounted 13 challenges to Republican incumbents in Dallas County, they were unable to defeat a Republican incumbent. Republicans in Dallas County, on the other hand, defeated 12 Democratic judges in Dallas County out of 21 races. Most of the other counties in Texas at this time had no incumbent defeats, and only two other counties in the state, Bexar (San Antonio) and Tarrant (Ft. Worth), had more than three challenges to incumbents. Turnover due to the electoral process on the major trial courts in Texas was generally a phenomenon restricted to the most urban counties.

As is the case with the major trial courts, two-party competition for judicial positions had primarily been in the three most populous courts of appeals (intermediate appellate courts). Two of those districts included Harris County and the third included Dallas County. When Hill was first advocating reform, it was only in those areas where Republican strength had been great enough to defeat a Democratic court of appeals judge. Indeed, seven of the eight Democratic court of appeals judges who were defeated were beaten in the heavily Republican court of appeals district that includes Dallas County. In other court of appeals districts where incumbents had been defeated, it was often the appointees of Governor Clements who could not withstand a Democratic challenge in traditionally Democratic counties.[12]

One Republican appointee to the Texas Supreme Court, Will Garwood, was defeated in 1980. Until the appointment of Tom Phillips, no other Republican in modern times had served on the state's two highest courts.

Because of straight ticket voting, a strong showing by a candidate at the top of the ticket can have a tremendous impact upon candidates for lesser offices, such as judicial offices. A candidate with great strength at the top of the ticket, like Lloyd Bentsen in 1982 or Ronald Reagan in 1980 and 1984 can affect the outcome of judicial races. Nineteen eighty-two was a banner year for Democratic judicial candidates in Texas, and, at the top of the ticket, Lloyd Bentsen carried 59.1 per cent of the two-party vote against Jim Collins, the Republican challenger. Ronald Reagan's victory in 1980 was still during the early stages of Republican efforts to gain judicial offices in Texas. While Reagan's coattails were a valuable boost for Republican judicial candidates in 1980, it was in 1984 that his coattails were particularly powerful. In 1984, Ronald Reagan garnered an amazing 64.1 per cent of the two-party vote, and Republican judicial candidates did exceedingly well. In 1986, there was a great deal of split-ticket voting in Texas due to a close race for the governorship in which the Republican, William Clements, defeated Mark White, the Democratic incumbent. Then there was a reversal in voting with a strong vote for incumbent lieutenant governor, Democrat William Hobby, which was followed by a very narrow victory for Democratic Attorney-General Jim Mattox. As a result, neither party swept judicial races in that year.

The development of a two-party partisan system of judicial elections in Texas, however, led to questions about whether a popular senatorial or presidential candidate should affect state judicial races. Additionally, it led to questions about whether political partisanship is appropriate for the judiciary. Finally, concerns have been raised about whether able judges were being defeated solely because of their party affiliation and whether the defeats of incumbent judges were affecting the stability of the judiciary.[13]

Beginning in the 1970s, however, a less-noticed event was occurring in Texas politics. The bar was becoming increasingly specialized and fragmented, and that led to the second great pressure for judicial reform.

Specialization of the Bar

In years past, Texas lawyers tended to be general practitioners; however, increasingly over the past quarter century there has been specialization and sub-specialization. Two segments of the bar have a particular interest in the Texas Supreme Court—the insurance defense bar which represents insurance companies which are subjects of litigation and the insurance plaintiffs' bar which represents injured individuals who seek to collect damages from insurance companies. A small number of defense firms and a small number of plaintiffs' lawyers tend to handle the very large judgment cases that are appealed to the Texas Supreme Court.

At the beginning of Hill's reform movement, there were more than 48,000 members of the Texas bar; statistics vary, but at most only 2.6 per cent classified themselves as defense lawyers, and only 9.3 per cent were members of the Texas Trial Lawyers Association, whose members are largely plaintiffs' lawyers. An even smaller number of lawyers tend to be the Supreme Court appellate specialists in the big ticket cases. Those lawyers, of course, have strong interests in Supreme Court decisions. The plaintiffs' bar, in particular, has strong economic interests in Supreme Court decisions since their income is mostly derived from contingent fees. If they lose the case, they don't get paid. Defense lawyers also like to win cases, and their continued employment by business and insurance companies probably requires some reasonable level of success in litigation, but they are paid by the hour regardless of whether they win or lose. As a result, the plaintiffs' lawyers have the strongest economic interest in Supreme Court outcomes.[14]

Traditionally, the Texas Supreme Court had a reputation for being defense oriented. By 1980, however, the election of Texas Supreme Court justices had become a battleground for plaintiffs' and defense lawyers, each trying to elect candidates favorable to their perspective. Supreme Court races began to get expensive in that year. For the three open seats on the Texas Supreme Court in 1980, $1,800,000 was raised.[15] Until 1988, with the exception of the race between Republican incumbent Will Garwood and Democratic challenger C. L. Ray in 1980, the struggle between the plaintiffs' and defense bar was largely within the Democratic primary. For statewide races below the governorship, Republican candidates then tended to only rarely mount strong races, and none had mounted successful races. As a result of this increased competition within the Democratic primary, campaign contributions for the Texas Supreme Court increased dramatically.

With several strong Republican candidates for the Texas Supreme Court in 1988, campaign contributions went to record levels, amounting to million-dollar campaigns in several races. Just a few years earlier, it was possible to run a strong race for the Texas Supreme Court with $100,000 or less. Charles Barrow, for example, claimed he spent about $100,000 in his unsuccessful 1976 race against Don Yarbrough.[16]

People who contributed to judicial races tended to be lawyers or potential litigants. Thus, the base of contributors was very small. In 1983–84, for example, C. L. Ray received $1,043,879 in contributions. The list of contributors is 195 pages long. However, 76 donors gave slightly over one-half of the justice's campaign fund, and many of those 76 persons were either related to or were affiliated with the same law firms.[17] One unsuccessful Supreme Court candidate in 1982, Woodrow Wilson Bean, received over $200,000 from a potential litigant, Clinton Manges. That sum amounted to over 90 per cent of Bean's total contributions.[18] About one-third of the money contributed on behalf of Ted Z. Robertson in 1982 also came from Clinton Manges.[19]

As Supreme Court campaigns got more expensive, the amounts of contributions from some lawyers and litigants became distressingly large. One of the problems was that the base of contributors to judicial races is small, and so at times there seems to be an unhealthy dependency between the judicial candidates and large contributors. The campaign finance wars between plaintiff and defense lawyers have even now not yet filtered down to all courts of appeals races or district court races, but battles do occur there. Joe Jamail, for example, was criticized by Texaco lawyers for the $10,000 contribution he gave to Anthony Farris, the first district court judge in the Texaco-Pennzoil trial.[20]

Pat Maloney, a well-known San Antonio plaintiffs' lawyer, recruited and financed a justice of the peace who proceeded to defeat an 18-year judicial veteran after that court of appeals judge ruled against Maloney and his clients in a $3,000,000 slander case. Maloney stated, "[J]udges now realize that he [Maloney] will back politically what he believes in legally." He added, "I think that message has gotten across pretty substantially... We have a pretty good court now.... We seem to have their undivided attention."[21]

The Growth of Urban Counties

In 1985, there were approximately 15 million residents of Texas. That represented almost a doubling of the state's 1950 population of 7.7 million. Texas moved from being the sixth largest state in 1950 to the third largest in 1980. Houston, in particular, grew dramatically. In the 1970s Houston was the fastest growing metropolitan area in the nation, growing by 45 per cent to almost 3 million. The next fastest growing metropolitan area was Denver, half Houston's size with a growth rate of 30 per cent.[22] Although Dallas County has not experienced the growth of Harris County and Houston, it too has experienced significant growth. In 1950, Dallas County had approximately 615,000 residents; in 1960 it had nearly 952,000 residents, in 1970 over 1.3 million, and in 1980, nearly 1.6 million.[23]

As a result of the growth and size of Dallas and Harris Counties and the election of judges for the courts of appeals and the district courts in these areas on a district-wide basis, judicial candidates have huge numbers of voters to canvass. Even uncontested district court races in these counties in those days could draw over 200,000 voters, and contested district court races commonly attracted from 400,000 to 700,000 voters. At least one contested judicial race in Harris County in 1984 attracted over three quarters of a million voters. In contrast, some of the rural judicial districts attracted fewer than 10,000 voters for uncontested races and fewer than 20,000 voters for contested races. Additionally, voters must be aware of a large number of judges in Dallas and Harris Counties. There were 59 district court or criminal district court judges in Harris County and 36 in Dallas County. Dallas County had 13 judges on its court of appeals, and there were 18 judges on the two Harris County-based courts of appeals.[24]

When Hill first talked of judicial reform, voters in Harris and Dallas counties might face ballots with over 70 judicial positions, such as occurred in Harris County in 1982. Harris County voters in that year saw half of those races contested. In 1984, Dallas County saw 14 contested races at the district court level or higher. The result was that, contrary to the rural counties, it was difficult for the judicial candidate to know his/her constituents or to be known by them. There was a belief that ballots tended to be cast in those counties on the basis of name familiarity or party affiliation.[25] Interestingly, one of the two Democratic judicial candidates to win election to any bench in Dallas County in 1986 was Judge Ron Chapman, who had the highest name recognition of any judge in the county, probably because Ron Chapman is the name of a popular local radio personality.[26]

The Strength of Minorities

Related to the vast growth of Texas and its urban counties was the increased political power of African Americans and Hispanics. One also was seeing increased political power of women. In 1990, some scholars have claimed, it was women voters who defeated the Republican candidate for governor, Clayton Williams, largely because of disgust over his public and often sexist statements and his ungentlemanly behavior.[27] One study that was widely publicized by Hill in an effort to show that partisan election of judges worked to the detriment of women and minorities found that of 470 judges in Texas, only 29 judgeships were held by women, only 3 by blacks, and only 37 by Hispanics. Hill used the study to argue that partisan election was not benefiting women and minorities, but that merit selection would do so.[28] Indeed, that was the conclusion of the study, which was later shown to be inaccurate based on a multivariate analysis of the same data.[29]

Hill needed to make that argument because of a persistent concern, at least among leaders in the minority community, that merit selection would not benefit their interests and that Hill was trying to change the system of selection just as minorities (and women) were making political gains in the state.

Judicial reforms in Texas had been discussed for years, but these pressures for reform were building, and John Hill seemed to step into the battle at an opportune time. Not only was Hill an important Texas political leader, but he was working within an environment where there were pressures for reform as a result of the development of a two-party system, pressures as a result of plaintiffs' and insurance defense lawyer tensions, pressures from the growth of Texas, and pressures for more power in the judicial branch from women and minorities.

Hill's vehicle for reform was the Committee of 100, a group of citizens appointed by the chief justice, the speaker, and the lieutenant governor to examine judicial reform. However, the speaker and lieutenant governor played only minor roles. Given the vast power of these two officials in Texas government, their inactivity was to prove a bad omen. Adopting a proposal of a state bar committee, Hill proposed what was essentially the Missouri Plan for Texas. It applied to all courts at the district court level and higher. He then went on a statewide speaking tour to receive citizen comment on the proposal, called the "Texas Plan," and to generate public support for it.[30]

As opposition to the plan emerged, various modifications were made, but the essence of the plan remained. Under the plan a commission would name at least three nominees, one of whom would be chosen by the governor. That appointee would be confirmed by the state senate and would serve for one or two years. Afterwards, he or she would run in a retention election and would be elected to a six year term. Every six years, the judge would run in another retention election. Chief Justice Hill heralded the plan as a modern mechanism for judicial selection and as one which was non-political. He argued that it would allow a judiciary to be selected on its merit rather than on the basis of partisanship or money.[31]

Opposition

Opposition to the plan emerged from several sources. Most notable was opposition from the other members of the Texas Supreme Court. Because the chief justice was on the appellate selection commission in one of the earliest versions of the "Texas Plan," Justice Franklin Spears accused Hill of trying to be a king-maker in selecting other justices. That charge led Hill to modify the plan to remove the chief justice from the selection commission. A successful candidate for the Supreme Court, Oscar Mauzy, accused Hill of using judicial reform as an issue for a try for the governorship in 1990.[32]

A fundamental question raised by the plan was, "Who picks the pickers?" That is, how are the commissioners chosen? If the plan was to result in nonpolitical judicial nominees, it was asked, why were the chairmen of the state political parties selecting members of the selection commissions? Other questions were asked about the partisanship of the elected officials who were selecting commissioners. It was also noted that the requirement of senatorial confirmation would perpetuate a political judiciary since state senators in Texas practice senatorial courtesy, and senators could be expected to oppose nominees who were not allied with the senators.[33]

Minorities and women, particularly Hispanic leaders, opposed the plan out of concern that it would lead to further Anglo male domination of the state judiciary. The argument was made that at a time when minorities and women were just beginning to win elective offices in the state, including judicial offices, a new system of selection was being developed. That system, it was argued, was dominated by Anglo males in other states and would be in Texas. A study distributed by the Committee of 100 which argued that minorities and women benefited from merit selection in other states was subjected to heavy criticism for misclassifying state systems of selection and for being misleading.

Although Hill tried to quell doubts by stressing that he would not support a discriminatory plan, that did not work. He then suggested that the number of commission nominees to the governor could be increased from three to five in order to increase the chances that a minority member or a woman would be on the list. Finally, the Texas Plan was modified to include an admonition that supported nondiscriminatory selection of nominees. Some minority leaders argued that the plan should require proportionate representation of minorities on the judiciary. Hill, however, argued that only considerations of merit should enter into the selection process.[34]

Largely through the efforts of the Democratic Party chairman of Travis County (Austin), Charles Herring, an organization opposing the Texas Plan came into being. That organization, initially called the Committee of 250, with heavy membership from Democratic and Republican County chairs, lobbied in favor of a continuation of the partisan elective system. It argued that the Texas Plan and the Committee of 100 were elitist and, arguing that retention elections were meaningless, that the plan would take away the right to vote for judges. Six members of the Texas Supreme Court joined the Committee of 250, and some spoke in favor of the partisan election system.[35]

Leading plaintiffs' lawyers, apparently fearful that the Texas Plan would take away hard-won gains in Texas tort law by leading to the appointment of defense-oriented judges, opposed the plan. They were joined by organized labor and an official in the Texas Civil Liberties Union.[36]

Some Republican leaders challenged the plan, fearful that it would take away Republican gains. Rural Democrats such as the state Democratic Chair, Bob Slagle, also opposed the plan, fearing that it would lead to Republican gains in the rural Democratic strongholds.[37] Since rural Texas has not yet experienced growth of a two-party system and since rural districts are small enough for judges to know their constituents and to be known by them, there seemed little interest in changes in those areas of the state. For rural Texas, there were no sweeping changes occurring which were creating pressures for judicial reform. As a result, Hill proposed that there be discussions about whether counties could choose to not participate in merit selection. Although many states with merit selection exclude rural areas from coverage under the plan, the point was made that in Texas, the counties that were experiencing problems tended to be counties with Republican strength; the rural counties were Democratic. Thus, counties which were likely to not be covered under the plan were Democratic; counties with the likelihood of coverage were heavily Republican Dallas County or increasingly Republican Harris County. Thus, by allowing rural counties to remain unreformed while urban counties were being reformed, the plan began to appear to be increasingly partisan. Republicans asked why there was a need for reform only when Republicans started winning elections.[38]

Other Problems

Hill was faced with a problem with social science evidence as well. Although his speeches indicate that he deeply believed it, he could not provide conclusive evidence that the Texas Plan would lead to the appointment of more meritorious judges. Opponents of the plan enthusiastically cited Henry Glick's *University of Miami Law Review* article, which concluded that there were no significant differences in the characteristics of merit selection and partisan-elected judges.[39]

At the same time that Hill was claiming that merit selection would reduce "politics" in the judicial process, charges of improprieties in the merit selection system in Missouri were being aired. In 1982, the governor and the chief justice had manipulated the merit selection system in Missouri in order to appoint three Missouri Supreme Court justices who were friendly to them. Allegations were also made that a youthful political crony of the governor had been appointed to the Missouri Supreme Court in 1986 under the merit selection plan.[40]

To counter these criticisms of the Missouri Plan, Hill brought his personal friend, Missouri's Chief Justice Andrew Jackson Higgens, to speak in favor of the Missouri Plan. Higgens spoke in several Texas cities, including Austin, Dallas and Ft. Worth. He assured his audience that whatever problems that had existed under the Missouri Plan had been solved, and he insisted that the Missouri Plan worked well and that it had produced a better judiciary in Missouri; however, his assurances were insufficient to quell the continuing comment that something had been rotten under the Missouri Plan.[41]

Additionally, Chief Justice Rose Bird and two other Supreme Court justices were defeated in retention elections in California.[42] It was clear that retention elections could be expensive elections and that special interest groups with commitment and money could defeat judges in these elections. A new argument against merit selection began to be made: Retention elections didn't work because only 1.6 per cent of judges had been defeated under retention elections,[43] but retention elections could lead to big money races that defeated incumbent judges.

In Texas, Hill was faced with another problem—not many judges were defeated in 1986. In comparison with 1982 and 1984, there seemed to be no strong coattail effect which swept incumbents out of the courthouse and replaced them with judges of the same party as the candidate at the top of the ballot. Thus, it was argued that the problems of instability in the judiciary were obviously temporary and that those problems had been resolved by 1986. What was not stressed was that 1986 was a close election at the top of the ticket and that there was widespread ticket splitting. It could just as easily have been argued that 1986 was simply inconsistent with the trend begun in the 1980 elections and that judicial instability would begin again as soon as an unusually popular candidate at the top of the ticket appeared. However, the lack of widespread defeats in judicial races lessened the sense of urgency in Hill's call for reform.[44]

For some time there had been rumors of improprieties involving several Supreme Court justices, but it was not possible for most people to separate partisan and bar bickering from legitimate concerns over the integrity of the judiciary. During 1986, the Texas Commission on Judicial Conduct began looking into some of these charges, and several papers and a leading magazine in the state published articles about the improprieties. However, the Commission on Judicial Conduct did not act during the regular legislative session. In fact, it did not issue an admonishment against Justice William Kilgarlin and a reprimand against Justice C. L. Ray until June 9, 1987, after the close of the regular legislative session and at a time when the state was primarily concerned about a projected budget deficit and worried about the prospects of a tax increase. As a result, Hill and the reform movement could not even reap much benefit from the scandal on the Texas Supreme Court. Initially, the Texas Supreme Court scandal received minimal attention because the public was preoccupied with the SMU football scandal which had heavily involved the governor.[45] SMU and Governor Clements got the front-page coverage. When the governor called for the resignations of the two sanctioned justices, Justice William Kilgarlin had a ready reply, "My reaction to his request is that Governor Clements is certainly a fine one to be discussing matters of morality and ethics in light of his involvement with paying athletes when he was at Southern Methodist University."[46] The reform movement did not even get its legislation out of committee, although in an effort to get enough votes for reform, the reform proposal was modified so that merit selection would be limited to the appellate bench—a proposal which enhanced the view that merit selection was a cover for reshaping Texas law into being defense-oriented law since it was the appellate bench, especially the Texas Supreme Court, which was responsible for the new plaintiffs' orientation in Texas law.

New Life

Not even Chief Justice Hill's resignation from the Supreme Court in order to pursue judicial reform seemed sufficient to produce an incentive for reform. Hill was unable to convince Governor Clements to appoint his successor through a commission system voluntarily used by the governor.[47] However, with a "60 Minutes" broadcast on the Texas judiciary, new life seemed to be breathed into the reform movement. With large contributions to the Texas Supreme Court by lawyers, especially Pennzoil lawyers, in the multi-billion dollar Texaco-Pennzoil case and the refusal of the Texas Supreme Court to hear Texaco's appeal in the Texaco-Pennzoil case, the *Wall Street Journal*, *U.S. News*, the *New York Times*, and *Time* all ran critical stories on the Texas judiciary. The stories were so critical that the Texas press and Texas judges began to refer to the commentary as "Texas bashing" by the national media. Governor Clements expressed support for merit selection of appellate judges on the grounds that he had become convinced that the Texas appellate courts were issuing decisions that were bad for the Texas business climate.[48]

A state committee, the Joint Select Committee on the Judiciary, was appointed by Governor Clements to make recommendations about the Texas judiciary. The committee was loaded with lawyers with defense-oriented practices. It held hearings for most of 1988 and concluded its work in October. It recommended judicial campaign finance reform, voter information pamphlets, and removal of judicial races from straight-ticket voting. It also recommended nonpartisan elections for the trial bench and a modified version of Hill's "Texas Plan" for the appellate bench. Hill also established a committee, The Committee for Merit Election, to campaign for reform, and he established a PAC called MeritPAC to support candidates interested in reform.[49]

In late February, 1988, John Hill revealed another modification of his reform plan, one endorsed by the Joint Select Committee on the Judiciary.

Commission selection would only apply to the appellate courts and responding to the perception that Texas retained the populist desire to vote for public officials, Hill proposed that a selection commission would choose a panel of nominees after holding public hearings and the governor would choose one of those nominees. After the nominee was confirmed by the state senate, the nominee would run in a confirmation election prior to taking office. The confirmation election would be like a retention election where the judge would not have an opponent. Unlike the retention election, the judge would have no judicial record and would presumably only run on the basis of his or her qualifications. After being confirmed, the judge would serve in office until it was time to run in a regular retention election.[50] By this point it was clear that Hill and his forces were settling in for a long battle. Merit selection would not be an easy victory.

The Lieutenant Governor's Committee

Lieutenant Governor Bob Bullock, a Democrat and one of the most powerful and effective politicians in the state, concerned about the role of money in judicial elections and the possibility that the Department of Justice would refuse to approve the creation of any more courts in Texas (on the grounds that the current system discriminated against minorities), created a committee in 1994 to explore the possibilities of developing a judicial reform proposal. The composition of the committee was such as to give key interests a voice in developing the proposal. Three Democratic state senators and three Republican senators were appointed. One of the Democratic state senators was an African American who had close ties to civil rights groups in Houston that advocated greater representation of African Americans on the bench. One of the Democratic state senators was Hispanic and had close ties to civil rights groups in San Antonio that advocated greater representation of Hispanics on the bench. Four members of the committee were judges: one Republican and three Democrats. Three of the judges were Texas Supreme Court justices, and one was the Presiding Judge of the Court of Criminal Appeals. All were well respected in the legal community.[51]

The President of the Texas Trial Lawyers Association, the major plaintiffs' attorney organization in the state, regularly attended the meetings; another participant was a public relations specialist who represented business in political and legislative matters. Although there were complaints that the meetings were closed to the public, that there were no public or consumer representatives on the committee, that there were no lower court judges on the committee, and that no members of the Texas House of Representatives were there, important interests in judicial politics were represented.[52] Notably, John Hill was not invited to attend the meetings. Bullock claimed that Hill had wanted to be on the committee, but that Hill had become a political lightning rod, which made it impossible for him to serve. Nevertheless, at least one state senator, the Chief Justice, and the business representative were strong supporters of merit selection.

It soon became clear to the committee that there were no easy solutions to the politics of judicial selection wherein all competing interests could be readily accommodated. Some sort of compromise would have to be reached. Minorities were willing to support modifications of the appellate courts in exchange for greater representation of minorities on trial courts. While minorities believed that it would be possible to draw smaller districts within counties to increase minority representation, they knew that appellate court districts were so vast that small districts for appellate courts would generally still be so large that minorities would benefit little. Business interests saw an opportunity. They would support greater minority representation on the trial court bench in exchange for an appointive system such as merit selection. Plaintiffs' lawyers saw their grip on appellate courts weakening. It would not make much difference whether Republican governors appointed conservatives to the appellate bench or voters elected conservative Republicans to the bench. Smaller trial courts, however, opened up the possibility that at least some pro-plaintiff trial judges could continue to be elected.

One problem with merit selection was that, among minorities and plaintiffs' lawyers who had long fought it, the system was perceived as so evil that it could not be supported. Republicans had fought very small judicial districts, and judges were uncomfortable with the idea of small districts as well. As a result, creating a compromise was difficult. However, the committee agreed on a compromise wherein appellate judges would be appointed by the governor. Trial judges in urban areas would be elected from county commissioners' precincts. After serving for a time they would run county-wide in retention elections. They would later have to be reelected from county commissioners' precincts. In order to depoliticize the judiciary, judges were to be elected in nonpartisan elections, which would protect judges from the party sweeps of recent elections.

The compromise seemed to have something for everyone. Business was given an appointive system. Because the governor would appoint appellate judges, they would have greater career security and no worries about campaign funding. In addition, an appointive system enhanced the power of incoming Governor Bush. Minorities and plaintiffs' lawyers got smaller trial court districts, which would allow for the election of more minorities and some plaintiff-oriented judges. Judges were protected from party sweeps. All of these interests seemed to be accommodated without resorting to merit selection commissions and the worries over "Who picks the pickers?" or the formation of very small electoral districts.

However, not everyone was happy with the accommodations. Although African Americans were very supportive of the compromise, Hispanics were not. The two largest counties in Texas—Harris and Dallas counties—elected a total of 96 of the 386 district court judges then in Texas. Thus, those counties were the most important in any plan that would increase minority representation on the bench. Each county in Texas is divided into four county commissioners' precincts. Under the compromise, one-fourth of Harris County and Dallas County judges would be elected from each county commissioner's precinct in that county. Harris and Dallas counties had three white county commissioners' precincts and one African American precinct. Hispanics believed this indicated that the compromise would not promote the election of more Hispanic judges. To achieve their objective, they felt that considerably smaller districts would be needed.

The political parties also opposed the compromise. Nonpartisan elections might protect the interests of judges, but nonpartisan elections weakened the political parties. In addition, an appointive system for appellate judges reduced the number of elective offices and thus reduced the role of the parties. Governor Bush, although his powers would benefit from an appointed appellate judiciary, opposed the compromise, probably because he did not want to oppose the Republican Party.

The compromise passed the Texas senate because Bullock had such influence over the state senate that any legislation he backed had a high probability of success. In the Texas House, however, the plan had opposition. Unlike Bullock, Speaker of the House Pete Laney did not give priority to judicial selection reform. Party opposition, especially the opposition of the Republican Party and Governor Bush, emboldened dissenters. Hispanic House members also opposed the compromise, but offered an alternative, which was to elect district judges from state representative districts rather than from county commissioners' precincts. That proved unacceptable: business and Republicans could not approve of a smaller constituency for judges. Another chance to change the way judges were selected in Texas was gone.[53]

The Exceptional Reform: 1995

In 1995, a remarkable event happened in the battles over judicial reform: A successful reform effort developed. Unlike other efforts to reform the Texas judiciary, this reform was not a change in the system of selection; rather, it was an incremental reform within the partisan election system. The reform was the Judicial Campaign Fairness Act, which placed limits on judicial campaign contributions. Individual contributions to statewide judicial candidates were limited to $5,000, and individual contributions to other judicial candidates were limited to between $1,000 and $5,000 depending on the population of the judicial district. Limits were also placed on contributions from law firms and members of law firms as well as on contributions from political action committees. Contributors had to be reported and identified by name, address, and job title. Voluntary expenditure limits were also established by which the opponent of a candidate exceeding the expenditure limits was not bound by contribution limits.

The law grew from the convergence of several events. First, Governor George W. Bush announced his opposition to changing the system of electing judges but did not reject other reform ideas. Second, in 1994 nearly $4.5 million was spent by two candidates in a vicious Democratic primary campaign, and that race focused attention on the huge sums that were going into judicial races. Third, by 1995 there was no longer the possibility that smaller judicial districts would be imposed on the state by the federal courts, and thus attention could be focused on issues other than judicial subdistricts and smaller districts. Additionally, with the election of Governor Bush, Republicans were gaining more influence in Texas government and with them came greater support for tort reform. One of the leading tort reform groups, Texans for Lawsuit Reform, supported limits on judicial campaign contributions. Another supporter of judicial campaign contribution limits was Democratic state senator Rodney Ellis, who had previously unsuccessfully backed legislation on contribution limits. Wisely, Ellis reached out for support to a stalwart Republican state representative, Jerry Madden. With Madden's backing the judicial campaign finance proposal became a bipartisan one. Madden then cultivated the support of judges who tended to see the legislation as beneficial to their interests. And, in the wake of the vicious and extraordinarily expensive Democratic primary campaign for the Texas Supreme Court, both the plaintiffs' bar and the defense bar were ready to support campaign contribution limits.

The law is by far the most significant judicial reform in Texas in modern times. Chief Justice Tom Phillips saw it as a "first step," but Representative Madden quickly noted that the reform had gone "as far as it needs to go." Soon the battles returned to the old issue of changing the system for selecting judges in Texas, and judicial reform efforts again began their old pattern of failure.[54]

The 1996–1997 Effort

Buoyed by the passage of judicial reform legislation in the senate as a result of Lieutenant Governor Bullock's initiative, the Texas Supreme Court appointed task forces to develop proposals for improving the Texas judiciary. One of those task forces examined judicial selection, but its effort was doomed to failure. The task force expressed its concerns about the current system for selecting judges, but its members were unable to agree upon an alternative judicial selection system.[55]

Chief Justice Tom Phillips, long an advocate of judicial selection reforms in Texas, again tried to push the issue in his State of the Judiciary address, in which he severely criticized the partisanship of the current system, the role of money in judicial races, and lack of minority representation on the bench.[56]

As the 1997 legislative session entered the home stretch, however, the prospects for reform remained slim. In the senate, one proposal provided for the appointment of appellate judges and the election of district judges in nonpartisan elections. Both appellate and trial judges would then run in retention elections, although trial judges would run in regular nonpartisan elections after two retention elections. In counties of more than one million, district judges would be elected from county commissioners precincts. The other major senate proposal provided for the appointment, election, and retention of appellate judges and eliminated straight party voting for appellate and district judges. Appellate judges would have to run in partisan elections following the expiration of their appointed terms and then would be subject to retention elections.[57]

Of these two proposals, the first bill was sponsored by state senator Rodney Ellis, an African American Democrat from Houston, but he admitted that it did not have enough support from non-minority legislators to pass. The second proposal was by a white Republican from Lubbock, state senator Robert Duncan. Minorities threatened to oppose the Duncan plan on the grounds that it did not provide increased chances for minority representation on the bench. Senator Ellis, for example, threatened to filibuster the Duncan bill, and the chairman of the Mexican-American Legislative Caucus, Representative Hugo Berlanga, a Democrat from Corpus Christi, claimed the plan was going to meet very stiff resistance.[58] Minority leaders were especially adamant that any judicial selection change include both trial and appellate judges. Their hope was that some compromise would develop to allow them to get smaller trial judge districts and therefore more minority judges in exchange for an appointed appellate judiciary, which would be favored by business interests. If the Duncan bill passed, minorities feared business interests would gain their objective of changing the way appellate judges were selected and then would never support the minority group objective of smaller trial court districts.[59]

After considerable posturing, senators Ellis and Duncan agreed to a compromise bill by which appellate judges would be appointed. District judges would also be appointed, but the districts would be county commissioners' precincts. The appointed judges would then run against opponents in the next primary elections. However, all candidates would run in all primaries, creating a nonpartisan primary election. If a candidate did not receive 50 percent of the vote, there would be a run-off in the general election. The winner would serve four years and would then run in a nonpartisan retention election.[60] The compromise plan, however, still did not resolve the concerns of Hispanics, and many incumbent judges were uncomfortable about the plan as well. Without sufficient support, judicial reform was postponed again.

The 2003 Effort

In the 2003 legislative session, still another major effort was made to change the Texas system of judicial selection. Aware of the problems John Hill had in earlier years with a judicial selection commission and the "Who picks the pickers?" issue, state senator Robert Duncan introduced a bill which would have district court judges and appellate judges appointed by the governor with the consent of the Texas Senate. Afterward, the judges would run for office in retention elections. One of the strongest supporters of the bill was Texas Chief Justice Tom Phillips. Just as had occurred when Lieutenant-Governor Bob Bullock took an interest in judicial selection; the Duncan bill cleared the Senate, only to die in the Texas House.

The bill did have bipartisan support, including significant Republican support. A Republican group, Make Texas Proud, was formed to support the bill, and its leader was a long-time Midland Republican. Membership in the organization included former Governor Bill Clements, former Republican National co-chairwoman Anne Armstrong, and three former state party chairs. Perhaps the support from Republicans had something to do with Phillips' efforts to show that demographic changes in urban counties would soon bring about a Democratic resurgence in those areas. Indeed, that might also explain the continued opposition by some Democrats and especially by the Mexican American Legal Defense and Education Fund. But many Republican leaders, including the current leadership of the state Republican Party, opposed judicial selection reform. For many, politics relates to the here and now, not future demographic changes. And, the Texas Republican Party mounted a mighty effort against the bill.[61]

In killing the bill, the Texas Republican Party attacked one of their own; Chief Justice Phillips was attacked by the Republican Party Chairwoman, Susan Weddington, who claimed the bill was Phillips' idea and that he was the one "very out front on this." Phillips argued that the strategy of the state party was to convince people that the bill was just his idea, making the bill easier to defeat. And, Senator Duncan, the author of the bill, said that "Justice Phillips is suffering the price for providing leadership on this issue."[62]

The Texas Republican Party's website even contained a petition that visitors could sign "to protect Texans' right to elect their judges!"[63] Supporters in the House were lobbying colleagues, and Chief Justice Phillips along with associate justices Craig Enoch and Harriet O'Neill was seeking the support of House members. The bill was about to be voted out of the House Judicial Affairs Committee with majority support. Suddenly, staff members of new Republican Speaker Tom Craddick told the chairman of the committee to pull the bill from consideration. Although Craddick refused to comment on his action, the spokesman for the Republican Party claimed that it was not pressure from party leadership that caused Craddick to kill the bill, but that "it was a bad bill that the majority of House members opposed." The Democratic Party had also opposed the bill, but it was the adamant opposition of the state Republican Party that had the real impact. The state Republican Party had even sent out an e-mail to party members urging them to contact lawmakers to oppose the bill.[64] It was a dramatic turn from the earlier position of the Texas Republican Party, a position when it was not in power, that Texas should abandon the partisan election of judges.

Why Texas Still Has Partisan Elections

It is important to understand that there are many factions involved in the debate over judicial selection. One has to examine the key special interest groups in order to determine the selection system each believes is in its best interests.

The Political Parties

The Democratic and Republican parties in Texas need to maintain their numbers and power. In part, that is done by having a large number of partisan offices that can be political rewards for the party faithful, which in turn encourage people to get involved and to work on behalf of the party and its candidates. A large number of partisan offices can also be a source of pride and prestige for a political party successful enough to capture many of those offices.

Judgeships in Texas are not only numerous, they are also prestigious and pay fairly well. If the partisan election of judges was abandoned in favor of another system of selection, such as nonpartisan election or an appointive system, it would be contrary to the interests of the political parties. As a result, both the Democrats and Republicans can be expected to resist change. Interestingly, when Hill first proposed reforms, the Democratic Party was still dominant and was especially hostile to moving away from partisan election of judges. Within the Republican Party, there was much support for merit selection. That changed when the Republican Party became the dominant party in Texas. Now the Republican Party is among the strongest supporters of partisan election of judges.

The Plaintiffs' Bar

Texas is, in general, a conservative state with a pro-business environment. There is a tendency to elect conservative, pro-business governors, who appoint conservative, pro-business judges. As a result, plaintiffs' lawyers, those who sue on behalf of injured parties, often against businesses, historically have supported partisan election of judges. Their fear has been that Texas would move toward an appointive system, such as merit selection, for selecting judges.

When the Democratic Party was dominant or at least competitive in state-wide races, the plaintiffs' bar was allied with the Party in its opposition to merit selection. With the partisan election system, plaintiffs' lawyers might exert some influence over the selection of judges by contributing generously to judicial campaigns.

However, political influence of the plaintiffs' bar is far less now that the Republican Party has ascended to power. Lawyers who sue businesses obviously have little influence in a Republican Party that is a conservative, pro-business party. And, in the current political scene with a Republican governor, a Republican-controlled legislature, and an entire Supreme Court that is Republican, the plaintiffs' bar's once-booming voice in judicial selection politics has been stilled. All that this interest group can now hope for is the maintenance of elected trial judges in places such as South Texas, where there is still sympathy for the plaintiffs' viewpoint.

Insurance Defense Lawyers, Business Interests, and Medical Interests

Businesses and professional groups, especially physicians, are likely to be sued and are represented by defense lawyers. These defense interests have long worried about the influence of plaintiffs' lawyers and their contributions in judicial races. Not only have they contributed great amounts of money in judicial races to counter the contributions of the plaintiffs' bar, but they believe that they have suffered in the courts at the hands of plaintiff-oriented judges who were chosen under a partisan election system. As a result, these defense interests have traditionally supported merit selection as the appropriate system of selection for judges. Not only is it likely that the appointing governor will have a conservative, pro-business perspective, but because no one runs against a judge in a retention election, these elections are usually inexpensive, and the importance of plaintiffs' lawyers contributions is minimal.

However, this traditional support for merit selection of judges among defense interests is declining as those defense interests, especially in the aftermath of the 1994 elections, see more conservative, pro-business Republicans being elected to office. Partisan election of judges in Texas, in other words, is not the threat to their economic interests that it once was except perhaps in the more pro-plaintiff areas of the state such as South Texas.

Thus, while there remains significant business interest support for merit selection of judges, like the activities of business interests in a number of other states, one sees an increasing willingness to enter the political fray and elect judges more sympathetic to their viewpoints.

Minorities

Minority groups want to elect more African American and Hispanic judges to the bench. The current system of partisan elections has led to the election of relatively small numbers of minorities to the bench, and in 1994, eight of the ten minority judges in Harris County were defeated. As a result, minority interest groups concerned about judicial selection do not like the system in which the districts are county-wide or larger.

Some have argued that minorities would be better off with a nonpartisan election system. Because minorities in Texas are overwhelmingly Democratic voters, and because large numbers of minority judicial candidates who have been defeated have been Democrats, it may be that in a nonpartisan system, the recent tendency in Texas to vote Republican would not affect judicial races, and more minorities would win judgeships. However, the counterargument is that minorities tend to vote straight Democratic tickets, and the elimination of the party label in judicial races would vastly reduce minority voting in those races.[65]

Minority groups involved in judicial selection in Texas dislike appointive systems because of a concern that governors would not appoint many minorities to the bench. Because Texas is increasingly Republican and minorities provide little of the electoral base of the Republican Party in Texas, it seems unlikely that minorities could expect many appointments from Republican governors.

Minorities do not trust the current elective system, have concerns about a nonpartisan system, and are hostile toward an appointive system; therefore, minorities have tended to support the partisan election of judges from small districts. Civil rights groups have argued that district court judges (the major trial court judges in Texas) should be elected from districts about the size of state representatives' or county commissioners' districts. One proposal has been that in a county such as Dallas, the county would elect its district judges from eighteen districts instead of the current system of electing those judges county-wide. Because several state representative districts have large minority populations, minorities believe that African American and Hispanic judges can be elected from those districts. Texas minority groups have been unsuccessful in enlisting the federal courts in supporting their position that these minority districts should be created because the current system violates federal law, however. The Republican Party would, of course, likely lose judgeships to the Democratic Party under a smaller district system. And, business interests fear that smaller districts might create pro-plaintiff havens. Thus, the push for smaller districts—especially given the absence of federal intervention—seems unlikely to succeed.

Judges

Judges have a key interest in the battle over judicial selection. Their main concern is political security. In addition, sitting judges have a considerable amount of power. Within the legal community and within county politics, judges are often well-connected and influential figures. Thus, if there were an appointive system such as merit selection, judges would want to be "grandfathered" into the system so that they would reap the benefits of retention elections. With retention elections they would run for office and have no opponents, and probably no need for significant fund-raising efforts. Because only about 1.6 percent of judges are defeated in retention elections,[66] some sort of system that includes retention elections would be very attractive to judges. However, judges would also want to avoid the risk of being screened out by the merit selection commission or not being appointed by the governor.

There might be some judicial support for nonpartisan elections. Incumbent judges would have a political advantage in a nonpartisan election and would not be subject to the partisan sweeps, where judges have been voted out of office simply because they had the wrong party label for that particular election year.

Most judges who are in office because they have been elected from a large district will not support the formation of smaller districts. If they suddenly have to campaign in a much smaller district, they are in danger of losing. And it is likely that most judges support the status quo. They are opposed to change because they have been successful under the current system and might not be successful under an alternative system. Additionally, as Texas has increasingly become a one-party Republican state, many judges have tied their careers to the fortunes of the Republican Party. They would be unlikely to support reforms opposed by the party since damage to the party might damage their careers and since their loyalty to the party will be considered for future appointments to higher judicial offices. Indeed, Dallas County judges have been the most adamant opponents of judicial selection changes.

The Amalgam of Competing Interests

The problem that has occurred from the amalgam of competing interest groups is that the key interests in judicial selection politics are very different. The political parties—especially the Republican Party—have no doubts: they want partisan election of judges. The Democratic Party would, because of its strong minority constituency, be more tolerant of smaller districts than would the Republican Party. The Republican Party would oppose smaller districts because such a system would provide Democrats with the means to break the Republican stronghold on large counties. Republicans are currently winning with larger districts and would prefer the status quo. An appointive system is risky. In spite of the state's increasing Republican representation, a Democrat could be elected governor. Therefore, Republicans see the current system as providing them the most benefit in terms of controlling the state's judiciary.[67]

Plaintiffs' lawyers have no major problems with the smaller districts promoted by minorities. They have increasingly mixed feelings about the value of partisan elections in general, a system they have strongly supported in the past. However, plaintiffs' lawyers oppose an appointive system such as merit selection, because conservative, pro-business judges would be selected. And, the plaintiffs' bar is far from being the political powerhouse it once was in Texas, given conservative Republican control of all branches of state government.

Defense interests have traditionally supported merit selection, although with increasing Republican strength in Texas, they are more satisfied with the current system of selection. Defense interests do not want significantly smaller judicial districts in Texas. In at least some urban counties smaller districts would break conservative Republican control of the courthouse. It is more important, however, that, as theories of politics from the days of James Madison have suggested, the smaller the constituency, the more sensitive the elected official must be to that constituency. An elected official in a small district cannot play one interest against another simply because, unlike in a larger district, the constituents are more likely to be homogeneous. Thus, business interests fear what lawyers call "home cooking"—judges who are very responsive to the demands of constituents. Business interests remain concerned with areas of South Texas which are very pro-plaintiff areas; they would not want such areas to also exist within the urban centers of Texas.

Judges don't want any change in the system which will endanger their jobs. Since they have been successful with partisan elections, many judges wish to keep that system. If there is a change, their ideal would be a system that made their jobs more secure. Thus, for judges, retention elections are especially attractive, while significantly smaller districts are threatening to their careers.

The problem with judicial reform has been two-fold: (1) with the exception of Lieutenant Governor Bullock and Chief Justice Tom Phillips, state-wide elected officials in Texas have not chosen to make judicial reform part of their agenda; and, (2) there are so many competing interest groups with divergent concerns in the debate over reform that change in the way judges are selected seems unlikely.

What does the future hold? The problem remains in accommodating the various interest groups involved in this issue. The interest group struggle has created a policy-making deadlock concerning reform. The result of this deadlock is that the existing system, despite its many flaws, will likely continue for want of an acceptable alternative.

Conclusion

At this point it is difficult to imagine that merit selection of judges in Texas is in the offing. Judith Haydel found that support of the bar is almost essential for judicial reform movements to succeed.[68] In Texas, the bar is too split between plaintiffs' and defense lawyers to even take an official position on reform. Additionally, even the Democratic Party is split over reform with rural Democrats tending to support the status quo, and many urban

Democrats tending to support reform. The state Republican Party is vehemently opposed to reform. Minorities and women, particularly Hispanics, question why reform is needed at a time when they are beginning to gain entry into judicial ranks.

Additionally, there is the traditional Texas populism which leads Texans to vote for innumerable public officials from governor to attorney general to railroad commissioner to constable. Although the question has a biased wording, it is instructive to note that in the March 1988 Democratic primary, 86 per cent of the voters were "For" the referendum question, "Texans shall maintain their right to select judges by a direct vote of the people rather than to change to an appointment process created by the Legislature."

While an influential Texan, John Hill, made judicial reform his cause, he was hindered by the opposition of most of the rest of the Texas Supreme Court. Not even the Ray-Kilgarlin Supreme Court scandal and the Texaco-Pennzoil case brought reform to the forefront. The Ray-Kilgarlin scandal did not involve criminal behavior and was at a time when the governor's role in the Southern Methodist University football scandal had captured public attention. It was hard to turn the Texaco-Pennzoil case into a vehicle for reform since the decision in the case was based on a jury verdict and since the Texas Supreme Court did not decide the case and therefore issue an opinion that could be criticized. Additionally, the problems of the 1986 California Supreme Court retention elections and the 1982 and 1986 Missouri Supreme Court problems, coupled with the lack of evidence that merit selection results in the election of meritorious judges, all made it difficult to show that the proposed alternative would result in improvement of the Texas judiciary.

Problems with the Texas judiciary are likely to remain, and instead of trying to work out viable solutions to those problems, Texans for some time will likely debate the value of some form of merit selection versus partisan election. Ironically, the reform movement may itself inhibit reform by focusing on merit selection (or at least retention elections) as a reform alternative instead of far more feasible but more incremental reforms. At the same time, the struggle for judicial reform will remain, if only because the reform and anti-reform bandwagons cloak important political and social interests which seek influence over the Texas judiciary.

Notes

[1] John Hill, A Time of Challenge: Judicial Reform in Texas, 52 *Texas Bar Journal* 165, 168–69 (1989).

[2] The description of Hill's unsuccessful race for governor is from Benjamin Ginsberg, et al. *We the People: An Introduction to American Politics* 881–883 (3rd ed., Texas ed., 2001).

[3] Anthony Champagne, The Selection and Retention of Judges in Texas, 40 *Southwestern Law Journal* 53, 91 (1986).

[4] One indication of the tension on the Supreme Court which was produced by Hill's reform proposal is Linda Ponce, Justices Divided on Plan, *Texas Lawyer*, December 1–5, 1986, at 1.

[5] The ethics complaint was dismissed by the Commission. Justice Franklin Spears, one of Hills strongest opponents, filed the complaint in reference to Hill's appointment of a judge to hear a case that involved the firm to which he was moving after resigning from the court.

[6] Anthony Champagne, Judicial Reform in Texas, 72 *Judicature* 146, 151–153 (1988).

[7] Id., 156–157.

[8] Id., 158.

[9] The above material is from John L. Hill, Jr., The Texas Plan: Merit Selection of Judges in Committee of 100 for the Merit Selection of Judges (ed.), *The Texas Plan: Merit Selection of Judges* 7–12 (1986).

[10] Champagne, supra note 3 at 66–67.

[11] Bancroft Henderson & T. C. Sinclair, The Selection of Judges in Texas, 5 *Houston Law Review* 441–442 (1968).

[12] Champagne, supra note 6 at 147.

[13] Hill, supra note 9 at 8–10.

[14] Champagne, supra note 3 at 90.

[15] Roy Schotland, Elective judges' Campaign Financing: Are State Judges' Robes the Emperor's Clothes of American Democracy?, 2 *Journal of Law and Policy* 57, 60 (1985).

[16] Charles W. Barrow to Wiston Bode, May 19, 1976, Charles W. Barrow papers, W. R. Poage Congressional Library, Baylor University, Waco, Texas.

[17] Champagne, supra note 3 at 89.

[18] Id., 84.

[19] Id.

[20] Thomas Petzinger, *Oil and Honor: The Texaco-Pennzoil Wars*, 285–286 (1987).

[21] Fish, Flashy Lawyer Dabbles in Politics for Fun, *Dallas Morning News*, May 9,1982, at 1AA.

[22] Ron Briggs, The Demography of a Sunbelt State in Champagne and Harpham, *Texas at the Crossroads* 16, 35 (1987).

[23] Champagne, supra note 6 at 151.

[24] Id.

[25] Id., 151.

[26] See the discussion of the significance of having a readily identifiable name, including the political value of the "Ron Chapman" name in Steve McGonigle, Name Recognition at the

Heart of Judge Candidates' Game Plan, *Dallas Morning News*, November 3, 1984, at 34A.

[27] Ginsberg, supra note 2 at 884–886.

[28] E.g., Hill, supra note 9 at 10. The study was prepared by M. L. Henry, Jr., et al. for the Fund for Modern Courts. It is titled, *The Success of Women and Minorities in Achieving Judicial Office: The Selection Process* (1985).

[29] Nicholas O. Alozie, Distribution of Women and Minority Judges: The Effects of Judicial Selection Methods, 71 *Social Science Quarterly* 315 (1990).

[30] For a discussion of the Texas Plan, see Champagne supra note 6.

[31] Hill, supra note 9 at 11–12.

[32] One indication of the tension on the Supreme Court which was produced by Hill's reform proposal is, Ponce, supra note 4 at 1.

[33] Champagne, supra note 6 at 152.

[34] Id..

[35] See, "Citizens to Protect Our Right to Elect Texas Judges," Press Release, January 29, 1987.

[36] Charles Herring, Written Testimony of Charles Herring, Jr. Before the Joint Select Committee on the Judiciary, mimeographed, undated; James Harrington, Letter to the Texas Senate Committee on State Affairs, March 13,1987; Texas AFL-CIO, Friends of Labor Prevail in Court Races, *Labor News*, March, 1988, at 1; Robert Elder, A Year of Scandal and Ambivalence, *The Texas Lawyer*, December 14,1987, at III-4.

[37] Champagne, supra note 6 at 152–153.

[38] Id., 153,

[39] Henry Glick, The Promise and the Performance of the Missouri Plan: Judicial Selection in the Fifty States, 32 *University of Miami Law Review* 520 (1978).

[40] For example, Citizens to Protect Our Right to Elect Texas Judges, supra note 35 at 2–3.

[41] Champagne, supra note 6 at 154.

[42] Id., 154–155.

[43] Susan Carbon & Larry Berkson, *Judicial Retention Elections in the United States* 23 (1980).

[44] Champagne, supra note 6 at 155.

[45] Id., 155–156.

[46] Ratcliffe & Moran, Embattled Justice Raps Clements' Ethics, *Houston Chronicle*, June 12, 1987, at 1.

[47] Champagne, supra note 6 at 157.

[48] Id.

[49] Id.

[50] Id. at 158.

[51] Anthony Champagne, Judicial Selection in Texas: Democracy's Deadlock, in Anthony Champagne & Edward J. Harpham (eds.), *Texas Politics: A Reader* 100 (1998).

[52] An example of these complaints that additional interests should be represented on the committee is in Robert Elder, Jr. & Walter Borges, A Bullock in a China Closet? Group Tackles Judge Selection, *Texas Lawyer*, August 15, 1994, p. 1.

[53] Champagne, supra note 51 at 101–102.

[54] This discussion of the 1995 reforms is taken from an excellent selection of case studies of reform in the states by Daniel Becker and Malia Reddick, *Judicial Selection Reform: Examples from Six States* 1–9 (2003). The chapter on Texas is titled, "Campaign Finance Reform in Texas."

[55] Texas Commission on Judicial Efficiency, *Governance of the Texas Judiciary: Independence and Accountability*, Volume 1 23–24 (1996).

[56] Thomas R. Phillips, State of the Judiciary Address, February 24, 1997 (mimeographed).

[57] Texas Senate Research Center, Comparison of Selected Judicial Selection Legislation, February 24, 1997 (mimeographed).

[58] Sam Attlesey, Standoff between Judicial Reformers Stalls Legislation, *Dallas Morning News*, April 20, 1997, 48A.

[59] Id.

[60] Texas Judges, *Dallas Morning News*, 2 May 1997, 32A.

[61] An excellent treatment of the Republican split on the bill is, Max B. Baker, Groups push for judicial reform, DFW*com, April 21, 2003, http://www.dfw.com/mld/dfw/news/legislature/5681053.htm?templ...

[62] Discussion of the attack on Chief Justice Phillips is found in Mary Alice Robbins, Texas Chief Justice Takes Heat for Judicial Selection Stance, *Texas Lawyer*, May 1, 2003, 1.

[63] Republican Party of Texas, Sign the petition to protect Texans' right to elect their judges!, www.texasgop.org/judges/.

[64] Monica Wolfson, Bill changing judicial election process dies, Caller.com, May 27, 2003, www.caller.com/ccct/cda/article_print1,1983,CCCT_876_1992186_ARTICLE-DET...   and Max B. Baker, Outlook Bleak for Judge Bill, *Star-Telegram*, May 25, 2003, http://www.dfw.com/mld/dfw/news/legislature/5942485.htm?template=contentModules/pri...

[65] Chapman reports that more than 90 percent of African American voters and between 60 and 70 percent of Hispanic voters vote Democratic. See Ronald W. Chapman, Judicial Roulette: Alternatives to Single-Member Districts as a Legal and Political Solution to Voting-Rights Challenges to At-Large Judicial Elections, *SMU Law Review* 457, 482 (1995).

[66] Carbon & Berkson, supra note 43 at 21 (1980).

[67] Conservative columnist William Murchison expressed a widespread Republican view of judicial reform when he wrote, "The Democratic-inspired idea behind judicial reapportionment is to unhorse Republican judges, replacing them with black or brown Democrats grateful to the party establishment." See William Murchison, Why Morales Deserved to Lose, *Texas Lawyer*, September 6, 1993 at 8. Although former Republican Governor William Clements and Republican Texas Chief Justice Tom Phillips supported judicial reform in a jointly written newspaper opinion piece, they recognized that many Republicans felt otherwise and wrote, "After 31 Democratic state judges lost in November's election, many Republicans are reluctant to reform Texas' judicial election process. They see a basic unfairness in changing the judicial system just when it seemingly begins to favor them." See Bill Clements and Tom Phillips, GOP Sweep Shouldn't Obscure Need For Texas court reform, *Dallas Morning News*, January 27, 1995, p. 29A.

[68] Judith Haydel, Explaining Adoption of Judicial Merit Selection in the States, 1950–1980: A Multivariate Test (1987) (unpublished dissertation in University of New Orleans Library).

Chapter VII

Coming to a Judicial Election Near You: The New Era in Texas Judicial Elections

The Texas Judiciary at the Forefront

As quickly as it had arrived, it dissipated: Texas judicial politics calmed down. Texas Supreme Court contests still involve a lot of money, but it is much less now than over a decade ago.[1] A judicial candidate's party label is still important but in a different way. Now to win a statewide election or election in counties such as Dallas or Harris, one has to be a Republican. In the 2000 elections, there was not even a Democrat who ran for one of the three seats on the Texas Supreme Court. There is now no Democrat on either the Texas Supreme Court or the Texas Court of Criminal Appeals. And in the two most populous counties in Texas, Dallas and Harris, the countywide judiciaries are nearly Democrat-free.

The era of party sweeps has come to an end. That was an effect of the transition to a one-party Republican state, where there were elections that swept in Republicans one year and Democrats in the next election cycle. Now Republican nominees are regularly swept into office.[2] The result, of course, is a period of calm in Texas judicial politics. There is still considerable money in judicial races, but it is far from the frenzied fund-raising and giving of that earlier era. Judicial campaigns, while not the sleepy low-key affairs of the earlier era, have relaxed considerably. Texas seems back to the more stable times of one-party judicial politics. Even a second visit of "60 Minutes" presented a somewhat more relaxed view of the Texas judiciary.[3]

However, there are signs on the horizon that the current calm in judicial elections is only a brief one. Texas' judicial politics in the late 1970s and early 1980s turned out to be a bellwether for what was about to happen in much of the rest of the country.[4] While Texas judicial elections have cooled, judicial elections in the rest of the country have gotten "nastier, noisier, and costlier."[5] And there is every indication that the "nastier, noisier, and costlier" campaigns of much of the rest of the nation will soon come to

Texas. That will happen because the state's demographics are soon going to make the parties in Texas competitive again. While that might be a desirable thing for those who believe in a competitive two-party system in the political branches of government, highly competitive judicial elections may be considerably less desirable.

First, we will examine what has happened in the rest of the country during this period of relative judicial political calm in Texas. Then, let us turn to why this new competition in judicial politics is about to hit Texas.

And You Thought Judicial Politics in Texas Were Wild?

Today's judicial politics are far from the quiet affairs of the recent past. As one newspaper article explained,

> This ugly transformation of judicial politics has come as some of the nation's most divisive disputes have come before the courts. State Supreme Courts now decide the future of school funding; policies affecting guns, tobacco and the environment; and the rules that make it easy, or difficult, to sue corporations and doctors for damages. With such enormous stakes, the battle lines are stark: Trial lawyers and unions seek judges who will side with individuals and embrace new legal theories. Businesses want judges who'll protect them and the status quo.[6]

That transformation in judicial politics occurred quickly. Judicial elections moved from a time when they were "about as exciting as a game of checkers played by mail,"[7] to a new high (or perhaps a new low) in hard-fought, bitter campaigns in the 2000 elections.[8]

There were numerous hints, of course, that we were moving toward bitterly divisive campaigns. Over twenty years ago a California candidate who had campaigned simply as a believer in judicial independence suddenly one week before the election flooded his county with fliers proclaiming, "The Issue Is Rape."[9] Another incumbent in California published a flier claiming that he had "sent more criminals—rapists, murderers, felons—to prison than any other judge in Contra Costa County history."[10] In 1990 in North Carolina the state Supreme Court's Democratic justices were attacked for being too liberal. The governor called for replacing the three Democrats up for reelection with Republicans who would create a conservative majority.[11] In one decision, the court had awarded a teacher damages for being fired in a dismissal hearing that was biased, and that decision was affirmed by the state's Supreme Court. "You're going to love this," claimed the governor. "There was a driver education instructor over in Hickory who had a bad thing about taking indecent liberties with teenage girls....The liberal Democratic majority...said, 'That's all right, he can have $78,000'.... Maybe it was the little girl who should have gotten the $78,000."[12] In a separate television commercial, the Republican state chairman attacked the court for overturning a murder conviction. Said the chairman, "The judges on our Supreme Court are more interested in criminal rights than in victim rights."[13] It made little difference, of course that these opinions were not written by any candidate but rather by a justice praised by the governor as the most conservative member of the Court.[14]

In 1996, in North Carolina, a candidate addressed a roomful of potential voters saying, "I'm a Republican from the conservative side. I'm pro-life."[15] In an Alabama Supreme Court election in the 1996, a television ad even portrayed a candidate as a skunk.[16] And in 1998, a newspaper ad was run stating, "'Maximum Marion' Bloss: You do the crime, you do the time" and at the bottom of the ad was a picture of her opponent—a person of color.[17] In a 1998 race for the Georgia Supreme Court, a candidate accused an incumbent of believing that traditional moral standards were "pathetic and disgraceful," that she favored licensing same-sex marriage, and that she had called the electric chair "silly."[18] Even in a state like Wisconsin, a state not generally known for intensely fought judicial campaigns, a television ad was run against a Wisconsin justice who was portrayed as "pro-child molester" by her opponent. The ad used the grandmother of a murdered child against the justice even though the justice had not been involved in the case.[19] That 1999 race cost over $1,000,000.[20]

Nor were concerns over judicial elections building simply because of unsavory campaign tactics. Concerns over campaign contributions, at least as disturbing (if not more so) than the big money contributions to Texas Supreme Court candidates in the early 1980s, appeared in other states. One of the most disturbing was in Ohio. There was a suit for damages against Conrail as a result of an accident that killed 16-year-old Michelle Wightman when she was hit by a train. Wightman had driven onto a grade crossing despite closed gates and flashing lights. The proceedings involved three trials: a jury trial for compensatory damages, a bench trial for punitive damages, and after appeal, a jury trial for punitive damages. There was then another appeal and then an appeal to the Ohio Supreme Court. The Supreme Court agreed to hear an appeal by both sides after the second jury had awarded punitive damages of $25,000,000, reduced by the trial judge to $15,000,000. The plaintiff was represented by Murray & Murray Co., a firm that included nine members of the Murray family. Before the Ohio Supreme Court agreed on February 18, 1998 to hear that appeal, campaign contributions were made to two justices by that firm, by the nine Murrays in the firm, and by seven Murray spouses. Contributions were made to one justice on February 9 and to another between January 19 and January 21. Each contribution of $25,000 was lawful, and their campaign reports indicated that the contributions turned out to be 4.4% of one justice's total contributions and 4.7% of the other justices. Both justices ran for reelection in November 1998. And, both justices participated in oral arguments on November 10, 1998. Conrail filed a motion seeking the recusal of each justice, but in October 1999, without the Court or either justice addressing the motion, the Court decided in favor of the plaintiffs. Conrail then made the facts of these contributions a basis for the appeal for review by the U.S. Supreme Court, but they were turned down.[21] Big money in judicial elections elsewhere was raising the same concerns it had earlier when it had entered Texas judicial politics.

Concerns over this new era in judicial elections were not limited to competitive—that is, partisan and nonpartisan—elections. In 1986, the defeat of Chief Justice Rose Bird and two other justices in retention elections in California showed that even retention elections could exhibit rough campaign tactics.[22] However, it was a retention election in Tennessee that showed just how harsh judicial retention elections could be. And that election showed judicial retention election politics could prove a brutal game outside of the unique situation involving Rose Bird and the politics of California. In Tennessee a Supreme Court justice was defeated in a retention election in part because of the opposition of the Republican Party and of Republican leaders but also because of interest group opposition. Six weeks prior to the retention vote, the headline of a Nashville newspaper read, "Court Finds Rape, Murder of Elderly Virgin Not Cruel. Tennessee Conservative Union Says 'Just Say No to Justice White.'"[23] The court had unanimously agreed with the appellate court that the defendant in this case was entitled to a new sentencing hearing.[24] Three justices, including the defeated justice, commented that the evidence was insufficient to show an aggravating circumstance beyond a reasonable doubt as required by state law. That case, however, became the mechanism for interest group and political party efforts to make the justice the first in Tennessee to ever be defeated in a retention election. A mailing sent by the Tennessee Conservative Union opened with a description of the crimes of Richard Odom:

> 78-year-old Ethel Johnson lay dying in a pool of blood. Stabbed in the heart, lungs, and liver, she fought back as best she could.
>
> Her hands were sliced to ribbons as she tried to push the knife away.
>
> And then she was raped.
>
> Savagely...
>
> But her murderer won't be getting the punishment that he deserves.
> Thanks to Penny White.[25]

In the supposedly nonpartisan retention election in which White ran, the Republican Party sent voters a message with the party's name and logo saying: "If you support capital punishment, vote NO [sic] on Penny White."[26] In early voting, the Republican governor commented that he had voted "no" on White's retention since she "did not share the views of the average Tennessean."[27] That criticism was followed by similar remarks from both of the state's Republican senators.[28] Another justice listed as a top target of groups that opposed Justice White announced the year after White's defeat that he would not seek another term.[29]

The stakes are large and the battles are intense. In the 2000 judicial elections, about $45,000,000 was raised by Supreme Court candidates, and records in campaign fund-raising were set in 10 states.[30] Especially notable in these elections was the use of independent expenditures by political parties and especially by interest groups.[31] In the five states with the most heated state Supreme Court elections, about $16,000,000 was spent on the races by non-candidates.[32] In Alabama, Illinois, Michigan, Mississippi, and Ohio, there were seventeen Supreme Court contests, and the average contest came to over $2,000,000.[33] It was a dramatic ratcheting in the scale of interest group involvement in judicial races and, by spending money on advocacy ads independent of a judicial candidate's campaign, the interest groups and the political parties avoided the restrictions of the Code of Judicial Conduct.[34]

In the 2000 elections, judicial politics went wild, especially in Mississippi, Alabama, Ohio and Michigan.[35] Independent expenditures became major factors in all four of these states—and while many of the candidate-funded campaign efforts could not be counted as pure—the independent expenditures by political parties and interest groups were more like hard-fought campaigns for legislative offices. But even judicial candidates' campaign efforts raised eyebrows in 2000. In Illinois, for example, one Supreme Court candidate touted his anti-abortion views in his campaign literature.[36] Another candidate for the high court accused his opponent of supervising a system that "sent innocent men to death row while killers walk the street."[37]

Alabama has traditionally had major battles for their supreme court between trial lawyer-backed candidates and business interest-backed candidates.[38] To that in 2000 was added a religious issue. Trial judge Roy Moore had achieved national note by posting the Ten Commandments in his courtroom. In 2000, he was a Republican candidate for Chief Justice, and he let the voters know of his stance, running a television ad, for example, in which he advertised his Ten Commandments display, which he bragged was done over the opposition of liberals and the ACLU. And he did not go unrewarded. One Christian conservative grass-roots group raised $177,000 for him in his Republican primary campaign.[39] When Moore became Chief Justice, he on his own authority erected a stone display of the Ten Commandments in the foyer of the state Supreme Court building.[40] It proved an action that eventually led to his removal as Chief Justice. From a political perspective, such action continued the connection to the strong fundamentalist Christian support that helped him achieve the Chief Justiceship.

Moore's main opponent for Chief Justice was Harold See, who ran a television ad that compared his record on crime with that of Judge Moore. That led to a state Judicial Inquiry proceeding against See in which the Commission charged that See's claim that "Moore let convicted drug dealers off with reduced sentences or probation—at least forty times" was misleading and false.[41]

Nor were only the Moore and See campaigns on the wild side in Alabama's judicial politics in 2000. One Supreme Court candidate, Lyn

Stuart, let voters know that she had sentenced two convicted murderers to death, that she had a 91% conviction rate in DUI cases, that she had a 20-year record in fighting crime as both a prosecutor and judge[42] and that "she respects law enforcement."[43]

And a business group told voters, "If you thought we finally got greedy trial lawyers out of Alabama politics, try again." They claimed the trial lawyers were funding four campaigns for the state Supreme Court, and that it was time to tell those candidates, "Democrats Laird, England, Cook, and Yates: Get trial lawyer money out of our court."[44] In an Alabama Democratic Party ad, Alabama's Republican Supreme Court was blamed for forcing arbitration on victims of "Firestone tires and Ford Explorers." "Firestone and Ford," the ad claimed, "like it but you shouldn't." Of course the way to resolve the problems was, according to the Democratic Party-funded ad, to "vote against Alabama's Republican Supreme Court."[45]

In neighboring Mississippi, the U.S. Chamber of Commerce spent about $958,000 on television "issue" ads on behalf of the Chief Justice, two other incumbents and one challenger.[46] And two trial lawyer-funded political action committees spent about $312,000 opposing the ads.[47] The chief justice and her challenger even asked the Chamber to stop running the ads, but the Chamber refused.[48] And, though there was litigation over the issue, the Chamber did not meet disclosure requirements because of their argument that their ads were "issue" ads and therefore free from disclosure.[49] Still, that ad campaign by the Chamber may have defeated the 18-year incumbent Chief Justice whose campaign was marred by allegations of intervention by outsiders.[50] An example of how the Chamber's activities provoked a reaction in the state—a reaction not very favorable to the image of the state's judiciary—was a candidate-sponsored ad by Chuck Easley.

Auctioneer: "I've got 300, now 320...."

Announcer: "A Washington D.C. special interest group has already pumped a half million dollars into TV ads backing its candidates for the Mississippi Supreme Court. They know their candidates, like Lenore Prather, are more likely to listen when the HMO's and big drug companies need a favor. The secretary of state has asked the attorney general to investigate these questionable expenditures. Do they think justice is for sale here?"

Auctioneer: "Sold."

Announcer: "Send these out-of-state meddlers a clear message that the Mississippi Supreme Court is not for sale."

Announcer 2: "On November 7, vote for the candidate who's not for sale, Chuck Easley."[51]

In the 2000 Michigan Supreme Court elections, the Republican Party aired a television commercial against a Democratic nominee, who in an appellate decision upheld a sentence of a man convicted of molesting a seven-year-old girl. The ad depicted the Democrat as soft on crime, and the original script said the candidate, then an appellate judge, "gave that repeat pedophile less than the minimum sentence, just a slap on the wrist." When several television stations objected to the word "gave" because the original sentence was handed down by the trial judge, the revised script said that the candidate "let that repeat pedophile off with...."[52] And, to make matters worse the word "pedophile" was flashed near the judge's name. In response to criticisms of the connection between "pedophile" and the judge's name, the GOP replied, "We don't call him [a pedophile]."[53]

As is often the case in judicial campaigns,[54] law and order proved to be a big issue. One justice running for reelection explained that he had thought "for too long our courts have really emphasized the rights of criminals at the expense of victims." An announcer explained that the justice "believes in protecting the rights of police officers, victims, and law-abiding citizens." The announcer added that because the justice believed, "Technicalities or loopholes shouldn't keep criminals on the street," 22,000 Michigan police officers endorsed Justice Taylor. Further reassurance was then offered by the justice, claiming, "I think police officers are really champions of our society."[55]

In Ohio, non-candidate expenditures amounted to more than $8,000,000,[56] and one of the toughest battles was over the reelection of Democratic Justice Alice Resnick. Resnick had trial lawyer and union support and was strongly opposed by the Chamber of Commerce. Among other attack ads, the Chamber ran an ad that backfired and contributed to her election victory.[57] In the ad, Lady Justice peeked underneath a blindfold as special interest money tipped the scales of justice. An announcer then claimed that Resnick ruled 70% of the time in favor of trial lawyers who have given her more than $750,000 since 1994. The announcer concluded,

"Alice Resnick. Is justice for sale?"[58] And in reaction to the anti-Resnick ads, the Ohio Democratic Party responded in kind:

> Announcer: "Why are corporate polluters and a big insurance company spending hundreds of thousands distorting Justice Alice Robie Resnick's record?"
>
> Announcer 2: "Maybe because she's taken on the special interests."
>
> Announcer 1: "Stood up for families by exposing Ohio's dilapidated schools."
>
> Announcer 2: "Fought for quality education for all Ohio's children."
>
> Announcer 1: "But in the same landmark decision, Debra Cook said no to education reform and no to our kids."
>
> Announcer 2: "Say no to special interests and no to Debra Cook.
>
> Announcer 1: "Alice Robie Resnick and Tim Black for the Ohio Supreme Court."[59]

Nor are the 2000 judicial elections the end of these "nastier, noisier, and costlier" elections. The U.S. Chamber of Commerce and its affiliated state organizations, the most active of the interest groups involved in the 2000 state supreme court races,[60] has expressed pleasure with its successes—12 of the 15 candidates it supported won election.[61]

In 2002, there was some drop-off in the amounts of money spent in judicial campaigns, but it remained substantial. One estimate of money raised by candidates by November 7, 2002, nationwide was $16.9 million,[62] and an estimate of television expenditures in nine states was $7.4 million.[63] Those numbers may be underestimates because in the Ohio Supreme Court elections alone, it was estimated that four candidates and four interest groups spent $5.6 million on airtime alone.[64] In Mississippi, judicial television ads cost four times more in 2002 than they did in 2000.[65] There were more independent interest groups involved in the 2002 races compared to the 2000 races, and more states did see reliance on television ads than in 2000 as well.[66] One article recently estimated that the Chamber of Commerce had spent $100 million since 2000 on judicial campaigns, although this amount seems quite high as did their claim that the Chamber spent $50 million in 2003.[67] However, the Chamber has been involved in 24 judicial elections in eight states, and the candidates it supported have won 21 of those races.[68]

The television ad blitz seen in the 2000 judicial elections continued in even more states in the 2002 elections. The Brennan Center was able to identify eighty-one judicial campaign ads in 2002, aired in Alabama, Idaho, Illinois, Michigan, Mississippi, Nevada, Ohio, Texas, and Washington.[69] Compared to the 2000 elections, numerous new third-party groups appeared and funded ads such as the American Taxpayers Association, Mississippi Citizens for Truth in Government, Mississippi Law Enforcement Alliance of America, Competition Ohio, Ohio Consumers for a Fair Court, Informed Citizens of Ohio, and the Washington First American Education Fund.[70]

An Alabama candidate's ad explained that his opponent had not only taken money from trial lawyers, but he had supported Al Gore over George W. Bush in the 2000 elections.[71] In another ad, the same candidate stressed that children were a gift from God, perhaps tapping into the influential Christian Right and anti-abortion vote.[72] And, in still another ad, the candidate let voters know that he "…stood up to attacks by liberal trial lawyers."[73] In an Idaho ad, a candidate derided his opponent as "very liberal" and pointed out such transgressions by the opponent as voting to hand Idaho water over to federal bureaucrats, supporting court-imposed tax increases, and support by leading trial lawyers in the state.[74] An Illinois candidate was described as working "with police, prosecutors and victims to put violent criminals and sexual predators in jail."[75] That candidate's opponent described a personal encounter with a sexual predator to suggest that the justice system was letting too many criminals roam free and that she should be elected to do something about the problem.[76] In another ad, the candidate presented a montage of police officers reporting on her work in keeping the streets safe, children safe from sexual predators, and keeping the police themselves safe.[77]

One of the more ironic ads was a Chamber of Commerce-sponsored ad in the Michigan Supreme Court race that deplored the negative effects of special interest group influence on the Supreme Court. Voters were told that Justices Weaver and Young have changed things for the better.[78] One of the odder ads presented a long list of special interest contributors to an opponent and then superimposed the opponent's image on the body of a cow that was stamped "approved" by corporations.[79] The Law Enforcement Alliance of America ran two different ads endorsing one Mississippi candidate's support of the death penalty, the right to bear arms, and law enforcement.[80] In Nevada, an ad painted a sympathetic portrait of one candidate who "stood up" to Las Vegas casinos who were attempting to take land from an elderly widow. The heroism of such action was emphasized by an image of an individual standing in front of a tank during the Tiananmen Square riots in China.[81] In Ohio, voters were told that a judicial candidate was known as the "Velvet Hammer" because she was tough in sentencing and was the daughter of American missionaries.[82] A third-party ad in Ohio promised that two candidates would "... put the court back on the side of workers and families" and that the candidates would "...hold large corporations accountable for wrongdoing."[83] Another third-party Ohio ad spoke of the support of two candidates for competition in phone service after it discussed the deregulation of phone service in Ohio and one service provider's attempt to double rates.[84] Still another third-party ad in the Ohio races discussed a class action suit involving DES, a drug supposed to prevent miscarriages. However, the daughters of women who took this drug developed cancer. Showing various maternal images, the announcer noted, "Eve Stratton said she had sympathy for the victims, but she gave sanctuary to the big drug companies." In a morbid play on words, the announcer concluded, "Eve Stratton's ruling is a miscarriage of justice."[85] Another third-party ad showed an empty doctor's office and a forlorn couple who have no doctor. There is a narration of the candidate's views on tort reform, noting "Justice Evelyn Stratton's record shows that she understands the need to stop lawsuit abuse."[86] Another ad by the same interest group presented two lawyers discussing hypothetical suits regarding a hubcap thief whose hand was rolled over by a car and a dog dying when it was put in the microwave. An image of the candidate then came on screen, and it is stated that frivolous lawsuits cost "your family" $2500 a year and that the candidate "...protects your family by fighting lawsuit abuse."[87] The same sorts of themes that appeared in the 2000 ads are replayed: crime control, family values, and tort reform.

Future elections will also see "nastier, noisier, and costlier" campaigns because of a 2002 U.S. Supreme Court decision, *Republican Party of Minnesota v. White*.[88] That decision invalidated certain state regulations of judicial campaign speech, in particular bans on candidates announcing views on disputed legal or political issues. In the same year, the 11th Circuit, in *Weaver v. Bonner*,[89] invalidated part of Georgia's Code of Judicial Conduct including restrictions on judges soliciting campaign funds, and in 2003 the federal district court for the Northern District of New York in *Spargo v. NY State Commission on Judicial Conduct* invalidated restrictions on the partisan activities by judges. Though that *Spargo* decision was overturned on appeal, it is likely that further litigation will result over New York's Code of Judicial Conduct.

Only the U.S. Supreme Court decision had a direct effect on Texas, and in Texas judges were not restricted from soliciting campaign funds. However, the cases do suggest that the federal courts increasingly are seeing distinctions between judicial and other elections as being insufficient to justify limits on the speech of judicial candidates. As a result, judicial candidates are likely to become more vocal in their campaign speech and more willing to pander to the political and legal goals of interest groups involved in state judicial politics.

Partisanship in Judicial Elections

Interestingly in the immediate aftermath of the 2000 elections, a National Summit on Improving Judicial Selection was called and made a number of recommendations regarding state judicial elections. The first recommendation was that "All judicial elections, whether direct or retention, should be conducted in a nonpartisan manner." It was clear to the Summit members, who included a number of state supreme court chief justices, that partisanship was a big problem in judicial elections. That partisanship showed up in Texas, of course, as the Republican Party gained strength against the long-dominant Democratic Party in the state. Partisanship, however, has long been troubling to many who study and have been involved in judicial elections.

"I was elected in 1916 because Woodrow Wilson kept us out of war—I was defeated in 1920 because Woodrow Wilson hadn't kept us out of war."[90] That was the claim of Judge Fred Williams of the Missouri Supreme Court long ago.[91] While political party involvement in judicial elections has long had its detractors, there are positive statements that can be made. Political parties may provide campaign workers for judicial candidates. They can also help provide campaign funding. Most importantly, the party label provides a significant political asset for candidates in low-visibility races such as judicial races. And for voters, the party label is a crucial source of information. As Professor Philip Dubois wrote,

> Voters' reliance on the partisan label choices is, in a very real sense, a rational act. This is not less true in judicial elections....Thus, research has repeatedly

demonstrated that where the partisan cue is available, judicial voters will rely upon it. The availability of the party label both prompts voters to exercise a choice, thereby increasing the percentage of the eligible electorate participating in the election, and results in the expression in the aggregate of the voters' preferences for the direction of judicial policy.[92]

The party label provides a cue to the attitudes and values of judges and ultimately to how they might decide questions of public policy that are presented in their courts. One recent analysis of 140 articles written on the link between judges' party affiliations and performance on the bench confirmed that "party is a dependable measure of ideology on modern American courts."[93] Party affiliation, however, as an indicator of judicial ideology is not uniform across the states. In a study of workers' compensation appeals decided by the Wisconsin Supreme Court over a ten-year period, David Adamany found some correlation between the party affiliation of the justices and their votes in favor of or against claimants, but the correlation was less than that found in Michigan. Adamany believed differences in partisanship of judicial campaigns in the two states, and thus differences in the states' political cultures, explained the discrepancies in the correlations.[94] Another study of partisan voting on eight state courts concluded: "Where judges are selected in highly partisan circumstances and depend upon a highly partisan constituency for continuance in office, they may act in ways which will cultivate support for that constituency, that is, exhibit partisan voting tendencies in their judicial decision making."[95]

Of course, just as there is value in party label voting, there is also a downside. Highly qualified judicial candidates can be defeated simply because, in a particular election year, they bear the wrong party label. After Republican straight ticket voting led to the defeat of nineteen Democratic judges in Harris County (Houston), Texas, and led to Republican victories in forty-one of forty-two contested judicial races, one law school dean commented: "[I]f Bozo the Clown had been running as a Republican against any Democrat, he would have had a chance."[96] Similarly, while the parties can help provide funding for judicial campaigns, in some places funding arrangements are the reverse. Judges are required to contribute money to their party in order to secure the party's endorsement in the general election.[97] Such endorsement payments have been made in New York City; Cook County, Illinois; Philadelphia; Delaware County, Pennsylvania; and no doubt in many other jurisdictions. The extent of political party contributions to judicial campaigns is limited in some regions of the country. A study of thirty-five competitive Pennsylvania Supreme Court elections from 1979–1997 found that only 3.1% of contributions over fifty dollars came from political party committees.[98]

In addition, sometimes the parties routinely expect a high level of party loyalty from their judicial nominees. In the 1970s, for example, when the Supreme Court of Michigan decided a state redistricting case favoring the Republican Party, the Democratic chief justice was denied nomination for the 1976 election. The state bar, however, rallied to support him, and he won the reelection as an independent.[99]

In the early 1990s, the Illinois Supreme Court first rejected a redistricting plan favorable to Republicans by a four to three party line vote. After some minor changes were made in the plan, one of the Democratic justices switched sides and voted with the three Republican justices to uphold the plan. A Democratic legislator alleged that the Democratic justice's vote change had been for political reasons, but the court rejected the legislator's allegations. One justice, however, dissented. He acknowledged that party line voting occurred in political cases, and he pointed out that the Democratic justice who had switched his vote had plans to run for the Illinois Supreme Court in 1992 as a Republican.[100]

Party label is also an imperfect indicator of the ideology of judicial candidates. In states that have moved from one party's control to the other's control, judges often switch parties in order to retain their offices. The attitudes and values of the judges do not change—only the party label.

Phillip Dubois' highly regarded book, *From Ballot to Bench*, published in 1980, is the classic defense of partisan elections and the importance of parties as an indication of the values of judges. Dubois excluded the South from his analysis because the Republican Party was then so insignificant in most Southern states that study of party competition there would have been futile. In recent years, however, the Republican Party has shown such growth in the South that partisanship has become especially important in the study of Southern judicial elections.

Voters can best use party affiliations as a predictor of the attitudes and values of judges when appellate court elections are involved. It is there that major policy questions are more likely to be decided than in trial courts, where more routine legal issues will be handled.

Keeping in mind that parties can and do play an important and even positive role in funding judicial elections, mobilizing voters, and providing cues or hints to voters about the policy preferences of judicial candidates, there are nevertheless some serious concerns about some of the involvement of parties in judicial elections. The problems of partisanship that led to the creation of nonpartisan and "Missouri Plan" systems of judicial selection are still with us.[101]

North Carolina was one of the Southern states where turmoil in judicial elections occurred with the growth of the Republican Party in the state. As the Republican Party gained strength and elected governors in 1972, 1984, and 1988, the path to a judgeship in the state became less clear. Incumbent Democratic judges began to retire at the end of their terms in greater numbers, and the Democratic legislature began to create judgeships that were filled by election rather than appointment when Republican governors were in office. [102]

By 1986, there were strong partisan battles for the state supreme court. These battles were joined by interest groups, such as the Citizens for a Conservative Court, that ran advertisements critical of a justice's decisions in capital murder cases and sponsored news conferences with families of murder victims who condemned the justice's decisions. And the stridency of the 1986 elections continued. In 1990, the Republican state chairman made television advertisements criticizing the Democratic court for being soft on crime and unduly supportive of civil plaintiffs. The Republican governor joined the chairman.[103] Partisanship had come to judicial elections in North Carolina as it came to much of the rest of the South that for years had actually had nonpartisan elections under the façade of a partisan system.

In partisan elections, judicial candidates run under a party label. The effect in competitive races is that low-visibility races such as judicial races benefit (or suffer) from voting for candidates at the top of the ticket. In Texas, Democratic judicial candidates in 1982 clearly benefited from the popularity of Democratic U.S. Senator Lloyd Bentsen. Furthermore, in 1984, Republican judicial candidates benefited from the presidential candidacy for Ronald Reagan. [104]

It is the party label rather than the ability of the judicial candidate that often determines the outcome of an election. In 1994, for example, the former chairman of the state Republican Party called on Republicans to take control of the Texas Court of Criminal Appeals after the reversal of a capital conviction. The Democratic incumbent was a conservative former prosecutor who had served on the court for twelve years. He had support from both prosecutors and the criminal defense bar. His Republican opponent campaigned in favor of greater use of the death penalty, greater use of the harmless error doctrine, and sanctions for attorneys who file frivolous appeals especially in death penalty cases. He had misrepresented his background, his experience, his record, and had almost no criminal law experience. The Republican won with 54% of the vote in large part because in statewide elections, Texas has become a one-party Republican state.[105]

Missouri continues to have partisan judicial elections in most of the state, although it is known for the Missouri Plan. One trial court judge there switched from the Democratic to the Republican Party and issued a press release that included an exceptionally ugly partisan appeal:

> The truth is that I have noticed in recent years that the Democrat party places far too much emphasis on representing minorities such as homosexuals, people who don't want to work, and people with a skin that's any color but white. Their reverse-discriminatory quotas and affirmative action, in the work place as well as in schools and colleges, are repugnant to me....I believe the time has come for us to place much more emphasis and concern on the hard-working taxpayers in this country.... That majority groups of our citizens seem to have been virtually forgotten by the Democrat Party.[106]

Regardless of the press release, however, it is the same judge with simply a different party label.

Partisan Nonpartisan Elections

One study of California judicial elections noted:

> Even in the context of nonpartisan elections, however, voters have always been able to rely upon partisan cues regarding candidates for nonpartisan offices. Even if political parties did not formally endorse candidates, voters could look for guidance to other individuals or organizations with recognized partisan leanings....In addition, state and local governmental officials with well-known political affiliations sometimes endorsed candidates for nonpartisan office (including judicial offices)....In short, the practical differences between a technically nonpartisan election and partisan election may be more imagined or perceived than real.[107]

Still, in spite of the author's belief that absent partisan cues on the ballot the voter in California can easily obtain information about the partisan affiliation of judicial candidates, the absence of those ballot cues at least complicates the search for information on partisan affiliations.

In Ohio's highly partisan supreme court elections, in recent years all-out battles have taken place. Democratic candidates are supported by trial lawyers and labor unions; Republicans by business interests. Much of the spending in these races has been independent advocacy spending by interest groups, which means that campaigning was not restricted by the Canons of Judicial Conduct, and thus the campaigning was especially intense and focused on the groups' political agendas.[108]

Michigan has nonpartisan ballots, but like Ohio, it has very partisan judicial races. In the 2000 Michigan elections, the Republican Party aired a television commercial against a Democratic nominee for the supreme court that criticized the candidate's role in a decision involving the sentence of a man convicted of molesting a seven-year-old girl. Democrats also objected to the GOP ad's mention of two other Democratic court nominees who were not involved in the case though Republicans responded that there was no suggestion in the ad that the other two candidates were involved.[109]

Retention Elections

Though the 1986 defeat of three California Supreme Court justices in retention elections are ascribed to the activities of interest groups such as Crime Victims for Court Reform, there was also a high level of partisan activity. Republican legislative incumbents campaigned against the three justices, but only some Democratic incumbents from safe districts supported them.[110] The Republican governor, having already announced opposition to the Democratic chief justice because of her votes in capital cases, publicly warned the two associate justices on the court who were also up for retention that he would oppose their retention unless they voted to uphold more death sentences.[111] The effects of such a retention battle can fuel opposition to other judges, and, of course, it can also induce judges to pause and consider political implications of their decisions in controversial cases. One Democratic California justice, speaking of his vote in a controversial 1982 decision shortly before his retention election, later commented: "I decided the case the way I saw it. But to this day, I don't know to what extent I was subliminally motivated by the thing you could not forget—that it might do you some good politically to vote one way or the other."[112]

What Is Happening with Partisanship and Judicial Elections?

Partisanship in judicial elections is nothing new. Political parties jockeying for power in the selection of state court judges is an ancient political rite. After all, the main goal of the parties is to gain and hold offices and that includes judicial offices. However, there is a new level of partisanship in many judicial elections. It is not limited to partisan judicial elections but can be found in nonpartisan systems and in retention elections as well. Part of that new partisanship may be reflected by the enhanced competitiveness of the political parties. Certainly that is true in the South, where there has been a dramatic rise in the fortunes of the Republican Party over the past twenty years. The result is that in the 1980s and 1990s, the sleepy affairs that used to pass for judicial elections in the South became pitched battles between the Democratic and Republican candidates.

It is important to note that modern partisanship in judicial elections is not limited to the party supplying workers, or funds, or even the all-important party label to candidates. There is viciousness, a stridency to many modern-day judicial elections that goes beyond routine maneuvering by the parties for greater representation on the bench. Judicial candidates are faced with hard-hitting, bitter attacks being waged by partisans using the mass media.

The mass media are becoming the way to reach voters. No longer can one successfully campaign for judicial office by speaking at civic clubs, shaking hands, and garnering a few newspaper and bar endorsements. One immediate effect of reaching voters in judicial elections is that costs increase dramatically because judicial candidates must advertise to reach voters through newspapers, radio, and, most expensively, television. And for expensive media such as television, the message must be brief. That requires focusing on simple themes that are attractive to voters. The result is that often the most effective mass media advertising focuses on "hot-button" issues that have strong voter affect.[113] The late California Supreme Court Justice Otto Kaus called these issues the "crocodiles in the bathtub."[114] They are the issues that most judges must deal with but which can be effectively turned against the judge in a short, simple media message. Such issues are crime, capital punishment, abortion, and voter initiatives such as term limits. All it takes in this era of mass media politics is for a judge to do something—

almost anything—such as an apparent low bail for a murderer or reversal of a death sentence on appeal. A thirty-second media message can turn that decision into a charge of coddling criminals that could ruin the judge's career.[115]

In judicial races, the parties will often cooperate with interest groups in presenting a message about that particular judicial campaign. In a race in which an interest group is, for example, supporting a Democratic incumbent judge, the interest group is a political asset to both the incumbent judge and the Democratic Party. Some interest groups may also develop long-term working relationships with a particular political party. For example, organized labor has traditionally been aligned with the Democratic Party, as have trial lawyers.[116] Business groups are often aligned with the Republican Party.[117] In some states in recent years, the Christian Coalition has been aligned with the Republican Party.[118] The result of the long-term intimate ties between the parties and certain interest groups is that their goals and objectives mesh.[119] In Texas, for example, it would be difficult, though not impossible, for a candidate opposed by trial lawyers to get the nomination of the Democratic Party for the Texas Supreme Court. Conversely, a judicial candidate known as having pro-choice views would have trouble getting the Republican nomination. In fact, two Republican judges on a Texas intermediate appellate court were rebuked by delegates to the Republican State Convention because of their decision to overturn a sodomy conviction. This action angered religious conservatives in the party.[120] Although the judges were Republicans, the delegates opposed their reelection and placed language in the party platform attacking "activist judges who use their power to usurp the will of the people."[121] Thus, interest group politics in the states affect party politics that in turn have an influence on who becomes a judge. Those interest groups with influence in the party are going to want their party's candidate to be sympathetic to their objectives, and, to get their support, the judicial candidate is going to have to show that he or she is friendly to the goals of the group.

Where the interest groups' goals become one party's goal and the opposing interest groups' goals become those of the opposing party, the stage is set for the strident, bitter judicial election campaigns that have been seen in numerous states. There is little room for moderation in races that pit labor-backed Democrats against business-backed Republicans, trial lawyer-supported Democrats against physician-supported Republicans, or pro-life

Republicans against pro-choice Democrats. An example of such a tie between interest groups, political parties, and the judiciary is suggested by a string of decisions by the Cook County, Illinois judiciary in 1996 that declared parts of the 1995 Illinois tort reform law unconstitutional.[122] Cook County's bench was a bastion for Democrats, and both the judges and the party were strongly backed by trial lawyers whose goals were contrary to the Republican legislature's efforts for tort reform.[123]

The parties have also become more ideologically separate in America. One study of the political feelings of voters shows that while the general public's feelings about "liberals" and "conservatives" have remained fairly stable from 1964 to 1994 with a slightly more favorable response to "conservatives," Democratic Party and Republican Party partisans were quite different.[124] Strong partisans make up about one-third of the electorate and are most likely to vote and to participate in party activities. Strong Republicans tend to have much more favorable feelings toward "conservatives," and strong Democrats have much more favorable feelings toward "liberals."[125]

These long-term trends have several important implications for judicial races. The greater ideological divide among the parties suggests that campaigns between the competing parties, including judicial campaigns, will be increasingly bitter and hard fought. Further, issues that are ideological "hot buttons" will prove increasingly effective in mobilizing the activists of both parties. Since judicial candidates must find ways to mobilize the strong partisans of their respective parties to succeed in elections, some candidates will approach the line, and possibly cross the line, of unethical political appeals. If the Christian Coalition is important to the party, what better way of building a strong base of support in the party than doing an act such as posting the "Ten Commandments" in the courtroom?[126] If prosecutors and victims' rights groups are powerful in another county's politics, an effective way of building support might be to act as one judge did when he taped a picture of Judge Roy Bean's hanging saloon on the front of his bench with his name superimposed over Judge Bean's and referred to the high court's judges as "liberal bastards" and "idiots."[127] Logically, these, and numerous other examples of grandstanding and political rhetoric, can generate publicity and support and, thus, aid a party's nomination and election of its candidate.

The role of political parties in judicial elections has long been criticized, and reforms such as nonpartisan elections and retention elections were designed to restrict the influence of the parties. Nevertheless, political parties retain a major role in all judicial elections. However, that role is not all bad. The parties do perform valuable functions in judicial elections, such as providing campaign workers, funds, and the party label to judicial candidates. No doubt it is the utility of the parties in these elections that explains the persistence of parties even in the face of anti-party reforms.

However, parties do have negative effects in judicial races. These effects are especially noticeable when highly qualified judges are defeated simply because they had the wrong party label in a year when a presidential nominee of the opposing party was unusually popular—hence, Judge Williams' explanation of his defeat eighty years ago in connection with the Warren Harding landslide.

There appears to be a new level of partisanship in many judicial races. One explanation for this and more vicious partisanship is that the parties in some states have become more competitive. In the South, that competitiveness has come about in the past two decades as the Republican Party has become a major force in the region. Another explanation for the new partisanship is the increased reliance on mass media for campaigning in judicial races. The nature of mass media campaigns is to attempt to saturate the media market with a simple message. For judicial races, that means that a successful media strategy is to use "attack ads" to focus on "hot-button" issues such as capital punishment, abortion, or crime.

Additionally, the parties in some states are closely aligned with competing interest groups. That entanglement of parties and interest groups leads the parties to adopt the groups' goals as their own. The result is a wider gulf between viewpoints of the two parties and the candidates of those parties. Since neither the independent advocacy expenditures of the parties nor their interest group allies are restricted by ethical constraints, their use of "hot-button" issues in the media can be particularly strident.

Finally, there are increasing ideological differences between strong partisans of the two parties. The greater the gulf between the third of the population who are most likely party activists and the most likely voters, the more ideologically extreme will campaigns become—including judicial campaigns. Moreover, more judicial candidates will be inclined to adopt ideologically extreme positions to appeal to the strong partisans and the interest groups allied with that party. That involvement of interest groups in judicial elections, however, is an important enough aspect of the new era in judicial politics that it deserves special mention.

The New Role of Interest Groups in Judicial Elections

Interest groups have long had a role in judicial politics. They provide necessary funding to reach voters. They also serve as intermediaries between judicial candidates and voters in the sense that they assist candidates in communicating with, and in mobilizing, voters. Interest groups can also provide important cues to voters about the attitudes and values of judicial candidates. For example, in the 2000 elections for superior court in California, one candidate obtained the endorsements of the Sacramento County Deputy Sheriff's Association and the Sacramento Police Officers' Association.[128] If a voter knew nothing else about the candidate—for example, did not know that the candidate had been a police officer for fourteen years or a prosecutor for fifteen years—those endorsements would provide a hint that the candidate was viewed as being pro-law enforcement. In states where the parties are not heavily involved in judicial elections, interest groups become crucial in providing cues to voters about the attitudes and values of judicial candidates and in mobilizing voters for the elections.

Although interest groups are often discussed in a pejorative manner, they are essential to the functioning of a pluralist democracy. Political scientists Theodore Lowi and Benjamin Ginsberg define interest groups simply as "a group of individuals and organizations that share a common set of goals and have joined together…to persuade the government to adopt policies that will help them."[129] Although interest groups are ordinarily examined in the context of legislative politics, interest groups have a role in all branches of government including the judicial branch.

The earliest texts on interest groups recognize that they attempt to influence courts. Interest groups do so for at least three reasons: (1) they believe they need to balance the views of other groups; (2) they wish to convince jurists to adopt their views as law; and (3) they wish to cut losses in the event they fail to persuade the executive or legislative branches to adopt their viewpoints.[130]

There have been several changes regarding interest group involvement in judicial elections. Interest groups are increasingly national in scope. Additionally, the number of interest groups and the amounts of money and other resources contributed by these groups to judicial candidates have vastly increased. In 1968 the *Encyclopedia of Associations* counted 10,300 interest groups; in 1988 it counted 20,600.[131] During World War II there were 500 registered lobbyists in Washington; in 2000, there were 25,000.[132] The number of political action committees registered with the federal government grew from 608 in 1974 to over 2500 in 1980 to about 4000 in 1994.[133] And something else has changed. As judicial races have become more competitive, campaign costs have risen dramatically. Judicial candidates need the substantial resources offered by interest groups to win.

Interest groups today often draw no distinction between achieving their goals through the courts or through the political process. The result can be an unhealthy dependence between judicial candidates and interest groups where interest groups back judicial candidates to secure their political agendas and candidates rely on interest group backing to achieve and retain judicial office. For some analysts of judicial politics, this new interest group involvement in judicial politics is more than unhealthy; it challenges the appearance of judicial impartiality. Some analysts go further and suggest that judges are becoming "captives" of influential interest groups.[134]

In an earlier era in judicial politics, to the extent that there was interest group involvement in judicial races, it was activity by competing segments of the bar. For civil court judgeships, trial lawyers might oppose a candidate supported by the defense side in civil cases; for criminal courts, prosecutors might support a candidate opposed by the criminal defense bar. However, even this interest group involvement was low budget and low key.

By the late 1970s and early 1980s, the nature of judicial elections was changing. The changes did not happen at the same time or in all states, but in several places judicial elections became more competitive and more expensive. Initially competing segments of the bar became more involved in judicial races—primarily through campaign contributions that were increasingly needed by judicial candidates for the advertising necessary for competitive campaigns.[135]

In Ohio there were also hotly contested, expensive contests for the state supreme court that involved plaintiff-defense interests.[136] Alabama soon began to receive media attention for the costly battles between trial lawyers and defense interests in Alabama Supreme Court elections. One scholar described Alabama as a "battleground between businesses and those who sue them."[137] That battle, he wrote, "is often fought in elections for the Supreme Court of Alabama."[138] In the 1994 Supreme Court elections, a rancorous battle occurred where trial lawyers and business groups backed opposing candidates for the five seats that were up for election.[139] A precipitating factor in this battle was a 1993 Alabama Supreme Court decision that had declared unconstitutional a package of tort reform legislation.[140] The result was a continuation of the trial lawyer-business interest battles every two years as seats came up for election.

Between 1986 and 1996, the cost of running for the Alabama Supreme Court rose 776%, and one journalist described the races as changing from "low-key races" to "expensive mud-wrestling contests."[141]

While there is greater interest group involvement in judicial races than plaintiff-defense interests and crime control interests, those interests have proven to be the most involved in judicial elections in most states. Trial lawyers and unions on the one hand and defense lawyers in civil cases, business groups, and professional groups on the other battle in judicial campaigns on civil law issues. In the criminal law, a judge worries about being branded "soft on crime." As former Justice Hans Linde of the Oregon Supreme Court put it,

> Every judge's campaign slogan, in advertisements and on billboards, is some variation of "tough on crime." The liberal candidate is the one who advertises: "Tough but fair." Television campaigns have featured judges in their robes slamming shut a prison cell door....Most judges may see themselves as umpires between the state and the citizen, but many citizens regard judges as part of law enforcement, and plenty of candidates will offer themselves for that role. A conscientious judge who imposes less than the maximum possible sentence in cases evoking public outrage invites a bidding war with future opponents.[142]

By the early 1990s, a look at judicial politics in the states showed that interest groups were taking a more active role in judicial elections in numerous states. Region of the country made no difference; population of the states made no difference, and it even made no difference if the judges were elected in partisan or nonpartisan elections. Although retention elections rarely result in the defeat of a judge, there have been notable exceptions that involved the activity of interest groups.

Former Federal Judge and Congressman Abner Mikva, commenting on the 2000 Illinois Supreme Court elections, noted that in Illinois judicial elections, "every special interest in the state—the insurance, the defense bar, everybody—is in there with big bucks to promote their candidates."[143]

Ohio has long faced intense interest group involvement in its judicial races, especially between business groups and the defense bar on the one hand and trial lawyers and unions on the other. The increased battling between these interests in Ohio has led to large increases in the costs of judicial elections. In 1980 the race for chief justice of the Ohio high court cost $100,000; six years later the race cost $2.8 million.[144]

Illustrative of the national links among interest groups involved in judicial elections is the creation of Michigan's M-Law, a pro-business organization that spends money for advertising and other public outreach in an effort to influence Michigan judicial elections. The Michigan Chamber of Commerce, the Michigan State Medical Society, and several Michigan trade associations created M-Law in the 1990s. However, also involved in its creation was a Washington, D.C.-based organization, the American Tort Reform Association, a national pro-business interest group. Borrowing from earlier efforts in Oklahoma, M-Law has published evaluations of both the Michigan Supreme Court and the Court of Appeals to determine the extent to which the judges reflect pro-business values. M-Law has also been significantly involved in making independent expenditures and has run noncandidate-specific education ads on television and on radio that highlighted such things as the financial contributions of trial lawyers to judicial campaigns.[145] M-Law is, of course, only a small part of the overall battle between competing interests in Michigan's judicial elections. However, it does show several important developments in interest group politics: (1) interest groups are no longer just local organizations but sometimes have national connections; (2) techniques developed in one state in judicial elections may be quickly taken up and used in other states, such as judicial evaluations by interest groups; and (3) independent expenditures by interest groups can be both large and influential in affecting judicial elections. Indeed, the continuing nationalization of state judicial elections is further shown by the U.S. Chamber of Commerce's efforts through the Institute for Legal Reform to support the election of pro-business judges in a number of states such as Alabama, Mississippi, Michigan, Ohio, and Illinois.[146]

Nor are interest group activities limited to the largest states or to tort law. In Mississippi in 1992, a justice was defeated in the Democratic primary by an opponent who "ran as a 'law and order candidate' with the support of the Mississippi Prosecutors Association."[147] A concurring opinion of the justice, one consistent with U.S. Supreme Court precedent, was used to attack the justice for his view that the Constitution did not permit the death penalty for rape where no loss of life had occurred.[148] The justice was also attacked, as claimed by his opponents, for believing that "a defendant who 'shot an unarmed pizza delivery boy in cold-blood' had not committed a crime serious enough to warrant the death penalty."[149] Actually, he had wanted to remand the case for a new sentencing hearing.[150] Two years earlier, another Mississippi justice was defeated for being "soft on crime," and the successful challenger in that race as well had the support of the Mississippi Prosecutors Association.[151]

While no Oklahoma judge has lost a retention election, there has been a pattern of lower percentages of favorable votes for judges. In 1986 the Oklahoma District Attorneys Association opposed a Court of Criminal Appeals judge because of a perception that he opposed the death penalty.[152] In 1996, Citizens for Judicial Review, an organization created by a Tulsa public relations firm with ties to conservative interests, spent $150,000 on election eve ads and news releases in opposition to a Court of Civil Appeals judge in a retention election.[153] In 1997 the public relations firm created Oklahomans for Judicial Excellence, which claimed support from fifty-two associations and corporations.[154] In 1998 this organization spent $250,000 on Oklahoma judicial elections and prepared "scorecard" ratings of judges, and the Christian Coalition distributed 1.4 million of these ratings.[155]

The Tennessee Conservative Union along with Republican leadership in the state successfully opposed Justice Penny White in a retention election. They made heavy use of a rape case in which White, along with two other justices, had commented that the evidence was insufficient to show an aggravating circumstance beyond a reasonable doubt as required by state law.[156]

Recent judicial campaigns in Nevada, a nonpartisan election state, have seen great involvement by casino and gambling interests. A few years ago, one Nevada justice received $80,000 in contributions from these interests.[157] In 1998 two members of the Nevada Supreme Court received nearly half their contributions from casino interests, and individual casinos were the judicial candidates' largest contributors.[158] It should not be surprising that gambling interests have a major role in Nevada elections, of course, any more than the coal industry in West Virginia, a partisan election state.[159]

In Idaho's May 2000 supreme court elections, a justice was defeated by a combination of factors. The justice authored a decision that upheld a federal reserved water rights claim in three wilderness areas.[160] That decision became the focal point in the election contest. Although officially nonpartisan, the two opposing candidates' parties were easily determinable— much as is the case with the nonpartisan elections in Ohio and in Michigan. The Democratic incumbent had been appointed by a Democratic governor, had married into a well-known Democratic family, and had been involved in liberal causes.[161] The Republican challenger launched his campaign by speaking at a Republican fund-raising banquet and was endorsed by state Republican Party leaders.[162] The Democratic incumbent's main interest group support was the Idaho Trial Lawyers Association; the Republican challenger's support included resource and agricultural interests as well as the Idaho Christian Coalition.[163] Substantial independent expenditures were involved, including a push poll against the incumbent that appears to have been funded by a South Carolina group.[164] One political action committee, the Concerned Citizens for Family Values, ran full-page newspaper ads on the Sunday prior to the election that proclaimed, "Will partial birth abortion and same-sex marriage become legal in Idaho? Perhaps so if liberal Supreme Court Justice Cathy Silak remains on the Idaho Supreme Court."[165] Other ads were run by gun advocates that suggested the justice would support gun registration. The justice was defeated by 60 percent of the vote.[166]

In Wisconsin, one study of supreme court elections in the past ten years found that the money for the races came overwhelmingly from a small number of contributors, most of whom were lawyers and lobbyists with a small number of large law firms. Recent spending for chief justice of the Wisconsin Supreme Court came to $1.3 million, twice the spending record set two years earlier and ten times the spending of a campaign twenty years earlier.[167]

Non-Campaign Contributions

While the extent of interest group activity in judicial races may only involve making campaign contributions to judicial campaigns, some groups play other roles. Some interest groups may make independent expenditures that benefit candidates for judicial office. These contributions are not reported in judicial candidates' contribution statements, and neither the funds nor the advertising they buy are in control of the candidate. From the candidate's perspective, such independent expenditures may not always be desirable since, for example, they may lead to advertising that goes "off-message" from the image the candidate would like to project. In the race for chief justice of North Carolina in 1986, for example, Citizens for a Conservative Court began running ads and holding demonstrations on courthouse steps in opposition to the challenger to the chief justice. The incumbent wrote of the organization's tactics,

> Some of their tactics…were offensive, and I asked them to discontinue them, but as they were in no way associated with my campaign, I had no means of controlling them. I have no idea whether their tactics had an overall positive or negative impact on the election results, but I know that they offended a large number of people. I also was unable effectively to dissociate myself from their tactics in the minds of some people, even after the election was over. A significant negative effect of their work was that some of the people whose financial support I had counted upon were influenced to make their contributions to the CCC instead of directly to my campaign….[168]

The Role of Ideology

The various segments of the bar and the clients they represent remain the leading interests involved in judicial elections. However, other interests do get involved, often mobilized by a "hot-button" issue with which the court has dealt. In 1996, for example, in Nebraska a supreme court justice was defeated in a retention election because he became a target of a $200,000 campaign by those opposed to the court's rejection of term limits for elected officials.[169] The justice had authored a unanimous opinion holding the term limits initiative invalid because it did not comply with a constitutional amendment that increased the number of signatures required to put the measure on the ballot.[170] The justice received only 32 percent favorable votes in the retention election.[171]

In 1990 the chief justice of Florida had to raise $300,000 to retain his seat against anti-abortion groups that sought to defeat him.[172] In 1992 anti-abortion groups challenged another justice who was also opposed by prosecutors and police organizations for her dissenting opinion in a death penalty case.[173]

In 1996 a district judge in Utah received only a 51 percent favorable vote after he was opposed by women's and gay rights' groups who campaigned against him on the grounds that he was soft on crimes against the two groups.[174] In Utah only one judge has ever been defeated in a retention election, and generally judges receive favorable votes in the 80 percent range.[175]

In 1998 a coalition of anti-abortion groups announced a $2 million campaign to defeat two California Supreme Court justices in retention elections.[176] Though the coalition never surfaced, justices were forced to raise money in an effort to fend off the threatened challenge.[177] The executive director of the Christian Coalition of Florida considered judicial elections to be "the next hot-button issue" for his group.[178] In Alabama the Christian Coalition recently surveyed judicial candidates prior to making endorsements. Some of the questions, according to the Judicial Inquiry Commission, called for the candidate to comment on issues likely to come before a judge or "embroiled the judicial candidate in political debate."[179]

One recent study of environmental issues in judicial elections recommended that environmental groups become involved in judicial elections by devoting time and resources to state judicial races and by educating their members and the public about the effects of judicial decisions on the environment. The study also recommended that environmental groups borrow from the business community and prepare evaluations of judges because, it is argued, "if the judicial selection process remains a political process, and if that process has direct and important implications for environmental policy, it is entirely appropriate for environmental groups to help voters educate themselves about the consequences of their choices in the voting booth."[180]

One recent comprehensive study of judicial elections in Pennsylvania strongly suggested that economic interests, however, seem to overwhelmingly dominate financial contributions to judicial races. Of $3,129,783 contributed by PACs and law firms to thirty-five Pennsylvania Supreme Court candidates from 1979 to 1997, only eighteen groups were labeled "ideological" groups, and they contributed only $25,053.[181] In contrast, groups categorized as "business" groups gave $1.5 million and consisted of 290 PACs and firms. Four hundred eighty labor PACs gave about $527,000.[182] However, a focus on financial contributions of ideological groups underestimates their importance, since these groups can provide volunteers for campaigns and most importantly mobilize their supporters to cast votes at the polls.

There are cases that raise concerns about the entanglement of interest groups and judges. In Louisiana, for example, a federal court addressed a challenge to rules that reduced the ability of law student legal clinics to practice in state courts.[183] Business groups had strongly opposed the activities of the Tulane Environmental Law Clinic and had written the court to express their opposition.[184] Business groups had also contributed substantial sums to supreme court candidates.[185] Although the court dismissed the plaintiffs' complaint, the judge noted the "close temporal relationship between the business community's expression of outrage and the subsequent changes" in court rules.[186] Wrote the judge, "[I]n Louisiana, where state judges are elected, one cannot claim complete surprise when political pressure somehow manifests itself within the judiciary."[187]

Interest groups will vigorously proclaim their goal of ensuring a level playing field in the courts and promoting fairness, but public opinion polls indicate that the public senses otherwise. The result is what appears to be a widespread belief that the new judicial politics introduces bias and unfairness into the state courts.

Yet the evidence points to continued expansion of interest group activity in judicial elections. There has already been a vast expansion of interest group involvement, a nationalization of that activity, and a recent call in academic research for a further expansion of interest group activity.[188] Additionally, it is clear that interest groups do have an impact on judicial races. In an era of thirty-second television advertisements, interest group advertising can hold considerable sway over the electorate, and the independent expenditures of interest groups can be especially hard hitting since they are free of ethical constraints. The result will be more and more interest group involvement in judicial elections in the future.

Minorities, Women, and the Texas Judiciary

Key interests in judicial politics in Texas and in other states in recent years have been women, ethnic, and racial groups. In large part, the concern of these interests has been with their under-representation on the bench. And while in recent years the representation of women has increased considerably; in Texas the representation of African Americans and Hispanics has not seen the same dramatic increases.

The first woman judge in Texas was Sarah T. Hughes who was appointed by Governor James Allred in the 1930s. There is no doubt that in

those days there was hostility to women in judicial offices. State Senator
Claud Westerfeld, for example, reacted to Hughes' judicial appointment by
saying that Hughes "ought to be home washing dishes."[189] However, as more
and more women have chosen law as a career, they have increasingly been
successful in gaining Texas judgeships. When Democrat Rose Spector first
ran for the Texas Supreme Court, she ran an ad noting that the Texas
Supreme Court was then all-male. However, as of September 2001, for
example, 30% of appellate judges were women as were 25% of district
judges.[190] And, unlike blacks and Hispanics who are disproportionately
Democrats in a Republican state, there are no partisan allegiances that
prevent women from obtaining judgeships in an era of Republican
domination. Thus, in modern Texas judicial history, one would likely not
find gender as a very important factor in explaining Texas judicial elections.

In contrast, one finds considerable argument that race and ethnicity are
important in explaining judicial elections in Texas. Civil rights groups have
long argued that there is inadequate representation of African Americans and
Hispanics on the bench in Texas. That view has been echoed by Chief Justice
Tom Phillips who in 1993 noted in his State of the Judiciary address the vast
disparity between the small numbers of minority judges and the large
minority population in Texas.[191]

Frustrated with the low percentages of minority judges in urban counties,
civil rights groups brought suit in 1989 in Midland, Texas's federal district
court. They initially challenged the elections of major trial court judges—
district judges—in forty-four counties in Texas. By trial, they reduced their
challenge to the election of judges in nine urban counties, arguing that the
countywide election of these judges diluted the strength of minority voters
and violated the federal Voting Rights Act.

The federal district judge who heard the case was Lucius Bunton, a
Carter-appointee and a former president of the Texas bar. After attempts at a
political solution failed, Bunton agreed with the plaintiffs and ordered that
district judges be elected in smaller-than-countywide judicial districts.
Interestingly, although not requested by the plaintiffs, Bunton also ordered
that the judges be elected in nonpartisan elections, an unsubtle signal that he
realized the importance of partisan voting in electing judges. One of the
defense arguments in the case had been that it was not racial or ethnic voting
that caused the lack of minority judges; it was partisan voting. That is,
minority judicial candidates were largely Democratic candidates, and in

urban counties in Texas, voters were casting Republican ballots and electing Republican judges who tended to be white. Thus, the defendants argued it was not race that explained the lack of minority judges; it was partisanship coupled with a lack of minority lawyers in the state.

The case was of vast importance and affected the basic structure of the Texas judiciary, and key political interests were affected. Minorities, of course, believed that smaller districts would improve the chances of electing minority judges. But the decision also had strong partisan overtones. With Republicans controlling the courthouse in most urban areas in the state, the decision was harmful to the interests of the Republican Party. Smaller judicial districts meant that Democrats would be able to win some judicial elections in urban counties that were now controlled by Republicans. On the other hand, Democrats saw gains from a decision favoring smaller districts. Plaintiffs' lawyers have tended to be allied with the Democratic party (or at least liberal factions of that party), and so they tended to support smaller districts as well since that would seem to lead to the selection of some judges who would be more liberal and more pro-plaintiff. The business community, on the other hand, was fearful that the decision would lead to pro-plaintiff pockets within Texas' urban counties. And, of course, incumbent judges in the affected districts were worried that their political base would be destroyed if they had to be elected from smaller districts.

The decision was blocked initially by the U.S. Court of Appeals for the Fifth Circuit on the grounds that the federal voting rights act did not apply to judicial elections, but then the case was taken to the U.S. Supreme Court, which held that the act did apply. The result was that the case was returned to the Fifth Circuit to determine whether minority voting strength was actually diluted and to determine the state's interest in maintaining countywide election of judges. Initially the Fifth Circuit heard the case in the usual manner—a panel of three judges—and two of the three judges decided in favor of the minority plaintiffs. The two judges affirmed Judge Bunton's findings for eight of the nine counties, excluding only Travis County (Austin), a Democratic stronghold.

For a while, there seemed to be a settlement of the dispute. The Democratic Attorney-General, Dan Morales, urged that the legislature change the way judges were elected. He proposed that judges be elected from smaller districts in all Texas counties that had populations greater than 100,000 and asked that a constitutional amendment be submitted to the voters allowing for such a change. However, given a lack of legislative support for the proposal, the Democratic Governor, Lt. Governor, and minority legislators urged Morales to accomplish the same result through a settlement agreement. Morales drafted an agreement that called for the election of most judges in the affected counties by subdistricts. Democratic officials who were parties to the suit agreed, but the Republican Chief Justice and two Republican judges who were interveners in the suit refused to agree. When the state senate was asked to approve the agreement, there was no quorum because eleven of the thirteen Republican state senators walked out. When the Senate then reconvened as a Committee of the Whole, not in formal session, a vote along party lines supported a resolution that expressed "sentiment" in support of the settlement. Voting in the House also broke along party lines. Failing to obtain more than a partisan expression of sentiment without the force of law from the legislature, Morales sought a remand to the district court for a hearing and entry of the consent decree. What Morales wanted was a system where 152 judges would be elected from subdistricts and 22 judges would continue to be elected at-large. The new subdistrict boundaries would mirror state representative districts in Dallas, Harris, Bexar, and Jefferson counties. Justice of the peace districts would be used in Tarrant County. In Lubbock, Ector, and Midland counties, judges would run from county commissioners' districts. To try to overcome the resistance of the two Republican district judges who were defendant interveners—no doubt because they distrusted a Democratic Attorney-General—the plan would allow those two judges to be elected county-wide. In that way, it was hoped that the two district judges would lose their standing to object. Morales then argued that the Republican Chief Justice, Tom Phillips, could not object to the agreement since the Attorney-General was the exclusive lawyer for the state, and Phillips was sued only in his official capacity.

Morales' effort was a bit too transparently partisan. The federal court of appeals, sitting en banc, did not accept Morales' view that he need not represent the views of the state's officials and that he could ignore their views as lawyer for the state and impose his own views. Indeed, given Morales' unsuccessful scrambling for support from the state legislature, his dramatic claim for power as attorney-general seemed notably false. Nor could Morales so easily exclude the two intervener judges from challenging his proposed settlement. The court noted that the interveners had played a major role in the litigation and even appealed Bunton's decision prior to the Attorney-General. Indeed, the Attorney-General had only seemed motivated to appeal because of Bunton's requirement that judges run in nonpartisan elections—an unpleasant thought for partisans regardless of their party affiliation. And, Bunton had essentially held that the two interveners had been illegally elected as judges. Additionally, they had intervened not only as judges but also as voters. In other words, Morales was not going to be allowed to exclude the judges as challengers to his settlement.

The result was that an appeal was made to the entire Fifth Circuit. The minority plaintiffs argued that the appeals court should respect the agreement out of respect for legislative will and state decisions. Of course, the problem with this argument was that the agreement was not a state decision but one of Democratic officials in the state. Nevertheless, if the district court's interpretation of legally significant racial bloc voting was correct, then there was a violation of the Voting Rights Act, and thus the electoral system was illegal. Bunton had held that if the plaintiffs could demonstrate that whites and blacks generally supported different candidates, there was legally significant racial bloc voting. Bunton ignored other explanations for the voting patterns. The problem, noted the appellate court, was that there was an important explanation other than racial animus for the voting patterns that had been found by the trial court. That explanation was partisan politics. Generally Republican judicial candidates won election regardless of the race of the candidate. Thus, if the Republican candidate was a member of a minority, the Republican candidate won just like white Republican candidates. Given that party affiliation was such a strong predictor of the election or defeat of judicial candidates, regardless of race of the candidates, the appellate court held that a finding of racial animus in voting could not be sustained.

Nor did the district court recognize other causes for the lack of minority judges. One obvious cause was the lack of minority lawyers. District judges must be licensed attorneys in Texas for four years and residents of the district for two years. The court noted that if there was a lack of eligible candidates, that went a long way toward explaining the absence of minority judges. In Ector County, one survey found only five eligible Hispanic lawyers and only one eligible black lawyer. In Lubbock County, there were no black lawyers eligible for a district judgeship, and there were only two black lawyers in the county. And in five of the counties in the litigation, the percentage of minority judges exceeded the percentage of minority lawyers who were eligible to run for district judge.

Added to the partisan voting pattern found by the appellate court and the lack of eligible minority candidates was a governmental interest in county-wide election of judges. The court noted the county was a basic governmental unit in Texas and that county-wide election encouraged accountability of judges.[192]

The issue of county-wide election of trial court judges was very much a partisan issue fought over in the courts with legal arguments. And, of course, because it was a partisan argument, it was also an argument involving key interest groups. In particular, the business community was concerned that sub-districts would increase the number of pro-plaintiff judges in urban areas; something plaintiffs' lawyers, of course, supported. However, without a federal court supporting sub-districting and with a strong and growing Republican base in Texas state politics, Texas' urban trial courts continued to be largely Republican and conservative.

Civil rights groups have continued to push for smaller judicial districts, and the numbers of minority judges remain small. As of September 1, 2001, only 4% of district court judges were African American and only 11% were Hispanic. Nor are the percentages for appellate court judges any better. Only 2% of appellate judges are African American and only 12% are Hispanic.[193] However, without the force of federal law behind them, civil rights groups have been unable to achieve their objective of smaller districts. Still, the changing demographics of the state will one day lead to a reemergence of the Democratic Party in Texas built largely on a Hispanic voter base. When that day emerges, many of the supporters of sub-districting will no doubt praise the wisdom of the federal 5th circuit's decision because the result will be more Democratic judges and more Hispanic judges. Republicans, on the other hand, will see how a major victory in the short term can prove to have long-term effects detrimental to their interests.

Demographics Drive Politics, Including Judicial Politics

In the media coverage of the 2000 Presidential election, one little judicial race in Dallas County was almost overlooked. Only one puzzled article on the race's results appeared in the *Dallas Morning News*.[194] A three-time Republican judge won re-election against a first-time Democratic candidate. That should have been no surprise. By the late 1980s, the only Democrat who could win a county-wide judicial race there was Ron Chapman, a Democratic judge who happened to share the name of the most popular disk jockey in the county.[195] In the early 1980s, there had been a wholesale rush of incumbent Democratic judges to the Republican Party. Though varying explanations were given by the party-switchers, perhaps the most honest and straightforward was by Judge Richard Mays, "My political philosophy about general things has nothing to do with me [sic] being a judge," he said. "That's not the reason I'm switching parties. The reason I'm switching is that to be a judge in Dallas County you need to be a Republican."[196] With Mays' switch in August 1985, 32 of the 36 district judges in Dallas County were Republicans, though none were Republicans before 1978.[197] It would, of course, not take long until all judges in Dallas County were Republican.[198]

So what was remarkable about that one District court race between a Democratic challenger and a long-time Republican incumbent, other than that a Democrat had the temerity to challenge an incumbent in a Republican bastion like Dallas County? Out of 560,558 votes cast, only 4,150 votes separated the two candidates. In other words, a three-term Republican judge with no scandal or other controversy surrounding his name won with only 50.3% of the vote. It is no wonder that the judge commented, "I'm thrilled to be serving again and duly humbled by the vote count."[199] And he admitted he could not explain his margin of victory.[200] Even more astounding, Judge Rhea's Democratic opponent, Mary Ann Huey, had run with no money, no political experience, and no support from the legal community. She ran in the same year that George W. Bush was the Presidential nominee, with no other Democratic judicial candidates on the ballot at the county level, and with little more than chutzpah on her side.[201]

Judge Rhea's humbling experience, of course, was not caused by his judicial performance but rather by demographic changes. The Republican base in Dallas County has moved to places like Collin, Denton, and Rockwall Counties.[202] That suburban growth has changed those traditionally Democratic Counties to Republican Counties, but the old Republican base— Dallas—was left with a larger African American and Hispanic population and is close to returning to the Democratic column that it left a little over twenty years ago. In 1996, Bill Clinton came within 5,000 votes of defeating Bob Dole. In 1998, Democrat Paul Hobby carried Dallas County in the race for comptroller. And, in 2000 George W. Bush only got 52% of the Dallas County vote.[203]

Those sorts of demographic changes will not only affect judicial politics at the county level, demographic changes will also be affecting judicial politics at the state level. In spite of much lower percentage turnout in the 2000 elections compared to the 1996 elections, Hispanic voting hit the 1,000,000-vote mark for the first time in Texas.[204] Even though Hispanic turnout dropped from 64.1% in 1996 to 51.4% in 2000; in actual numbers Hispanic votes increased by 21,000 statewide.[205] That decline in turnout seemed related to the lack of competitiveness in races in Texas and the lack of Democratic candidates seeking office. Even with the reduced turnout—with much of that reduction being Hispanics who would have voted Democratic if they had gone to the polls—nearly two-thirds (65.7%) of Hispanic voters voted for Al Gore and only 32.5% voted for George W. Bush.[206] That vote, of course, shows overwhelming Democratic support even though George W. Bush was much more popular among Texas Hispanic voters than the previous Republican Presidential nominee, Robert Dole, who only received 15.4% of Hispanic votes.[207] Nor did Bush's popularity (compared to Dole's) provide much of a coattail for candidates further down on the ballot. Only 22.5% of Texas Hispanic voters cast ballots for Republican Congressional candidates, although that was some improvement over 1996 when only 13.6% of Hispanic voters cast votes for Republican Congressional candidates.[208]

Additionally, among Texas Hispanic voters who have registered to vote most recently—registered since 1996—73.3% identified themselves as Democrats and 15.9% as Republicans.[209] Thus, the fastest growing ethnic group in the Texas population is overwhelmingly voting Democratic, and the newer these voters are to voting, the more likely they are to vote Democratic.

With a Hispanic candidate running for Governor of Texas in 2002, an exit poll of 838 Latino voters found that only 10% of Hispanics voted for the Republican candidate, Rick Perry. In contrast, 87% voted for the Democratic candidate, Tony Sanchez. In the 2002 lieutenant governor's race, Republican David Dewhurst also received only 10% of the Hispanic vote, and Democrat John Sharp received 85% of the Hispanic vote. Republican U.S. Senate candidate John Cornyn received 19% of the Hispanic vote compared to Democrat Ron Kirk who received 76%. In Congressional races, Republicans received 17% of the Hispanic vote and Democrats received 77%.[210]

Texas in 1990 had a population of 16,986,510 people.[211] In 2000, its population had grown to 20,851,820.[212] In 1990, 25.55% of the Texas population was of Hispanic origin.[213] In 2000, that percentage had jumped to 32%.[214] True, many Hispanics may not be citizens, and there is relatively low voting participation among Hispanic voters.[215] Nevertheless, the demographic trend of the past decade is overwhelming—there are now many, many more potential voters in Texas, and the vast majority are likely to be Democratic voters. In the fairly short run, that means judicial elections in Texas—like elections in general in the state—are about to become competitive.

Table 1 Projected Demographic Change in Bexar, Dallas and Harris Counties 2005 and 2010			
	Bexar	Dallas	Harris
2000 Pop.	1,392,931	2,218,899	3,400,578
2000 Hispanic Pop.	757,033	662,729	1,119,751
% Hispanic in 2000	54%	30%	33%
2005 Projected Pop. w/ Migration at Level of 1990s	1,487,546	2,435,493	3,757,387
2005 Projected Hispanic Pop. w/ migration at Level of 1990s	849,240	886,425	1,463,315
2005 % Hispanic w/ migration at Level of 1990s	57%	36%	39%
2010 Projected Pop. w/ Migration at Level of 1990s	1,581,048	2,697,280	4,188,014
2010 Projected Hispanic Pop. w/ Migration at Level of 1990s	943,643	1,160,691	1,890,345
2010 % Hispanic w/ Migration at Level of 1990s	60%	43%	45%

Source: These demographic projections (along with projections based on other assumptions) can be found at Texas State Data Center and Office of the State Demographer, Projections of the Population in Texas and Counties in Texas by Age, Sex and Race/Ethnicity for 2000–2040 (December 2001), http://txsdc.tamu.edu/cgi-bin/prj2001totnum.cgi

The most rapid demographic changes are happening in Texas' urban counties. In part that is because of the growth of the Hispanic population in those counties. However, it is also due to the movement of the white population to suburban counties. Thus, the first indications of the demographically induced political shifts in Texas will occur in its urban counties. Although Republicans currently and in much of the 1990s have dominated the district benches in Bexar, Dallas, and Harris Counties, that is about to change because of vast demographic changes occurring in those areas. Until the 1980s Democrats dominated these benches. Then, over a few short years, those judgeships became overwhelmingly Republican.[216] Now it appears than in a few short years, these district court positions will revert back to the Democratic Party.

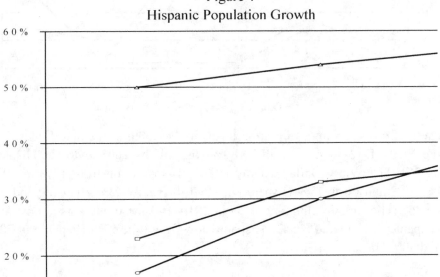

Figure 1
Hispanic Population Growth

Republican voters tend to be non-Hispanic white voters, while African American and Hispanic voters vote Democratic. Of these three racial/ethnic groups, it is the Hispanic population that is dramatically increasing in Texas. Thus, largely because of the growth of the Hispanic population, most counties in Texas have experienced a proportional decline in non-Hispanic whites by a percentage of 0–10%. Dallas and Harris Counties have experienced decreases of more than 10% because of the rapid increase in the Hispanic population but also because of a decline in the numbers of non-

Hispanic whites in those counties. The increase in Hispanics as a proportion of the population of Dallas, Harris, and Bexar Counties is projected to increase. Although demographic projections must always be treated with

Figure 2
Number of Contested Elections

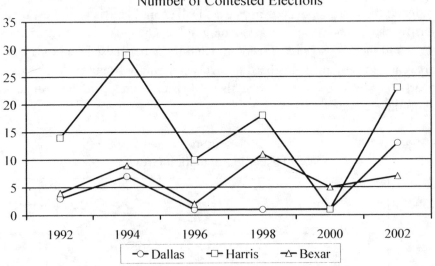

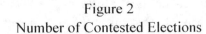

caution, if one assumes migration levels in the 2000s will equal the levels of the 1990s, Dallas County will be 39% Hispanic by 2005 and 45% Hispanic by 2010. Currently Dallas County is 30% Hispanic, up from 17% in 1990. Harris County was 23% Hispanic in 1990. It is now 33% Hispanic and will be 36% Hispanic in 2005 and 43% in 2010. Bexar County was almost 50% Hispanic in 1990 and is 54% Hispanic now. It will be 57% Hispanic in 2005 and 60% Hispanic in 2010.[217]

Dallas, Harris and Bexar County District Courts: The Numbers[218]

Dallas County has not had a Democratic district court candidate win an election since 1992. Yet in the past decade there have been twenty-six district court elections where a Republican candidate has faced a Democratic candidate (see Figure 2). Thus, from 1992–2002, Republicans have won twenty-five out of twenty-six contested district court elections (see Figure 3). And Democrats hardly bothered to run in Dallas County district court elections in 1996, 1998, and 2000. In each of those election years, only one district court race was contested. No doubt the strength of the one Democrat who ran for district judge in Dallas County in 2000 encouraged Democratic challengers in 2002, when thirteen district court races were contested. In other words, half of the Democratic candidates who ran in district court elections in the past decade ran in 2002. And, while the Democratic candidates did not win, their performance was impressive. Overall, Republicans received only an average of 52.40% of the vote against these Democratic candidates (see Figure 4). In contrast, in 1994, the last time that a substantial number of Democratic candidates ran for Dallas County district court seats, Republicans received an average of 56.1% of the vote.

Figure 3
Percentage of Democratic Victories
in Contested District Court Elections

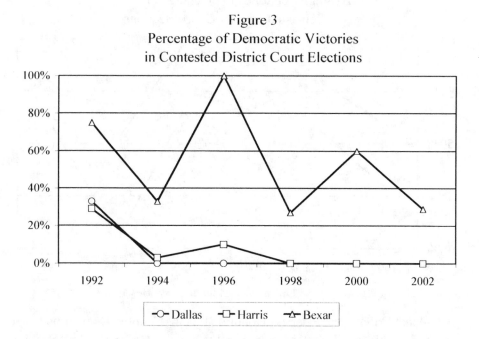

With the exception of the 2000 elections, Harris County has had more competition in judicial elections than has Dallas County. Since 1992 there have been 95 contested district court elections. However, no Democrat has been elected to the Harris County district courts since 1996, and there have only been six Democrats elected in the past decade. Like Dallas County, Democrats almost gave up running for the district bench in 2000 when only one ran in a contested election even though there were 14 contested elections in 1992, 29 in 1994, 10 in 1996, and 18 in 1998. In 2002, contested elections picked up dramatically with the highest number—twenty-three—since 1994. The average Republican vote in each election year has ranged from 51.84% in 1992 to 56.39% in 1994. In 2002, on average, the Republican district court candidate vote was 54.78%, which was considerably higher than in Dallas County. Unlike Dallas County's recent voting patterns which show Democrats on the edge of victory, Harris County Republicans have considerably more impressive vote margins. However, demographic changes are occurring there, and Republican successes may prove short lived.

Figure 4
Average Republican Percentage of Vote
in Contested District Court Elections

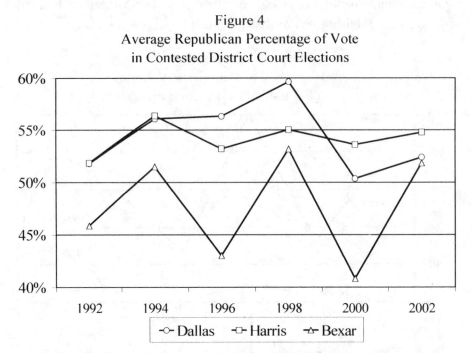

Unlike Dallas and Harris County, Bexar County Democrats have remained viable in district court races. Of course, Bexar County also has considerably higher percentages of Hispanics than does Dallas and Harris. In the past decade, there have been between two and eleven contested district court races in Bexar County, and Democrats have had election victories in from 27% to 100% of those elections. By 2010, the Hispanic population in Bexar County may well be 60%, and so those Democratic victories should increase. And, interestingly, by 2010 the Hispanic population in Dallas and Harris County will approach the Hispanic population in Bexar County in 1990 when Democrats continued to be competitive in courthouse races.

Conclusion

Demographics drive politics, and Texas' urban counties are undergoing a period of massive demographic changes where large increases are occurring in the Hispanic population. Since in Texas, Hispanic voters have been overwhelmingly Democratic, that demographic change should benefit the Democratic Party in district court races. In the 1980s, judicial politics in Texas moved from being one-party Democratic to competitive two-party to one-party Republican (in many parts of the state). A similar pattern is about to take place where the move will be from one-party Republican to competitive two-party to one-party Democratic.

With such a large and fast-growing group supporting Democrats, judicial elections should quickly become competitive again. And, with increased competition between Republican and Democrats, the types of campaigns we have been seeing in other competitive states should soon appear in Texas. Once the competition appears, the big money, the interest groups, and the independent expenditures cannot be far behind.

Notes

[1] Kyle Cheek and Anthony Champagne, Money in Texas Supreme Court Elections: 1980–1998, 84 *Judicature* 20 (2000).

[2] Of course there are parts of Texas where Democrats can still win elections, such as South Texas or the more rural parts of Texas. But statewide elections and the state's most urban (and suburban) areas tend to be overwhelmingly Republican.

[3] The program was broadcast on November 10, 1998.

[4] Anthony Champagne & Kyle Cheek, The Cycle of Judicial Elections: Texas as a Case Study, 29 *Fordham Urban Law Journal* 907, 908 (2002).

[5] Roy Schotland, Comment, 61 *Law & Contemporary Problems* 149 at 150 (1998) [Hereinafter Schotland Comment].

[6] See Campaign Contributions Corrupt Judicial Races, *USA Today*, September 1, 2000, at 16A.

[7] Schotland, Financing Judicial Elections, 2000: Change and Challenge, 2001 *Law Review Michigan State University–Detroit College of Law* 849, 850 (2001), quoting Bayne, Lynchard's Candidacy. Ads Putting Spice into Judicial Race, *Memphis Commercial Appeal*, October 29, 2000, at DS1. [Hereinafter Schotland Financing.]

[8] Deborah Goldberg & Mark Kozlowski, Constitutional Issues in Disclosure of Interest Group Activities, 35 *Indiana Law Review* 755 (2002).

[9] Schotland Comment, supra note 5, at 150.

[10] Id.

[11] Hans A. Linde, The Judge as Political Candidate, 40 *Cleveland State Law Review* 1 at 7 (1992).

[12] Id.

[13] Id.

[14] Id.

[15] Amy M. Craig, The Burial of an Impartial Judicial System: The Lifting of Restrictions on Judicial Candidate Speech in North Carolina, 33 *Wake Forest Law Review* 413 (1998).

[16] The Constitution Project, The Higher Ground Standards of Conduct for Judicial Candidates, available at http://www.constitutionproject.org/ci/standards_questions.html. See also Stephen J. Ware, Money, Politics and Judicial Decisions: A Case Study of Arbitration Law in Alabama, 15 *Journal of Law and Policy* 645, 658–659 (1999). Ware notes that personal matters, particularly the skunk-portrayed candidate's divorce, were also explored by his opponent.

[17] Schotland Comment, supra note 5 at 150.

[18] Steven Lubet, Judicial Discipline and Judicial Independence, 61 *Law and Contemporary Problems* 59, 63 (1998).

[19] Judith L. Maute, Selecting Justice in State Courts: The Ballot Box or the Backroom, 41 *South Texas Law Review* 1197, 1224 footnote 167.

[20] Id at 1205.

[21] Key points of this extraordinary case are discussed by Roy Schotland, Proposed Legislation on Judicial Election Campaign Finance, Ohio Forum on Judicial Selection Reform, Ohio

State University, Columbus, Ohio, March 6, 2003, http:moritzlaw.osu.edu/lawjournal/schotland.htm.

[22] John T. Wold & John H. Culver, The Defeat of the California Justices: The Campaign, the Electorate, and the Issue of Judicial Accountability, 70 *Judicature* 348–355 (1987).

[23] Stephen B. Bright, Political Attacks on the Judiciary: Can Justice Be Done Amid Efforts to Intimidate and Remove Judges from Office for Unpopular Decisions?, 72 *New York University Law Review* 308, 313 (1997).

[24] See *State v. Odom*, 928 S.W.2d 18, 21 (Tenn. 1996).

[25] Bright, supra note 23, at 313.

[26] Symposium, Breaking the Most Vulnerable Branch: Do Rising Threats to Judicial Independence Preclude Due Process in Capital Cases?, 31 *Columbia Human Rights Law Review* 123, 140 (1999).

[27] Id. at 139.

[28] Id. at 139–40.

[29] Stephen B. Bright, Can Judicial Independence Be Attained in the South? Overcoming History, Elections, and Misrepresentations About the Role of the Judiciary, 14 *Georgia State University Law Review* 817, 849 n. 195.

[30] Schotland Financing, supra note 7.

[31] Id.

[32] Id.

[33] Id.

[34] Id. Indeed, Schotland wrote of the 2000 judicial elections, "… the United States saw an unprecedented number of intensely fought campaigns, some described as "sleazy," "a national disgrace" and "rotten to the core," and many that were dramatically more costly than ever before. In these campaigns interest group activity was unprecedented, not merely an increase but a change in kind."

[35] Though the campaigns were less intense, other states saw significant interest group involvement. See, for example, Daniel C. Vock, Outside Voices Taking Role in Judicial Races, *Chicago Daily Law Bulletin*, November 7, 2000, p. 1.

[36] Daniel C. Vock, By Law and Ethics, Judicial Candidates Are Different, *Chicago Daily Law Bulletin*, October 17, 2000, 1 at 26.

[37] Id.

[38] Ware, supra note 16, 645, 656.

[39] Schotland Financing, supra note 7.

[40] Discussion of the erection of the Ten Commandments display can be found in Stan Bailey, Moore Puts Commandments Monument in Court Building, *Birmingham News*, August 2, 2001. Such grandstanding by judges is, of course, not limited to Chief Justice Moore. See Stephen B. Bright & Patrick J. Keenan, Judges and the Politics of Death: Deciding Between the Bill of Rights and the Next Election in Capital Cases, 75 *Boston University Law Review*. 760 at 813 (1995).

[41] Schotland Financing, supra note 7.

[42] The Chief Justice of the Nevada Supreme Court wrote in an opinion, "Judges should be judging crime not 'fighting' crime." See, *Nevius v. Warden* 114 Nev. 664 at 673 (CJ Springer dissenting) (1998). Often the current political rhetoric in judicial campaigns allies the candidate with law enforcement. See Hans A. Linde, Elective Judges: Some Comparative Comments, 61 *Southern California Law Review* 1995 at 2000 (1995). A wonderful explanation of the use of television ads in attacking a judge's record on crime control is offered by former California Supreme Court Justice Joseph R. Grodin: "And imagine the power of the 30-second television spot: here was a stomach-turning crime, committed by a person whose humanity was cloaked in blood; here is the mother, or the grandmother, or the daughter of the victim lamenting her loss, and suggesting, or implying, that the California Supreme Court, in its unalterable opposition to the death penalty, and in defiance of the public will, had in reliance upon some unidentified technicality set the defendant loose on the streets. Of course, it was no technicality, it was a matter of constitutional or statutory right, and of course the defendant was not turned loose, but returned for retrial—in fact by the time the opposition ran the principal ad I have described, the defendant in the case had already been retried, reconvicted, and resentenced to death. But try explaining all of that effectively in 30 seconds on television, or in any manner sufficient to offset the emotional impact of the opponents' appeal." See Joseph R. Grodin, Judicial Elections: The California Experience, 70 *Judicature* 365 at 366–367 (1987).

[43] I am grateful to the Brennan Center and especially to Craig Holman for providing me with a transcript of this ad.

[44] Id.

[45] Id.

[46] Schotland Financing, supra note 7.

[47] Id.

[48] Id.

[49] Goldberg & Kozlowski, supra note 8.

[50] Schotland Financing, supra note 7.

[51] See note 43.

[52] Anthony Champagne, Political Parties and Judicial Elections, 34 *Loyola of Los Angeles Law Review* 1411 at 1419 (2001).

[53] Schotland Financing, supra note 7.

[54] Linde, supra note 42.

[55] See note 43.

[56] Schotland Financing, supra note 7.

[57] Id.

[58] See note 43.

[59] See note 43.

[60] Goldberg and Kozlowski, supra note 8.

[61] Id., citing a U.S. Chamber announcement in April, 2001 and Katherine Rizzo, Chamber Ads Failed in Ohio, Worked Elsewhere, *Associated Press Newswire*, November 8, 2000.

[62] Justice at Stake Campaign, The Fall Campaigns: Some Early Results, http://www.justiceat stake.org. These estimates were as of November 7, 2002 and are based on judicial campaigns in 13 states. The numbers include some appellate and trial court races, along with state Supreme Court races.

[63] Brennan Center for Justice, Buying Time 2002: Television Advertising in State Supreme Court Elections, http://www.brennancenter.org.

[64] Brennan Center for Justice, State Supreme Court Races: Ten Out of Eleven Candidates With the Most TV Advertising Support Also Received the Most Votes, http://www.brennan center.org.

[65] Id.

[66] Brennan Center for Justice, More State Supreme Court Races Include Advertising; More Advertising by Interest Groups, http://www.brennancenter.org.

[67] Robert Lenzner & Matthew Miller, Buying Justice, Forbes.com, July 21, 2003. These figures, however, may include spending by the chamber on state attorneys' general races and legislative races as well.

[68] Id.

[69] Brennan Center for Justice, supra note 66.

[70] Id.

[71] Harold See ad for the Alabama Supreme Court in 2002 labeled "Anderson Misleading." This ad and those cited through footnote 87 can be seen on the Brennan Center website at www.brennancenter.org/programs/buyingtime_2002/storyboard_2002_index.html.

[72] Harold See ad for the Alabama Supreme Court in 2002 labeled "Family Man."

[73] Harold See ad for the Alabama Supreme Court in 2002 labeled "Keeping His Promise."

[74] Starr Kelso ad for the Idaho Supreme Court in 2002 labeled "Trout Liberal."

[75] Rita Garman ad for the Illinois Supreme Court in 2002 labeled "Tough on Crime."

[76] Sue Myerscough ad for the Illinois Supreme Court in 2002 labeled "Crime."

[77] Sue Myerscough ad for the Illinois Supreme Court in 2002 labeled "Police Endorsements."

[78] Chamber of Commerce ad for the Michigan Supreme Court in 2002 labeled "Weaver & Young Common Sense."

[79] Chuck McRae ad for the Mississippi Supreme Court in 2002 labeled "Dickinson Special Interests."

[80] Law Enforcement Alliance of America, ads for the Mississippi Supreme Court in 2002 labeled "Dickinson McRae" and "Dickinson Strong Leader."

[81] Don Chairez, ad for the Nevada Supreme Court in 2002 labeled "Stood Up."

[82] Evelyn Stratton, ad for the Ohio Supreme Court in 2002 labeled "Velvet Hammer."

[83] Citizens for an Independent Court, ad for the Ohio Supreme Court in 2002 labeled "Black on Our Side."

[84] Competition Ohio, ad for the Ohio Supreme Court in 2002 labeled "O'Connor & Stratton Phone."

[85] Consumers for a Fair Court, ad for the Ohio Supreme Court in 2002 labeled "Stratton No Justice."

[86] Informed Citizens of Ohio, ad for the Ohio Supreme Court in 2002 labeled "Stratton Endorsement."

[87] Informed Citizens of Ohio, ad for the Ohio Supreme Court in 2002 labeled "Stratton Lawsuits."

[88] 122 S. Ct. 2528 (2002).

[89] 309 F. 3d 1312 (11th Cir. Ga.) (2002).

[90] Philip L. Dubois, *From Ballot to Bench: Judicial Elections and the Quest for Accountability* 7 (1980).

[91] Id. at 258 n. 12.

[92] Philip L. Dubois, Accountability, Independence, and the Selection of State Judges: The Role of Popular Judicial Elections, 40 *Southwestern Law Journal* 31, 44 (1986).

[93] Daniel R. Pinello, Linking Party to Judicial Ideology in American Courts: A Meta-analysis, 20 *Justice System Journal* 219, 243 (1999).

[94] David W. Adamany, The Party Variable in Judges' Voting: Conceptual Notes and a Case Study, 63 *American Political Science Review* 57 (1969).

[95] Dubois, supra note 90, at 148.

[96] Bright & Keenan, supra note 40, at 780.

[97] See Scott D. Wiener, Popular Justice: State Judicial Elections and Procedural Due Process, 31 *Harvard Civil Rights—Civil Liberties Law Review* 187, 196 (1996). The Cook County Democratic Party requires all slated candidates, including judicial candidates, to contribute money for printing and mailing campaign literature. See Aaron Chambers, How High the Bar?, *Illinois Issues* 14, 19 (2000), available at http://illinoisissues.uis.edu/bar.html. Marlene Arnold Nicholson and Bradley Scott Weiss found that Republican judicial candidates also gave money to party committees in Cook County. They believed, "The standard sums given by partisan judicial candidates appear to be assessments that are necessary for obtaining a place on the party slates." Marlene A. Nicholson & Bradley S. Weiss, Funding Judicial Campaigns in the Circuit Court of Cook County, 70 *Judicature* 17, 24 (1986). In 1982, the Brooklyn Democratic Party chairman rejected an offer from the Republican Party to endorse seven Democratic candidates running for newly created judicial seats. The offer was declined because a cross-endorsement would have eliminated the incentive for the candidates to fund raise and campaign for the rest of the ticket. Without cross-endorsement, funds raised by the judicial candidates would be diverted to the Brooklyn Democratic organization campaign for use by all Democratic candidates. See Roy A. Schotland, Elective Judges' Campaign Financing: Are State Judges' Robes the Emperor's Clothes of American Democracy?, 2 *Journal of Law and Policy* 57, 65 (1985).

[98] James Eisenstein, Financing Pennsylvania's Supreme Court Candidates, 84 *Judicature* 10, 15 (2000).

[99] See Wiener, supra note 97, at 196.

[100] Jackson Williams, Irreconcilable Principles: Law, Politics, and the Illinois Supreme Court, 18 *Northern Illinois University Law Review* 267, 285–87 (1998).

[101] See generally, Michael Wallace, The Case for Partisan Judicial Elections, at http://www.fed-soc.org/judicialelections.html.

[102] James C. Drennan, Judicial Reform in North Carolina, in *Judicial Reform in the States* 19, 27 (Anthony Champagne & Judith Haydel eds., 1993).

[103] Id., 19–49.

[104] L. Douglas Kiel et al., Two-Party Competition and Trial Court Elections in Texas, 77 *Judicature* 290 (1994).

[105] Bright, supra note 29, at 847.

[106] Id., 850.

[107] J. Clark Kelso, Judicial Elections: Practices and Trends, 11–12, at http://www.mcgeorge.edu/judicial_elec_prac.html.

[108] Spencer Hunt, Judicial Races Stretch Ethics: Ads, Agendas Tarnishing Impartiality, *Cincinnati Enquirer* (Sept. 24, 2000), http://www.enquirer.com/editions/2000/09/24/loc_judicial_races.html.

[109] Id.

[110] John H. Culver & John T. Wold, Judicial Reform in California, in *Judicial Reform in the States* 139, 155 (Anthony Champagne & Judith Haydel eds., 1993).

[111] Bright & Keenan, supra note 40, at 760–761.

[112] Culver & Wold, supra note 110, at 156 (quoting Justice Otto Kaus).

[113] Lawrence R. Jacobs & Robert Y. Shapiro, *Politicians Don't Pander: Political Manipulation and the Loss of Democratic Responsiveness* 49 (2000).

[114] Gerald F. Uelmen, Crocodiles in the Bathtub: Maintaining the Independence of Supreme Courts in an Era of Judicial Politicization, 72 *Notre Dame Law Review* 1133, 1133 (1997).

[115] Id, 1133–37.

[116] See, e.g., Ann Devroy, Clinton Leans Left on Bias Rules: Speech Energizes Liberal Loyalists, *Chicago Sun-Times*, July 20, 1995, A22.

[117] See, e.g., David Nitkin, You Can Count on State Tax Cut: Times Are Good, So GOP Leaders Want to Give You a Break. But Should Florida Be Saving Instead?, *Orlando Sentinel*, Mar.1, 1999, at A1.

[118] See, e.g., Kurt Erickson, Christian Coalition Chairman Seeks Bipartisanship, *The Pantagraph*, June 21, 2000, at A3.

[119] Jeffrey M. Berry, *The Interest Group Society* 44–54 (3d ed. 1997).

[120] See Julie Mason, Bizarre Double Standard Permeates State GOP Convention, *The Houston Chronicle*, June 25, 2000, at A32.

[121] People for the American Way, Right-Wing Attacks on Judicial Independence in the States in 2000, Sept. 25, 2000 at 5, available at http://www.pfaw.org/issues/right/rwwo/rwwo.000925.shtml.

[122] See Williams, supra note 100, at 313–14.

[123] Id.

[124] Jacobs & Shapiro, supra note 113, at 35.

[125] Id.

[126] See Bright, supra note 29, at 833.

[127] See Bright & Keenan, supra note 40, at 813.

[128] These endorsements (along with other interest group endorsements) are found in Gary Delsohn, Spending, Integrity Hot Issues in Judge Race, *Sacramento Bee*, Sept. 10, 2000, at B1.

[129] Theodore J. Lowi & Benjamin Ginsberg, *American Government: Freedom and Power* 307 (6th ed., 2000).

[130] See Williams, supra note 100 at 296 (1998) (paraphrasing Lee Epstein, Interest Group Litigation During the Rehnquist Court Era, 9 *Journal of Law and Policy* 639 (1993)). Epstein provides a bibliography of works on interest groups and the law in Lee Epstein et al., *Public Interest Law* (1992).

[131] See G. Calvin MacKenzie, The Revolution Nobody Wanted, *Times Literary Supplement*, Oct. 13, 2000, at 12 (citing the *Encyclopedia of Associations*).

[132] Id.

[133] See Berry, supra note 119 at 24; MacKenzie, supra note 131.

[134] See American Friends Service Committee–Northeast Ohio Office and Ohio Religious Leaders for Campaign Finance Reform, Ohio Supreme Justice for Sale (Jan. 2000) (unpublished manuscript); see also Texans for Public Justice, Payola Justice: How Texas Supreme Court Justices Raise Money from Court Litigants, at http://www.tpj.org/reports/payola/summary.html.

[135] Chambers, supra note 97.

[136] Schotland Financing, supra note 7.

[137] Ware, supra note 16, at 656.

[138] Id. at 657.

[139] See id.

[140] See *Henderson ex rel. Hartsfield v. Alabama Power Co.*, 627 So. 2d 878 (Ala. 1993).

[141] Ware, supra note 16, at 659 (quoting Sheila Kaplan, The Very Best Judges That Money Can Buy, *U.S. News & World Report*, Nov. 29, 1999, at 35).

[142] Linde, supra note 42 at 2000–01 (1988). Melinda Hall found that reelection concerns have influenced liberal justices to join conservative majorities in death penalty cases in four states. See Melinda Gann Hall, Electoral Politics and Strategic Voting in State Supreme Courts, 54 *Journal of Politics* 427 (1992). Earlier studies found no statistically significant relationship between judicial selection methods and judicial decisions in the treatment given governmental, criminal, corporate, or "underdog" litigants. See Williams, supra note 100, at 296–97. However, a recent study found that awards in cases with out-of-state defendants are much higher in states with partisan elected judges than in states with other systems of selection. See Alexander Tbarrok & Eric Helland, Court Politics: The Political Economy of Tort Awards, 42 *Journal of Law and Economics* 157, 186–87 (2000).

[143] Mark Schauerte, Fund-raising for Supreme Court Primaries Breaks Records, *Chicago Lawyer*, Mar. 2000, at 10.

[144] See Mark Hansen, A Run for the Bench, 84 *ABA Journal* 68, 69 (1998).

[145] For a discussion of M-Law and other interest group involvement in judicial campaigns, see John D. Echeverria, Changing the Rules by Changing the Players: The Environmental Issue

in State Judicial Elections, 9 *New York University Environmental Law Journal* 247–55 (2001).

[146] Id.

[147] Bright, supra note 23 at 316.

[148] Id. at 316–18.

[149] Id. at 318.

[150] Id.

[151] Bright & Keenan, supra note 40, at 764–65.

[152] Robert Darcy, Conflict and Reform: Oklahoma Judicial Elections, 1907–1998, 26 *Oklahoma City University Law Review* 519, 531 (2001).

[153] Id.

[154] Id. at 537.

[155] Id.

[156] *State v. Odom*, 928 S.W.2d 18, 21 (Tenn. 1996).

[157] Sheila Kaplan & Zoe Davidson, The Buying of the Bench, *The Nation*, Jan. 26, 1998, available at http://past.thenation.com/1998/980126.htm.

[158] Shannon Davis, Courting the Casinos: Judicial Elections in Las Vegas and Nevada, Center for Investigative Reporting, at http://www.muckraker.org/stories/991123-justice/cs-nevada.html .

[159] Kaplan & Davidson, supra note 157.

[160] In re SRBA, 1999 Ida. Lexis 119 (1999).

[161] Echeverria, supra note 145.

[162] Id.

[163] Id.

[164] Id.

[165] Id.

[166] Id.

[167] Alexander Wohl, Justice for Rent, *American Prospect*, May 22, 2000, at 34.

[168] E-mail from Rhoda Billings to Anthony Champagne (Oct. 16, 2000).

[169] Hansen, supra note 144, at 68, 70.

[170] Uelman, supra note 114, at 1134.

[171] Id.

[172] Id. at 1140.

[173] Id.

[174] Stephen Hunt, Judicial Elections Offer Few Thrills but Get Job Done, *Salt Lake Tribune*, Oct. 15, 2000, at A1, available at http://www.sltrib.com/200/oct/10152000/nation_w/33478.htm.

[175] Id.

[176] Hansen, supra note 144 at 69.

[177] Id.

[178] Kaplan & Davidson, supra note 157.

[179] Politics and Judges, *Birmingham News*, Sept. 13, 2000, available at http://www.al.com/news/birmingham/Sep2000/13-politics.html.

[180] Echeverria, supra note 145.

[181] Eisenstein, supra note 98 at 17.

[182] Id.

[183] *S. Christian Leadership Conference v. Sup. Ct. of La.*, 61 F. Supp.2d 499 (E.D. La. 1999).

[184] Id. at 501.

[185] Mark Kozlowski, The Soul of an Elected Judge, *Legal Times*, Aug. 9, 1999, at 15, available at http://www.brennancenter.org/presscenter/oped_1999_0809.html.

[186] Id.

[187] Id.

[188] Echeverria, supra note 145.

[189] Some of that early opposition to women judges can be seen in a letter from W.R. Hegler to James V. Allred (the Texas governor who appointed Sarah Hughes as a state district judge), February 5, 1935, Texas State Library & Archives Commission, http://www.tsl.state.tx.us/governors/personality/allred-hughes-2.html. Hegler wrote, "...a woman is always a woman first and Governor or Judge or this or that next." In reference to Sen. Westerfield's remark, see the commentary with Business & Professional Women's Club to Allred, February 6, 1935, Texas State Library & Archives Commission, http://www.tsl.state.tx.us/governors/personality/allred-hughes-1.html.

[190] Benjamin Ginsberg et al. *We the People: An Introduction to American Politics* 994 (4th ed., Tex. ed. 2003).

[191] Thomas R. Phillips, State of the Judiciary, February 23, 1993, available at www.tomphillips.com/state3.htm.

[192] The above discussion of the case is from the U.S. Fifth Circuit Court of Appeals decision in *United Latin American Citizens, Council No. 4434 v. Clements*, 986 F. 2d 728, 5th Cir. (Tex.), Jan. 27, 1993.

[193] Lowi et al. supra note 190 at 993.

[194] Terri Langford, District Judge Fends off Democratic Rival's Challenge, DallasNews.com, November 9, 2000, http://www.dallasnews.com/campaign/102000/210364.

[195] Anthony Champagne and Greg Thielemann, Awareness of Trial Court Judges, 75 *Judicature* 271, 272 (1991).

[196] Anthony Champagne, The Selection and Retention of Judges in Texas, 40 *Southwestern Law Journal* 53, 80 (1986).

[197] Id.

[198] The Democratic survivor, Ron Chapman became an appellate judge. Democratic Governor Ann Richards' appointees were, as might be expected, Democrats. However, they were defeated if they did not switch to the Republican Party.

[199] Langford, supra note 194.

[200] Id.

[201] Mark Donald, The Lazarus Effect, www.dallasobserver.com/issues/2001-08-30/news3.html. One explanation for Rhea's weakness in the election was that he did not do

much campaigning. Still, with every judicial office in Dallas County Republican, with only one Democratic Dallas County judicial candidate on the ballot, and with a popular Republican governor of Texas running for President at the top of the ticket, such a low victory margin even for an inactive campaigner is surprising.

[202] Id.

[203] Id. The article notes that the Republican chairman tried to explain Bush's Dallas County performance by saying that the Bush campaign had allocated no money to Dallas County, Bush had not campaigned there, and the phone banks in Dallas were used to call Arkansas. Nevertheless, it should not be overlooked that George W. Bush was a popular Republican governor from Texas, and Dallas County is commonly thought of as a Republican bastion.

[204] This was about 15.6% of total votes cast in Texas in 2000. In 1996, Hispanic votes accounted for 17.5% of total votes cast in Texas. See, William C. Velasquez Institute, Latino Vote Hits 1 Million in Texas, http://www.wcvi.org/files/pdf/00_tx_newsletter.pdf.

[205] Id.

[206] William C. Velasquez Institute, Gore Carries Latino Vote in Texas as Republicans Make Significant Gains in 2000 Presidential Elections, http://www.wcvi.org/files/pdf/00_tx_newsletter.pdf.

[207] Id.

[208] Id.

[209] William C. Velasquez Institute, Texas Latino Vote in the 2000 Presidential Election Since 96's Profile, http://www.wcvi.org/files/pdf/00_tx_newsletter.pdf.

[210] William C. Velasquez Institute, Texas Exit Poll Results (updated Nov. 19th, 2002), http://www.wcvi.net/press_room/press_releases/tx/exit_results02.html.

[211] U.S. Census data available at http://census.tamu.edu/data/census/2000/demoprof/county/cntab-1.txt.

[212] Id.

[213] U.S. Census data available at http://census.tamu.edu/data/census/2000/demoprof/county/cntab-66.txt.

[214] U.S. Census data available at http://census.tamu.edu/data/census/2000/demoprof/county/cntab-64.txt.

[215] Courting the Hispanic Vote, www.owlnet.rice.edu/~adaml/mip/history.html.

[216] For a study of the changes in judicial politics in Texas in the 1980s, see Champagne, supra note 196, 53–117.

[217] These demographic projections (along with projections based on other assumptions) can be found at Texas State Data Center and Office of the State Demographer, Projections of the population in Texas and Counties in Texas by Age, Sex and Race/Ethnicity for 2000–2040 (December, 2001), http://txsdc.tamu.edu/cgi-bin/prj2001totnum.cgi. Projections based on varying assumptions are in five-year intervals to 2040. Of course, the further forward in time the projection, the more cautious must be the interpretation.

[218] The data on district court elections in this sections are calculated from Texas Secretary of State, Election and Voter Information, Historical Data, Historical Election Results (1992–current), www.sos.state.tx.us/elections/historical.index.shtml. This website is also the data

rrent), www.sos.state.tx.us/elections/historical.index.shtml. This website is also the data source for Figures 2, 3, and 4.

Chapter VIII

Judicial Elections: Present and Future

Introduction

It is an unavoidable conclusion that judicial elections are inherently political. This is neither a novel conclusion, nor is it the chief contribution of this book. What is not so obvious, though, is whether judicial elections should be treated as blatantly political events or whether the goal of reform should be to mute the effects of politics to the extent possible. And the preceding explication of judicial elections in Texas does not answer that question. What the Texas story offers, though, is a clearer understanding of the seminal events that gave rise to the new judicial politics and a better understanding of the multifaceted considerations that must inform any attempt at reform. That one recent commentator[1] finds it disturbing that works such as this question *whether* judicial elections accomplish their ostensible goal of promoting accountability only exemplifies the degree to which efforts to *describe* the dynamics of judicial elections are overshadowed by a sometimes mindless normative debate. In fact, judicial selection reform has been something of a Quixotic quest for much of American history precisely because reform efforts were premised on an oversimplification of the complex environment in which judges are selected. It is the aim of this work to reestablish an empirical grounding for the judicial selection reform debate.

What, then, does the future hold for judicial elections? Will the new politics of judicial elections continue on its current trajectory toward "noisier, nastier and costlier" campaigns? What effect will recent campaign-speech holdings have on that trajectory? Should special-interest involvement in judicial races be tempered? If it should be tempered, can it be? The lessons that emerge from Texas' bellwether experience with judicial elections suggest that these races are not likely to settle back into the sleepy, low-key affairs they once were. As in Texas, judicial elections in other states may have active and restrained eras, but judicial elections will not likely enter a permanent dormant state.

The Texas experience does offer valuable lessons as judicial reformers look toward the future. And it is with an eye to the future of judicial elections that the Texas judicial selection experience is particularly valuable. Texas' experience not only typifies the current state of judicial elections in the states but, in fact, has provided the blueprint for the emergence of this new era of judicial selection politics. To that end, it is fitting to consider next what effects the new judicial politics has had in Texas, how it has impacted public confidence in the state judiciary and, finally, what lessons the Texas experience has to offer for the future of judicial selection.

The Effects of the New Judicial Politics

One of the chief criticisms leveled against the popular election of judges is that the integrity of courts suffers when judicial candidates are forced to engage in election campaign politics.[2] The chief concern remains largely the same in Texas and elsewhere—that elected judges will be overly responsive to electoral pressures,[3] that they will not administer justice impartially, and that the public confidence in the legitimacy of the judiciary will suffer. It is argued that the integrity of courts is heightened when judges are perceived as impartial and not beholden to interests whose cases they may be called upon to hear.[4]

Given the potential for electoral politics to create the appearance of undue influence on judicial decisions, it is not surprising that one of the chief effects of the new judicial politics in Texas has been heightened media attention to the state judiciary. As judicial elections have become more high profile, media coverage has also increased, and the scrutiny has become more intense.[5] On December 6, 1987, that scrutiny landed Texas' judicial elections in the national spotlight. Texas was shaken when the national television news program "60 Minutes" featured the Texas Supreme Court in a story titled "Is Justice for Sale?," questioning whether Texas' judges were being exposed to undue political influence by deep-pocket interests who were contributing heavily to judicial candidates whom they perceived as friendly to their interests. Current Chief Justice Tom Phillips concedes that the story "had a tremendous impact on Texas judicial politics"[6] while his predecessor, John Hill, has argued that "[t]hese news reports only reflect a growing belief among many citizens of Texas that our state's legal system no longer dispenses evenhanded justice."[7]

Eleven years after the first "60 Minutes" story brought Texas' judicial politics to national attention, Texas was again cast into the national spotlight. On November 10, 1998, two days before election Tuesday, "60 Minutes" revisited the state of judicial selection in Texas and concluded that the judicial politics of 1987 were still pervasive in 1998. All that had changed, according to the story, was the primary source of campaign contributions.[8] Where trial lawyers had contributed the lion's share of money to judicial candidates in the 1980s, defense interests had become the primary contributors by 1998. Former Chief Justice John Hill, who had resigned from the Texas Supreme Court in 1987 to pursue judicial selection reform, defended the Texas judiciary in the 1998 "60 Minutes" story. He conceded though that efforts at judicial selection reform since the first story had been insufficient and that further reforms were needed. Current Chief Justice Tom Phillips, who advocates replacing partisan judicial elections with a merit appointment-type system, also conceded that although some reforms had been made, "much more needs to be done."[9] In his next State of the Judiciary Address after the "60 Minutes" story, he renewed his call for judicial selection reform, noting that "The current judicial selection system has long since outlived its usefulness."[10]

In the years between "60 Minutes" stories, government watchdog groups also began to focus on the electoral politics that had become pervasive in Texas' judicial races, most often pointing to the appearance of compromised fairness raised by a system that requires judges to campaign with funds donated by interests with cases before the state's courts. Early efforts focused on the sources of contributions to Texas Supreme Court candidates,[11] showing that high court races in the 1980s and early 1990s tended to pit plaintiff and civil defense-backed candidates against one another. Since then, Texans for Public Justice has issued reports probing in greater detail the linkage between the decisions of Texas Supreme Court justices and the donors who contribute to their campaigns.[12] One report that examined the linkage between donations and decisions by the court, *Payola Justice*, concluded:

> [W]hile the faces and ideologies of the justices and their paymasters have changed[,] justices continue to take enormous amounts of money from litigants who bring cases before the court. The fact that the parties who finance the justices' campaigns repeatedly reappear on the court's docket documents the extent to which justice is still for sale in the Texas Supreme Court.[13]

In another report,[14] Texans for Public Justice examined the correlation between donations and the acceptance of cases for review by the Texas Supreme Court. Although charges of a direct connection between donations and case outcomes were tempered,[15] the report nevertheless emphasized the higher acceptance rate among law firms that contributed heavily to the campaigns of the high court justices, suggesting that campaign donations at least provide an entrée to the court's docket.[16] Chief Justice Tom Phillips responded, however, that the report failed to prove that campaign donations had any effect on the acceptance of cases for review, noting that the large donor firms likely handled more of the types of cases that the Supreme Court deemed important to resolve.[17]

Perhaps more important than the linkages between donations to judicial campaigns and the decisions rendered by Texas courts is the simple fact that the manner in which Texas selects its judges remains at the center of media attention. The first "60 Minutes" story, rather than prompting serious reform, seemed instead only to encourage harsher and more constant criticisms of the Texas courts. However, the reluctance of Texas to provide serious judicial election reforms, other than the Judicial Campaign Fairness Act, combined with the perception of bias created by the present judicial campaign finance system, increases the likelihood that Texas' process for selecting judges will remain the focus of attention.

Perception of the Courts

The new judicial politics in Texas—replete with scandal, the embarrassing election of an unqualified Supreme Court justice, the appearance of impropriety raised by large campaign contributions, and the attention of the national media and interest groups—might well be expected to have caused significant erosion of public confidence in the courts. Largely in response the these concerns, Texas' Office of Court Administration commissioned a survey of the Texas public as well as of the Texas legal profession to determine what perceptions the public actually has of the Texas judiciary.[18] The results of the survey of the general public were generally positive, although they reveal concern among Texans over effects of the new judicial politics on the fairness of Texas judicial system.

The survey respondents' overall impressions of the Texas judiciary were generally positive. Over 50% expressed either a somewhat positive or very positive overall impression of the Texas judiciary.[19] Sixty-nine percent of the respondents believed that Texas' courts in general are somewhat or very honest and ethical[20] while 77 percent believe the same of the Texas Supreme Court.[21] Seventy-three percent of the respondents believed that "judges and court personnel are courteous and respectful to the public."[22] The same percentage believes that they would be treated fairly "if they had a case pending in a Texas court."[23]

In spite of the good overall impression of the Texas courts, the survey revealed concerns about the fairness of Texas courts in four general areas: gender, race, socio-economic status, and judicial campaign finance. With regard to gender, only 50 percent of respondents agreed that men and women are treated alike in the Texas courts while 62 percent believed that there are too few female judges in Texas. Texans expressed even greater concern about fairness with regard to race, with only 41 percent reporting that "the courts treat all people alike regardless of race" and 55 percent believing that there are too few minority judges. [24]

The greatest concerns by Texans, though, involved the influence of money in the Texas courts—either the effects of socio-economic status on fairness and court access or the effects of campaign contributions on judicial decisions. Only 21 percent of Texans agree that "the courts treat poor and wealthy people alike" while 69 percent do not believe that court costs and fees are affordable.[25] Texans' greatest concern about Texas courts, however, involves the effects of campaign contributions on judicial decisions. When asked whether judges in Texas are influenced by campaign donations, 83% indicated that campaign contributions influence the decisions made by judges.[26]

Painted in broad strokes, the attitude of Texans seems to be one of generally high regard for the state's courts but overall dissatisfaction with the composition of the courts and distrust of the role of money in the judicial process. However, in spite of Texans' overall belief that race, gender, socio-economic status and campaign finance are all problematic issues for Texas' court system, an overwhelming majority of Texans expressed a desire to retain the current elective method of judicial selection.[27] This reluctance to embrace wholesale reform of the state's judicial selection method suggests strongly that the only realistic opportunity for selection reform in Texas must occur within the current context of judicial elections.

In the survey to ascertain the legal profession's view of Texas courts, judges and lawyers had moderately consistent opinions about the courts and judicial selection. Both tended to have a positive view of the Texas courts,[28] but both also reported some degree of inequity based on race, gender, or socio-economic status. Among judges, 51% did not believe that Texas courts show racial bias[29] and 56% did not report gender bias.[30] However, only 42% of the responding judges reported equal treatment of the poor and wealthy.[31] Among lawyers, 42% reported the courts to be free of racial bias[32] while 37% reported no gender bias.[33] Only 19% of lawyers, though, felt that the poor and wealthy are treated equally in Texas' courts.[34]

With regard to judicial campaign finance, the opinions of judges and lawyers tend to diverge. Judges were nearly evenly split over the influence of campaign donations on court decisions with 48% reporting at least some influence of donations.[35] In contrast, nearly 80% of lawyers believed that campaign contributions have at least some influence on judges.[36] Judges and lawyers tend to agree, however, in their preferred judicial selection method. Fifty-two percent of judges and 42% of lawyers indicated a preference for judicial election, albeit on a nonpartisan basis.[37] In contrast, there was equal, though substantially weaker, support among judges for partisan elections and gubernatorial appointment systems, each being preferred by 21% of the responding judges.[38] Among attorneys, gubernatorial appointment with retention elections ranked a close second as the preferred method of judicial selection at 35%[39] while partisan election was supported by only 11%.[40] Both judges and attorneys agreed that judicial selection ranks as one of the most important issues facing Texas' court system, with judges ranking judicial selection as the feature they would most like to change about the Texas courts.[41] One conclusion that can be drawn from the desire among judges for selection reform, coupled with the concerns of Texans about the influence of campaign donations to judges, is that at least limited reform efforts would enjoy support. Clearly, though, Texans do not appear ready to give up judicial elections, and any reforms that occur will have to take place within the context of a popularly elected judiciary. This Texas pattern seems similar to that of other elective states—that is, changes in the system of selection are unlikely; although more incremental reforms within an elective system could occur.[42]

Texas Judicial Politics Now and Its Lessons for Judicial Elections Elsewhere

Since the advent of its new judicial politics, Texas has been a bellwether for emerging trends in other states that maintain elected judiciaries. In just over two decades, the Texas experience has completed a full cycle of change—from staid, one-party affairs dominated by initial appointment to the bench, to an era of true two-party competition in judicial contests. Currently, Texas has moved in the direction of the one-party dominance that defined its judicial politics just two decades ago. In the future, changes in the state's demographics suggest another shift in party allegiances to a competitive two-party system and then toward dominance by the Democratic Party. In the course of those changes in its judicial politics, Texas' judicial selection experience has produced valuable lessons for other states.

The most telling lesson from Texas' recent experience with judicial selection is that those interests most affected by the courts are willing to exert a great deal of influence in an attempt to shape the composition of state courts. It is at best misguided to argue that deep-pocket interests are attempting to buy decisions from individual judges. It is, however, equally naïve to suggest that those who stand to lose the most in the courtroom will stand idly by without attempting to influence the philosophical makeup of the courts.

In states with elective modes of judicial selection, influence on court composition is most easily achieved through campaign finance. So long as the perception exists that money buys electoral advantage, deep-pocket interests will donate heavily to their favored candidates. And even in the absence of real competition in a judicial race, there will be those who will continue to contribute, if for no other reason than to show their support for one judicial philosophy over another. On the other hand, so long as judges face the electorate for the right to serve on the bench, they will feel compelled to accept campaign contributions—even from those who have interests before their court. For judicial candidates who face no real competition in an election, a large campaign treasury may indicate to future challengers that they will face a formidable task. Even in an electoral environment that is dominated by one political party, a large campaign war chest may serve to stave off primary challengers—whether those challengers pose a real threat or are simply viewed as an inconvenience to the incumbent.

Money, although troublesome for judicial integrity, is not the fundamental problem in judicial elections. Money enters judicial politics because of the problem of name familiarity. Judicial races are typically low-profile affairs, and candidates for the bench seldom enjoy much name recognition among voters.[43] In order to run a strong campaign, judicial candidates must spend money to make themselves known to the voters. In local trial court elections in densely populated urban areas, this may still entail garnering recognition among tens of thousands of potential voters. In statewide elections, the problem is magnified to the size of the entire state electorate. Without other effective means of gaining familiarity with the voters, judicial candidates face little choice other than to raise large amounts in campaign contributions and then to spend that money on name recognition.

Party affiliation, of course, provides a critical cue to many voters.[44] Even in the absence of party labels on the general election ballot, candidates may enjoy partisan identification from their party's primary election.[45] When judicial candidates are also removed from nomination via party primary, parties may still prove invaluable to a candidate's campaign—often by providing campaign workers, publicity, or campaign funding. In states with real two-party competition, the presence of the party cue may serve to focus the importance of money's effect on independent voters.[46] Also, in truly non-partisan races with no party cue, it is likely in the new environment of judicial elections that money would only increase in importance since judicial candidates would not have their party base on which to rely.[47] In one-party states, non-partisan elections could present the opportunity for opposing economic interests to wage expensive campaigns to secure the election of their favored candidates since no candidate would be guaranteed electoral victory on the basis of party alone. Expensive judicial races—even if only a symptom of a deeper problem—are not likely to fade from the judicial landscape without broad, serious reforms to judicial campaign finance.

The Texas experience with expensive judicial races shows the deep institutional damage that can be caused to an entire judiciary by electoral politics. When fierce battles are waged between opposing interests to influence court composition, the public is likely to lose its sense that the courts will judge impartially. Rather, the opinion is likely to emerge that judges are in some way beholden to the interests that helped them win election to the bench. In the extreme cases, the new judicial politics may create opportunities not just for the appearance of impropriety, but for real judicial misconduct. While instances like the public disciplines of two Texas Supreme Court justices are infrequent, their existence only adds to the public sense that the electoral selection system renders justice to those who are able to gain influence by contributing to judges' campaigns.

Because judicial reform will invariably impact some interests adversely, the prospect of meaningful change in the way judges are chosen presents a formidable problem. In fact, an important lesson from the Texas experience is that reform may best be pursued in incremental steps. Wholesale reform efforts may pose major threats to established interests, but incremental reform may temper the severity of that threat, making reform easier to accomplish. Even in the wake of scandal and national scrutiny of the Texas judiciary in the late 1980s, wholesale reform efforts proved unsuccessful.[48] However, the same circumstances that led to calls for wholesale reform in Texas were the basis for later incremental changes in judicial campaign finance which limited the amount of campaign money that judicial candidates could receive from individuals, law firms, and political action committees.

A final lesson that should be taken from Texas' experience with judicial selection is that voters can be profoundly committed to selecting their judges in popular elections. In spite of the criticisms of popular judicial elections in Texas, national attention on perceived improprieties, the public mistrust of judicial campaign finance, and the low voter knowledge of judicial candidates, Texans still hold fast to voting for judges. This, coupled with the other difficulties of reform, makes it unlikely that Texas will abandon its elective process for selecting judges. It also serves to heighten the importance of incremental reform efforts.

In short, Texas' history of judicial elections illustrates vividly many of the oft-repeated criticisms of popular selection of judges. Perhaps more importantly, Texas' experience with judicial selection offers important lessons to other states of how to deal with the difficulties that are inherent in judicial elections. Certainly no other state wants to experience with its courts what Texas experienced in the 1980s. However, close attention to the Texas experience provides at the very least an outline for other states to consider as they find themselves emerging into the new era of judicial election politics.

Notes

[1] Luke Bierman, Comment on Paper by Cheek and Champagne: The Judiciary as a "Republican" Institution, 39 *Willamette Law Review* 1385–1395 (2003). It must be noted that Bierman thinks it is thinking creatively to argue that the "Republican Form of Government" clause in the Constitution makes judicial elections unconstitutional. Creative thinking such as this may explain why judicial reformers tend to fail.

[2] For a discussion of the concerns that led to the initial popularity of the Missouri Plan, see Richard A. Watson & Rondal G. Downing, *The Politics of the Bench and the Bar: Judicial Selection Under the Missouri Nonpartisan Court Plan* (1969).

[3] See Melinda Gann Hall, Electoral politics and strategic voting in state supreme courts, 54 *The Journal of Politics* at 427–446 (1992), for evidence that elected state supreme court justices may be more likely to rule in favor of the death penalty when facing an upcoming election.

[4] When presented with survey results showing that in Texas 83% of the public, 79% of lawyers, and 48% of judges think that campaign contributions affect judicial decisions, U.S. Supreme Court Justice Anthony Kennedy said, "This is serious because the law commands allegiance only if it commands respect. It commands respect only of the public thinks the judges are neutral," Pete Slover, Lawsuit Challenges Texas' System of Electing Judges, *Dallas Morning News*, April 4, 2000, at 28A.

[5] See, e.g., Richard Woodbury, Is Texas Justice for Sale?, *Time*, Jan. 11, 1988, at 74; Mary Flood, Justice Still for Sale? Clock Is Ticking on the Answer, *Wall Street Journal*, June 24, 1998, T1.

[6] See Flood, supra note 5.

[7] John L. Hill, Taking Texas Judges Out of Politics: An Argument for Merit Selection, 40 *Baylor Law Review* 342.

[8] See also Flood, supra note 5.

[9] Id.

[10] Thomas R. Phillips, State of the Judiciary, 76th Legislature, http://www.tomphillips.com/state76.htm.

[11] Texans for Public Justice, Checks and Imbalances, www.tpj.org/reports/checks/toc.html.

[12] Texans for Public Justice, Payola Justice, How Texas Supreme Court Justices Raise Money from Court Litigants, www.tpj.org/reports/payola.summary.html and Texans for Public Justice, Pay to Play, www.tpj.org/reports/paytoplay/index.html.

[13] Payola Justice, How Texas Supreme Court Justices Raise Money from Court Litigants, supra note 12.

[14] Pay to Play, supra note 12.

[15] Although the study conceded the difficulties of determining a cause and effect relationship between campaign donations and judicial decisions, the director of Texans for Public Justice argued, "The appearance that there is a cause-and-effect is undeniable. Money seems to get you in the front door," quoted in Pete Slover, Group Alleges Supreme Court Favors Donors, *Dallas Morning News*, April 25, 2001, at 23A.

[16] Pay to Play, supra note 12, found that petitions for review from large contributors were 7.5 times as likely to be accepted as those from non-contributors.

[17] Slover, supra note 15 at 28A. Citing another rationale for the high acceptance rate of large-donor firms, Chief Justice Phillips said, "Considering the amounts of money they charge, I'd be surprised if they didn't get good results."

[18] Supreme Court of Texas, Texas Office of Court Administration, and State Bar of Texas, Public Trust & Confidence in Texas Courts...A Summary Report, December 1998, http://www.courts.state.tx.us/publicinfo/publictrust/index.htm, The survey questioned 1,215 adults in Texas about their impressions of the state's courts. Among the questions asked by the survey, several focused on the overall perception of Texas courts and whether race, gender, or socio-economic status plays any role in the treatment of litigants in court. The survey also asked respondents whether campaign contributions influence court decisions as well as what method of judicial selection is preferable to most Texans. The sample size of 1,215 adults is sufficient to ensure, with 95% confidence, that the sample results are within 2.8% of the true percentage that would be determined by surveying the entire population of Texas.

[19] Id.

[20] Id.

[21] Id.

[22] Id.

[23] Id.

[24] Id.

[25] Id.

[26] Id.

[27] 70% of survey respondents "believed that judges should be elected by the people" while only 20% preferred gubernatorial appointment with retention elections. Id.

[28] 85% of judges and 63% of lawyers held either a somewhat or very high impression of the Texas courts, The Supreme Court of Texas, State Bar of Texas and Texas Office of Court Administration, The Courts and the Legal Profession in Texas—The Insider's Perspective: A Survey of Judges, Court Personnel, and Attorneys, May 1999, http://www.courts .state.tx.us/publicinfo/publictrust/execsum.htm

[29] Id.

[30] Id.

[31] Id.

[32] Id.

[33] Id.

[34] Id.

[35] Id. Judges in local trial courts, minority judges, and rural judges were more likely to indicate that campaign donations have at least some influence on decisions.

[36] Id.

[37] Id.

[38] Id.

[39] Id.

[40] Id.

[41] Id.

[42] National Summit On Improving Judicial Selection, Call to Action, 34 *Loyola of Los Angeles Law Review* 1353–59 (2001).

[43] Anthony Champagne & Greg Thielemann, Awareness of Trial Court Judges, 75 *Judicature* 271 (1991)..

[44] Phillip Dubois, *From Ballot to Bench: Judicial Elections and the Quest for Accountability* (1980).

[45] Kathleen L. Barber, Ohio Judicial Elections—Nonpartisan Premises with Partisan Results, 32 *Ohio State Law Journal* (1971), 762–789.

[46] For a discussion of the importance of money in judicial races as a means of securing the votes of those who are not guided strongly by party labels, see Kyle Cheek, The Bench, the Bar and the Political Economy of Justice: Texas Supreme Court Races, 1980–1994, (1996) (unpublished dissertation in The University of Texas at Dallas Library).

[47] One example of expensive campaigns occurred in California. In non-partisan, uncontested retention elections for three Supreme Court justices in 1986, record amounts—$11,400,000 in 1986 dollars—were spent in the retention elections. See Roy Schotland, Introduction: Personal Views, 34 *Loyola of Los Angeles Law Review* 1361, 1363 footnote 4.

[48] Anthony Champagne, Judicial Reform in Texas, 72 *Judicature* 146–159 (1988).

INDEX

Abortion issue, 144–145
Adamany, David, 8, 129
Alabama
    hard fought campaigns, 22, 43, 139–140
    1996 "skunk" ad, 119
    2000 Supreme Court elections, 122–123
    2002 Supreme Court elections, 126
Allred, James, 146
Arizona, 3
Adams, Randall Dale, 57, 59
Armstrong, Anne, 104
Attack ads, 137

Baum, Lawrence, 66
Baraka, Larry, 56, 59–60, 62–66
Bar associations, 3
Bar, specialization of, 88–90
Barrow, Charles, 56, 89
Bates, John, 84
Bayer, Karl, 42
Bean, Roy, 136
Bean, Woodrow Wilson, 90
Bentsen, Lloyd, 40, 46, 58–60, 62–66
    coattails of, 88, 131
Berlanga, Hugo, 103
Bloss, "Maximum Marion", 119
Boulter, Beau, 46
Briscoe, Dolph, 83–84
Brown, Joe B., 57, 59–60, 62, 66
Bullock, Bob, 98–102, 104, 110
    Bullock committee, 98–102
Bunton, Lucius, 147–150
Burke, Edmund, 11
Bush, George W., 73, 100–101, 152–153

California
    election fliers, 118
    hard fought campaigns, 22
    judicial elections, 132–133
    1978 Los Angeles campaign, 2, 22
    1986 Supreme Court elections, 2, 24, 95, 120, 133
    1998 Supreme Court elections, 145
Calvert, Robert, 83
Canales, Adolph, 57, 59–60, 62–66
Campbell, Robert, 39–41, 85
Chamber of Commerce, 123, 125, 141
Chapman, Ron, 57, 59, 61–66, 91, 151
Christian Coalition, 135–136, 145
Citizens for a Conservative Court, 131, 144
Clements, William, 66, 84–85, 88, 96–97, 104
    appointees to the bench, 87
Clinton, Bill, 152
Codes of Judicial Conduct
    Georgia, 30–31, 127
    Minnesota, 28–29, 127
    Republican Party of *Minnesota v. White*, 29, 127
    Michigan, 29–30
    New York, 31–32, 127
    Ohio, 133
Collins, Jim, 88
Committee of 100, 84, 92–94
Committee of 250, 84, 94
Committee on Merit Election, 97
Connally, John, 83
Cook County, Illinois
    judiciary, 136
    nonpartisan election of judges, 18

partisan election of judges, 18
Cook, Eugene, 42–43
Cornyn, John, 153
Courts as policy–makers, 6–8
Craddick, Tom, 104
Crime issue, 23, 140
Crime Victims for Court Reform, 24, 133
Crocodiles in the bathtub, 134
Culver, Barbara, 42

Dallas Morning News, 151
Declaration of Independence, 17
Dewhurst, David, 153
Doggett, Lloyd, 42
Dole, Bob, 152–153
Dubois, Phillip, 7, 8, 128, 130
Duncan, Robert, 103–104

Easley, Chuck, 123–124
Educational campaigns, 27
Ellis, Rodney, 101, 103
Encyclopedia of Associations, 139
Enoch, Craig, 104

Farris, Anthony, 90
Florida, 144
Fund for a Democratic Texas, 47

Garwood, Will, 70, 84, 87, 89
Ginsberg, Benjamin, 138
Glick, Henry, 95
Godwin, George, 56
Gonzalez, Raul, 41–43, 58–60, 62–65
Gore, Al, 153
Georgia
    codes of judicial conduct, 30–31

    election of judges, 18
    1998 Supreme Court campaign, 119

Haas, Rene, 43
Hall, Melinda Gann, 26–27
Hampton, Jack, 57, 59–60, 62, 65–66
Hance, Kent, 46
Haydel, Judith, 110
Hecht, Nathan, 41–43

Herring, Charles, 94
Higgens, Andrew Jackson, 95
Hightower, Jack, 42
Hill, John 41, 83–85, 91–97, 99, 103, 111, 172–173
Hobby, Paul, 152
Hobby, William, 88
Hot-button issues, 134, 137, 144
Howell, Charles Ben, 41–42
Huey, Mary Ann, 152
Hughes, Sarah, T., 146

Idaho,
    interest group involvement, 143
    judicial selection, 21, 25
    2000 Supreme Court election, 142–143
Illinois
    election of judges, 19–20
    retention elections, 19–21
Independent campaigns, 27
Indiana, 18
Interest group activity, 2
Interest groups, 138–139
Iowa, 3
Issue advocacy campaigns, 27

Joint Select Committee on the Judiciary, 97
Judicial accountability, 4, 8, 9–12
Judicial campaigns
    earlier era, 1, 22, 139
    low visibility, 27
    new era, 1, 22–24
    nastier, noisier, costlier, 1, 117, 171
Judicial campaign finance, 37–51, 177
    disclosure rules, 27, 44–45
    small contributor base, 44, 90
    top contributors in 1988, 48–49
    2000 state Supreme Court elections, cost of, 121
    2002 state Supreme Court elections, cost of, 125
    contributions, Pennsylvania political parties, 130
Judicial independence, 4

Judicial reform, 17–34, 32–34, 179
Judicial selection
    appointment of judges, 3, 17, 23
    election of judges, 3
    federal model, 3, 23
    gubernatorial appointment, 3, 17
    legislative selection, 17
    methods in the states, 20, 32
Justice, Department of, 98
Jacksonian democracy, 8
Jamail, Joe, 90
Jefferson, Thomas, 18
Judicial Campaign Fairness Act, 101–
        102, 174

Kaus, Otto, 134
Kilday, Patti, 44–45
Kilgarlin William, 41–43, 96, 111
Kirk, Ron, 153

Laney, Pete, 100
Lanphier, David, 24
Legal profession changes, 1
Light, Paul, 56
Linde, Hans, 140
Louisiana, 145–146
Lowi, Theodore, 138

M–Law, 141
Madden, Jerry, 101–102
Make Texas Proud, 104
Maloney Sr., Pat, 40–41
Manges, Clinton, 40, 90
Manges v. Guerra, 71
Marshall, John, 18
Mattox, Jim, 88
Mauzy, Oscar, 93
Mays, Richard, 152
MeritPAC, 97
Merit selection of judges, 19
    problems with, 21, 95, 99
Mexican American Legal Defense and
        Education Fund, 104
Michigan
    codes of judicial conduct, 29–30
    interest group involvement, 141

judicial selection, 21, 133
    2000 Supreme Court elections, 124
    2002 Supreme Court elections, 126
Mikva, Abner, 140
Minnesota
    codes of judicial conduct, 28–29
    judicial selection in, 25
    Republican Party of Minnesota v.
        White, 29
Mississippi
    Chamber of Commerce in, 24
    election of judges, 3, 18, 24–25
    interest group involvement, 141–142
    Prosecutors' Association in, 24,
        141–142
    2000 Supreme Court elections, 123–
        124
    2002 Supreme Court elections, 126
Missouri
    selection of judges, 19, 132
Missouri Plan, 3, 4, 19, 83
    problems with, 21, 95, 99
Moore, Roy, 122
Morales, Dan, 148–150
Murphy, Paul, 42
Murray & Murray, 120

National Summit on Improving Judicial
        Selection, 33, 128
Nebraska, 22, 24, 144
Nevada
    nonpartisan election in, 25, 142
    2002 Supreme Court elections, 126–
        127
New Mexico, 20
New York
    codes of judicial conduct, 31–32
    election of judges, 3, 18
Nonpartisan ballots, 3, 18–19
North Carolina
    hard fought campaigns, 22
    1986 Supreme Court election, 131,
        144
    1990 Supreme Court election, 118–
        119, 131
    1996 judicial campaign, 119

Ohio
    hard fought campaigns, 22, 43, 133,
        139
    interest groups involvement, 141
    judicial selection, 21
    Supreme Court, awareness of, 66
    campaign contributions, 119–120
    2000 Supreme Court elections, 124–
        125
    2002 Supreme Court elections, 127
Oklahoma
    interest group involvement, 142
    1986 judicial elections, 142
    1996 judicial elections, 142
    1998 judicial elections, 142
Oliver, Jesse, 57, 59–60, 62–64, 66
O'Neill, Harriet, 104
Organized labor, 135

Partisan ballots, 3
Party affiliation, as measure of judicial
        ideology, 129
Party endorsement, payment by judicial
        candidates, 129–130
Party loyalty, expectation from judges,
        130
Payola Justice, 173
Pennsylvania, 145
Perception of courts, 174–176
Perry, Rick, 153
Phillips, Tom, 41–43, 45–46, 50, 85, 87,
        102, 104, 110, 147, 149, 172–
        174
Political machines, 18
Political parties, cooperation with interest
        groups, 135, 137
Plaintiff–Defense conflicts, 37–51
Prather, Lenore, 123

Ray, C.L., 41, 89–90, 96, 111
Reagan, Ronald, 84, 88
    coattails of, 88, 131
Representation
    African-Americans, 146–151
    Hispanics, 146–151, 153–158

    women, 146–147
    minority judges, lack of, 146–151
    minority lawyers, lack of, 150
Republican primary in Texas, 50
Republican Party in South, 1, 25, 134
Resnick, Alice, 124–125
Retention elections, 4, 95
Rhea, Bill, 152
Robertson, Ted Z., 40–43, 45, 90
Roe v. Wade, 22
Ross, Kim, 47, 50

Sacramento County Deputy Sheriff's
        Association, 138
Sacramento Police Officers' Association,
        138
Sanchez, Tony, 153
See, Harold, 122
Sharp, John, 153
Silak, Cathy, 143
"60 Minutes" broadcast, 97, 117, 172–
        174
Slagle, Bob, 94
SMU football scandal, 96, 111
Spears, Franklin, 93
Spector, Rose, 147
State supreme courts
    Incumbents challenged and defeated,
        27
Straight ticket voting, 88, 129
Stratton, Evelyn, 127
Strauss, Annette, 58–60, 62–65
Stuart, Lyn, 122–123

Tennessee
    Retention election in, 21, 24, 120–
        121, 142
Texaco, 41
Texaco-Pennzoil trial, 90, 97, 111
Texans for Lawsuit Reform, 101
Texans for Public Justice, 173–174
Texas
    bellwether state, 2, 171, 176–177
    calm in judicial politics, 117
    Clean Slate candidates, 42

effects, demographic change, 118
effects, new judicial politics, 172–
    174
early judicial selection, 5–6, 39
emergence of Republican Party, 9
Hispanic population, 153–158
minority strength, 91
1988 elections, 37–51
one-party Republican, 132
party sweeps, 26, 117
party changes, 159
population growth, 153–158
populism, 111
pressures for judicial selection
    change, 86–93
reasons for continued partisan
    judicial elections, 105–110
Senatorial courtesy, 93
support for the Missouri Plan, 83
supreme Court battles, 22, 25–26
two-party system, 86–88
urban county growth, 90–91
voter knowledge, 10
Texas bashing, 97
    critical stories and broadcasts, 97
Texas Civil Liberties Union, 94
Texas Commission on Judicial Conduct,
    41, 84, 96
Texas Court of Criminal Appeals, 131
Texas Medical Association, 42–43, 45,
    47, 50
Texas Office of Court Administration,
    174
Texas Plan, 85, 92, 94, 97
    opposition to, 93–95
Texas Research League, 43
Texas Supreme Court elections, 69–80
    effect of political party, 71–72
    effect of incumbency, 72–73
    effect of campaign finance, 73–74
    effect of candidate demographics,
        74–76
    multivariate effects, 76–80
    task forces, 102–103
Texas Trial Lawyers Association, 89, 98
Third party interest groups, 126

Tort reform, 23, 136, 140
Trial lawyers, 135
Tulane Environmental Law Clinic, 146

U.S. Supreme Court Activism, 2, 22
Utah, 144–145

Voter cues, 10, 67, 129, 178
Voter knowledge, 26, 55–80
    Lubbock, Texas survey of, 55–56
    Texas Lawyer survey of, 56
    Dallas survey, 56–80
Voting Rights Act, 147–151

Weddington, Susan, 104
Westerfeld, Claud, 146
West Virginia, 142
White, Mark, 57, 88
White, Penny, 24, 120–121, 142
Wightman, Michelle lawsuit, 119
Williams, Clayton, 92
Williams, Fred, 128, 137
Wisconsin,
    campaign contributions in, 143
    judicial selection in, 25
    1999 Supreme Court race, 119

Yarbrough, Don, 39, 56, 90

TEACHING TEXTS IN LAW AND POLITICS ⚖

David Schultz, *General Editor*

The new series Teaching Texts in Law and Politics is devoted to textbooks that explore the multidimensional and multidisciplinary areas of law and politics. Special emphasis will be given to textbooks written for the undergraduate classroom. Subject matters to be addressed in this series include, but will not be limited to: constitutional law; civil rights and liberties issues; law, race, gender, and gender orientation studies; law and ethics; women and the law; judicial behavior and decision-making; legal theory; comparative legal systems; criminal justice; courts and the political process; and other topics on the law and the political process that would be of interest to undergraduate curriculum and education. Submission of single-author and collaborative studies, as well as collections of essays are invited.

Authors wishing to have works considered for this series should contact:

> Peter Lang Publishing
> Acquisitions Department
> 275 Seventh Avenue, 28th floor
> New York, New York 10001

To order other books in this series, please contact our Customer Service Department at:

> 800-770-LANG (within the U.S.)
> (212) 647-7706 (outside the U.S.)
> (212) 647-7707 FAX

or browse online by series at:

> WWW.PETERLANGUSA.COM